# PHILOSOPHICAL ANTHROPOLOGY IN ŚAIVA SIDDHĀNTA

# PHILOSOPHICAL ANTHROPOLOGY IN ŚAIVA SIDDHĀNTA

## With special reference to Śivāgrayogin

JAYANDRA SONI

MOTILAL BANARSIDASS PUBLISHERS
PRIVATE LIMITED • DELHI

*Revised and Corrected Edition: Delhi, **2018***
*First Edition : Delhi, 1989*



ISBN: 978-81-208-0632-0

*Also Available at*
MOTILAL BANARSIDASS
41 U.A. Bungalow Road, Jawahar Nagar, Delhi 110 007
1 B, Jyoti Studio Compound, Kennedy Bridge, Nana Chowk, Mumbai 400 007
203 Royapettah High Road, Mylapore, Chennai 600 004
236, 9th Main III Block, Jayanagar, Bengaluru 560 011
8 Camac Street, Kolkata 700 017
Ashok Rajpath, Patna 800 004
Chowk, Varanasi 221 001

*MLBD Cataloging-in-Publication Data*
Philosophical Anthropology in Śaiva Siddhānta :
*With Special reference to Śivāgrayogin* by Jayandra Soni
Includes Appendix, Bibliography, Index and Errata
ISBN: 978-81-208-0632-0
I. Philosophy II. Saivism III. Anthropology
IV. Soni, Jayandra

*Printed in India*

by RP Jain at NAB Printing Unit,
A-44, Naraina Industrial Area, Phase I, New Delhi–110028
and published by JP Jain for Motilal Banarsidass Publishers (P) Ltd.,
41 U.A. Bungalow Road, Jawahar Nagar, Delhi-110007

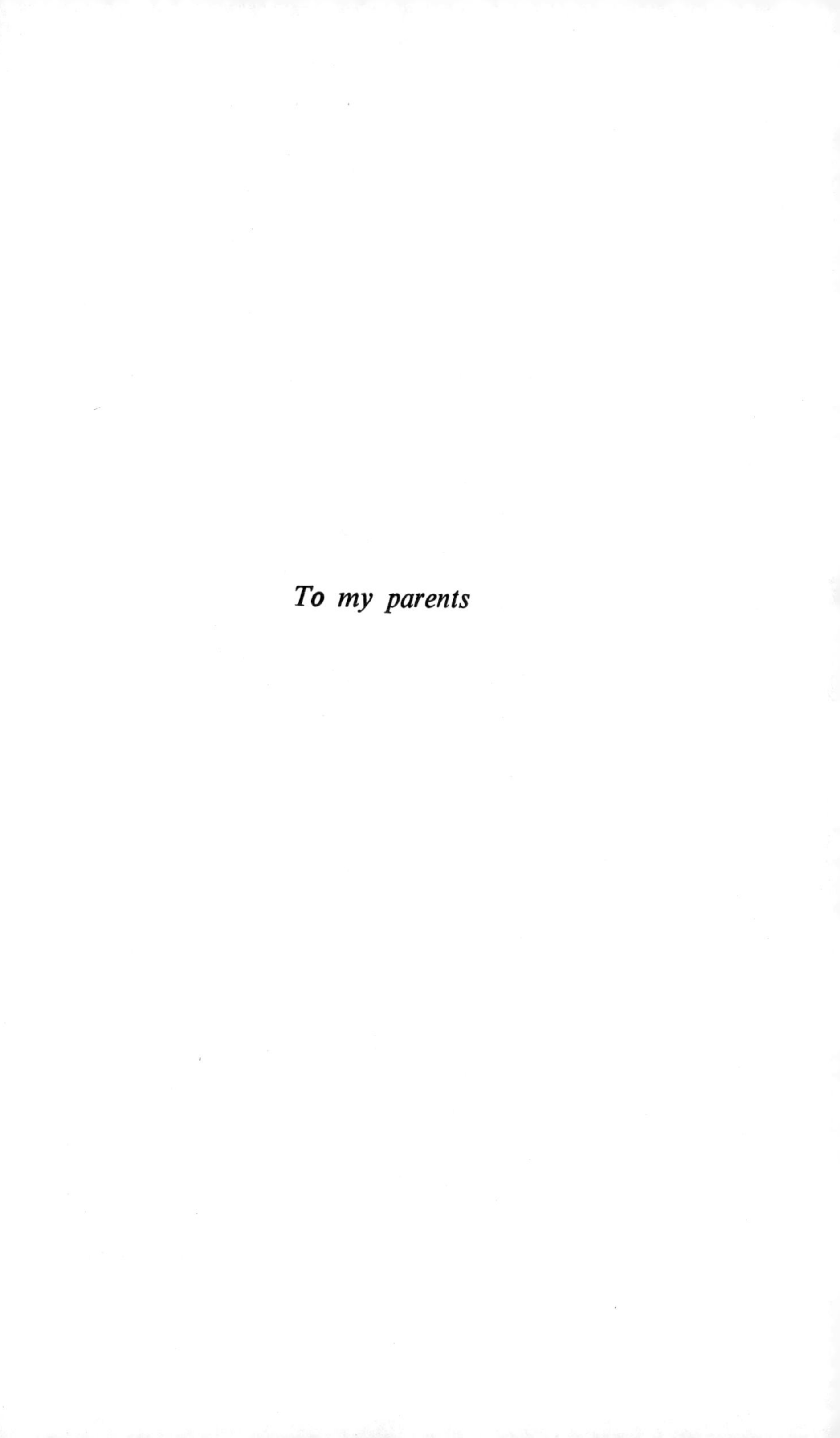

*To my parents*

# FOREWORD

*General*

Śaiva Siddhānta is a religio-philosophical system of Hinduism under the rubric of Śaivism. The origins of Śaivism are not very distinct, although the worship of Śiva is traceable to the Vedas.[1] The development of Śaivism is associated with the supreme position given to the god Śiva and, in the philosophical writings of the tradition, to the various interpretations of the relationship between the absolute principle called *śivam* and the individual beings in the world. A distinctive feature of Śaivism marking its development independent of the Vedic branch of Hinduism, is, among other things, the body of authoritative literature called the Āgamas.[2] Śaivism shares with Vaiṣṇavism and Śāktaism the possession of vast Āgama literature, which only since fairly recently has attracted the attention of scholars (due particularly to the efforts of the French Institue of Indology in Pondicherry, India).

The Āgamas of Śaivism have a traditional fourfold classification: the Soma Āgamas, the Lākula (or Nākula) Āgamas, the Pāśupata Āgamas and the Śaiva Āgamas. The last of these is further divided into three groups: the left-hand (*vāma*) Āgamas of the Aghoras, Kāpālas and Kālāmukhas (the works of the last two are apparently lost to posterity); the right-hand (*dakṣiṇa*) Āgamas of Kashmir Śaivism or the Trika system, based on the *Svacchanda* and other Āgamas; and the twenty-eight Āgamas of Śaiva Siddhānta beginning with the *Kāmika-Āgama*. Geographically the home of Pāśupata Śaivism is Gujarat; that of Vīra Śaivism (probably a continuation of the Kālāmukhas) is Karnataka; that of Kashmir Śaivism is Kashmir; and that of Śaiva Siddhānta is Tamil Nadu. The dating of the earliest Āgamas is a matter of great uncertainty but on the basis of the evidence in the extant Āgamas, the earliest ones may have been composed some time around A.D. 400.

The term Śaiva Siddhānta is used by the Āgamas themselves (e.g., *Kāmika Āgama* 1:1, 113 and 119; *Suprabheda Āgama* 1:56,

16 and 2:1, 12) to stand for the doctrine they teach and is especially adopted by the Tamil works which also form a substantial portion of the tradition's corpus of literature. The Āgamas of Śaiva Siddhānta have been preserved in Sanskrit in the Grantha script, a script invented by the South Indians and one which bears a close resemblance to the characters of the Tamil language. One of the most significant landmarks in the literary development of Śaiva Siddhānta is the emergence of the so called Meykaṇṭha *śāstra*, i.e., those works in Sanskrit and Tamil that were composed through the influence of Meykaṇṭha (twelfth century). He is credited with having composed a work in Tamil called the *Śivajñānabodham*. There is considerable debate over the origin of this work, viz., whether it belonged to the *Raurava Āgama* and thus was originally in Sanskrit or whether it is in fact a Tamil original (see also p. 38). In the absence of any conclusive evidence the matter cannot be finally decided at the present time. Nonetheless, the text is extant in both the Sanskrit and the Tamil with several voluminous commentaries in both languages. Śivāgrayogin's *Śivāgrabhāṣya* is one such commentary in Sanskrit on the Sanskrit version of the *Śivajñānabodham*.

### *Śivāgrayogin and his time*

Śivāgrayogin is reputed to have lived definitely in the latter half of the sixteenth century, although his exact dates are uncertain. He is one among the line of commentators who were well versed in both Sanskrit and Tamil with access to source material in both languages. It would seem that Śaiva Siddhānta philosophical fervour was particularly strong during his time with model expositions of the tradition being given by him and his contemporaries who left behind insightful treatises, especially Jñānaprakāśa, Maraijñāna Deśika and Nirambavalagia, the last of whom wrote only in Tamil. Like some of his contemporaries (e.g., Jñānaprakāśa) Śivāgrayogin shows clear evidence of the enormous influence of Vedānta on the Indian philosophical scene. It is in this context that the *Śivajñānabodham* takes on a significance in Śaiva Siddhānta which corresponds to the status given to the *Brahmasūtra* in Vedānta. Thus, for example, the scholastic differences evident in the brands of Vedānta arising from commentaries on the *Brahmasūtra* bear striking resemblances to those in Śaiva Siddhānta arising from the commentaries on the *Śivajñānabodham*. Hence, the view of Jñānaprakāśa, for instance, is regarded as Śivasamavāda because of his doctrine that the *ātman* is "equal" to *śivam* in all respects whereas Śivāgrayogin teaches the doctrine of *bheda-abheda*, a unity in difference.

The chief works by Śivāgrayogin used in this study are his *Śivāgrabhāṣya* and *Śaivaparibhāṣā*, two works in Sanskrit which in many respects complement each other in their ideas as commentaries to the Sanskrit version of the *Śivajñānabodham*. These works bear the mark of classical scholasticism in the compact and often difficult style characteristic of Indian philosophical debate. They evince a traditional training in Sanskrit with the merits of argumentation techniques that go with it (see also his other Sanskrit works listed on p. 54, n. 103). Śivāgrayogin's acquaintance with rival views are skilfully used to arrive at the established position (*siddhānta*) on all matters concerning *śivam*, i.e., Śaiva Siddhānta. Very often, as is common with several classical commentators, the rival positions are not mentioned by name and this leaves a great deal of scope for speculation. It is clear, for example, that he does not follow the metaphysical presuppositions of Kashmir Śaivism. He nowhere mentions this school by name in the above two works and one may come to the conclusion of his rejection of its views only indirectly through his refutation of *śivādvaita* (obviously referring to the views of Śrīkaṇṭha, eleventh century, in his commentary to the *Brahmasūtra*).

The Āgamas of Śaivism are a treasure-house of information concerning doctrine, liturgy, religious practice (including ritual), architecture of the Śiva temples, sculpture of the images, and art in general as well. By the seventh or eighth century 'a crystallization process was under way which led also to the formation of more or less defined Śivaite doctrines and systems. Texts reflecting this formative period ase however wanting.'[3] By the time Śivāgrayogin wrote in the sixteenth century there was already an ongoing debate about the validity of the Āgamas as revealed scripture (*śruti*), i.e., whether the Āgamas occupy the supreme and infallible status accorded to the Vedas (see p. 134). Therefore, one of Śivāgrayogin's chief tasks (as it was also for the commentators on the Vaiṣṇava Āgamas) was to philosophically justify the Āgamas as *śruti* and then to proceed scholastically to establish the doctrine of Śaiva Siddhānta. Whilst Śivāgrayogin accepts both the Āgamas and the Vedas as authoritative, it is noteworthy that he justifies his philosophical standpoint by referring almost entirely to the former. Indeed, there is a striking resemblance between Śaṅkara's method of establishing Advaita Vedānta and Śivāgrayogin's Śaiva Siddhānta: just as Śaṅkara comments on the *Brahmasūtra* by carefully selecting Vedic, and especially Upaniṣadic statements, Śivāgrayogin's commentary on the *Śivajñānabodham* is based similarly on a few specific Āgamas.

It seems that the *Śivajñānabodham* acquired its canonical status around the thirteenth century through the influence of Meykaṇṭha. The impact of Meykaṇṭha's stamp on the development of the Saiva Siddhānta tradition is so strong that it would not be incorrect to say that the tradition, as it has survived to this day, evolved through his apparent exclusive emphasis on the *Śivajñānabodham*. This impact permeates both the Sanskrit and Tamil literature as they have come down to us today. With the influence of Vedānta already mentioned, Śivāgrayogin establishes his brand of Śaiva Siddhānta in the style and manner of Vedānta commentators.

Apart from its unique status in the tradition, the *Śivajñānabodham* has the special feature of comprising only twelve verses, making it perhaps one of the shortest religio-philosophical treatises. Śivāgrayogin does not seem to have much problem in elaborating the ideas pregnant in the text. His voluminous commentary attests this fact. What this implies is that the basic ideas of the line of Śaiva teachers to which Śivāgrayogin belonged, the Skanda-paramparā, were already fairly well established during his time. It is to his credit that he was able, skilfully and scholastically to collate the prevalent ideas of his school, combined with his own penetrating insights, to elucidate the inherent meaning of the very compact *Śivajñānabodham*. What he does, in effect, is to develop the Śaiva Siddhānta system of thought entirely from this short, and often cryptic, text and quotes several Āgamas as the authoritative sources for his insightful ideas.

Although Śivāgrayogin's profound contribution to the Śaiva Siddhānta tradition is undisputed, not much, if any, special study has been made on what may be called his *magnum opus*, the *Śivāgrabhāṣya*. The present study is largely based on it, even though it deals with one specific problem of the entire system, viz., the notion of *ātman/paśu*, which comprises the tradition's philosophical anthropology insofar as it is directly related to what constitutes a definition of man in the world. In putting across his views he evidently attempts to furnish a definition which accounts for both man's situation in the world—a situation which evinces a condition of human limitation and human fallibility—and the condition of the possibility of unhindered expression and manifestation of man's essential nature. It is in this sense that Śivāgrayogin may be said to make a significant contribution to the basic issues of philosophical anthropology. This study is, therefore, an attempt to present Śaiva Siddhānta through Śivāgrayogin's ideas on the subject. It attempts to unravel crucial basic concepts and presuppositions of the tradition, over which there seems to be a great vacuum on account of the dearth of works dealing with the philosophical aspects of Śaiva Siddhānta. In terms of Śivāgrayogin's work as a whole and in terms of the entire tradition, this study is but a small contribution. However, there is such a wealth of untapped source material that even this study, it is hoped, will stimulate further interest in this relatively ignored area of research.

## NOTES

1. Cf. "Already in the Veda the god Rudra, primarily the representative of the uncultivated, dangerous and unreliable aspects of nature, was called Śiva, "the Mild or Auspicious One" when this aspect of his ambivalent character was emphasized." J. Gonda, *A History of Indian Literature*, vol. II, fasc., 1 *Medieval Religious Literature in Sanskrit*. Wiesbaden: Otto Harrassowitz, 1977, p. 153. See also C.V. Narayana Ayyar, *Origin and Early History of Śaivism*, Madras: University of Madras, 1939, p. 4 (reprint, 1974) and Sri Tribhuvan Prasad Upadhyaya (ed.), *Bhāskarī*, vol. 3, Lucknow: New Government Press, 1954, p. v of the Introduction.

2. Although Śaiva Siddhānta accepts the authority of both the Āgamas and the Vedas, this is not the case with all branches of Śaivism. For example, Kashmir Śaivism "does not recognize the authority of the Veda." J. Gonda, *op. cit.*, p. 161.

3. *Ibid.*, p. 163.

# ACKNOWLEDGEMENTS

This study would not have been possible without the expert guidance of Professor K. Sivaraman. It was undertaken as a thesis under the title 'Toward an Understanding of Man in Śaiva Siddhānta: A Study in Philosophical Anthropology' in the Department of Religious Studies, McMaster University, Hamilton, Canada for my second doctoral degree. It is with sincere appreciation that I acknowledge Professor Sivaraman's supervision, especially in introducing me to the complicated system of Śaiva Siddhānta with the clarity and authority of one deeply involved with the philosophical issues of the tradition. He entrusted me with his personal and valuable Devanāgarī manuscript of the *Śivāgrabhāṣya,* transliterated from the Grantha original, on which this study is largely based. It was this kind gesture, together with his unfailing encouragement, that facilitated this study.

Professor J.G. Arapura has been most helpful with many valuable suggestions and clarifications which only he as an expert in Indian philosophy could make.

Professors G. Vallee and G.B. Madison displayed a great deal of support through their useful ideas and comments.

The basic research for this study was done in Madras, India where I had the privilege of working with Professor M. Narasimhacary of Madras University. I appreciate the seriousness with which he undertook to read with me the entire *Saṅgrahabhāṣya* of the *Śivāgrabhāṣya* with thoroughness and much needed urgency. His expert handling of the Sanskrit, with extreme patience and didactic skill, unravelled the innumerable difficult constructions of scholastic Sanskrit. I especially note the informality with which he gave me a glimpse into the benefit and value of traditional learning in India.

The Adyar Library, Madras, provided the ideal academic atmosphere in which to work. I had the added benefit of fruitful discussions with Professor K. Kunjunni Raja, Sanskritist and Honorary Director of the Adyar Library. He always made himself immediately available to attend to my numerous querries with great expertise and patience. The Librarian, Mrs. Seetha Neelakanthan, and the Assistant Librarian, Ms. Yamuna, were extremely helpful and made available to me all the library facilities, including a private section of the library in which to work.

The Theosophical Society itself, in which the Adyar Library is housed, provided the serene atmosphere and convenient living conditions in which to pursue consistent and continued work and I acknowledge the Society with gratitude.

Professor R. Balasubramaniam, Director of the Dr. S. Radhakrishnan Institute for Advanced Study in Philosophy, was very helpful not only in making available to me the facilities of the Institute's Library but, also, in discussing several issues related to this study. Further, while in Madras I had the benefit of useful and elucidating discussions with Professors V.A. Devasenapathi and P. Thirujanasambandhan.

I wish to acknowledge the interest shown in my study by Pandit N.R. Bhatt of the French Institute of Indology, Pondicherry. I have had the privilege of discussing with him some crucial issues concerning Śaiva Siddhānta, and Śaivism in general, and to have been able to take note of his insights and observations which carry the authority of years of involvement with the tradition. I also appreciate having been able to use the facilities of the Institute. I note especially the free access given to researchers to the hundreds of manuscripts, either in original or in transcript form. One can hardly not be struck by the wealth of material there that still needs to be researched in the relatively virgin field of Śaiva Siddhānta, and especially, Āgama Studies.

*Hamilton, Ontario*
*Canada*

JAYANDRA SONI

# SCHEME OF TRANSLITERATION

| *Vowels* | *Consonants* | |
|---|---|---|
| अ – a | क – k | त – t |
| आ – ā | ख – kh | थ – th |
| इ – i | ग – g | द – d |
| ई – ī | घ – gh | ध – dh |
| उ – u | ङ – ṅ | न – n |
| ऊ – ū | च – c | प – p |
| ऋ – ṛi | छ – ch | फ – ph |
| ॠ – ṛī | ज – j | ब – b |
| ऌ – lṛi | झ – jh | भ – bh |
| ॡ – lṛī | ञ – ñ | म – m |
| ए – e | ट – ṭ | य – y |
| ऐ – ai | ठ – ṭh | र – r |
| ओ – o | ड – ḍ | ल – l |
| औ – au | ढ – ḍh | व – v |
| | ण – ṇ | श – ś |
| | | ष – ṣ |
| Anusvāra (.)-ṁ | | स – s |
| Visarga (:)-ḥ | | ह – h |

# CONTENTS

CHAPTER 1

# Introduction

## 1.1 *Some basic questions in philosophical anthropology*

The question whether there is indeed a concern in Indian thought of what comes under the theme of 'philosophical anthropology' is a moot one, especially since it has been said that the theme is conspicuous by its very absence.[1] If, however, the inquiry about the nature of man is 'the basic question or starting point of anthropology',[2] then access is provided into practically all the systems of thought in India for an investigation from the standpoint of philosophical anthropology. The problem of what exactly constitutes the essential nature or characteristic nature of man can be said to be common, *mutatis mutandis*, to all Indian systems of thought, even for those who deny—as the Buddhists and Cārvākas do—a permanent, unchanging principle in man. In this context there is no semantic difference between what constitutes self-knowledge and what concerns the inquiry into the nature of man. A study of man, among other things, must necessarily be a study of man in the world, of man in relation to the inalienable environment. Whilst man and the world have to be investigated together, indeed at one and the same time—insofar as man forms part of the world—both cannot be approached by the same mode of investigation:

> We cannot discover the nature of man in the same way that we can detect the nature of physical things. Physical things may be described in terms of their objective properties, but man may be described and defined only in terms of his consciousness.[3]

Whereas the description and definition of man through the mode of consciousness seems to be the proper formula for an inquiry into the nature of man, it seems also proper to say, in the context of man in the world:

> Contradiction is the very element of human existence. Man has no "nature"—no simple or homogeneous being. He is a strange mixture of being and non-being. His place is between these two opposite poles.[4]

The questions which are universally accepted in philosophical anthropology are the basic ones of epistemology, ethics and theology asked by Kant: 'What can I know?' 'What ought I to do?' 'What may I hope?'[5] This point, together with Feuerbach's claim that 'man can be used as the common denominator of philosophy,'[6] makes possible an investigation from the perspective of philosophical anthropology of any system of thought that attempts a description and definition of man in the world. Such an investigation would be meaningful even if—as is the case with several Indian schools of thought—the essential nature of man is ultimately contrasted with that of the physical, empirical world, through which, in fact, the former may be realized. Thus, one of the most significant goals of philosophical anthropology is its 'attempt to construct a scientific discipline out of man's traditional effort to understand and liberate himself.'[7] From the perspective of the Śaiva Siddhānta tradition, this goal is identical with the soteriological function furnished by the analysis of the system of categories which constitute our knowledge of the nature of ultimate reality, of which man's essential nature occupies a central position.

One of the notable features that characterized philosophical anthropologists in the western tradition was the 'conviction that the theory of knowledge had reached a desperate crisis' and that:

> Traditional theory of knowledge is seen by them as occupied only with one of the functions of consciousness; and consciousness, in turn, is understood to present only a part of the forces shaping human reason (as distinguished, in the Kantian sense, from understanding).[8]

Without stretching the argument too far, this point can be transferred to the Indian context where for such schools as Sāṅkhya, Yoga, and Vedānta, the nature of consciousness (*cit*) is considered to constitute the essential nature of man and, particularly in Śaiva Siddhānta, where consciousness is also not only the factor which makes knowledge as such possible but is the ultimate means by which cognition is possible as well. Further, in Śaiva Siddhānta, the manifestation of consciousness, evident in its epistemological operation in man, is but a limited expression of its powers—but through which, nonetheless, access can be provided to a knowledge of the full range of consciousness and its powers.[9] It is in this sense that Śaiva Siddhānta can be said to address the theme of contemporary philosophical anthropology, namely, 'to establish a complete picture of the potentialities open to man'.[10]

In contrast to things which always remain unchanged in our knowledge of them, it is significant to note at the outset of any philosophical anthropology 'one unusual and important fact: man's knowledge of man is not without effect on man's being'.[11] This point has a direct bearing on 'the influence of human self-interpretation on human self-formation'[12] and with this the theme, with its focus on the nature of the species 'man', is now transferred particularly to the individual of this species. It is in this context that such concepts as 'self-knowledge', 'selfhood', 'self-realization', 'self-consciousness', 'self-understanding' and the general concern with the problem of the 'self' become meaningful within the specific theme of man. A brief, concise description of what constitutes the ultimate significance of anthropology which captures the ongoing concern with it from the philosophical standpoint—applicable also within the Indian tradition—is given by Michael Landmann:

> Man does not, like other beings, simply exist, but he inquisitively asks about and interprets himself; the concept of man (*anthrōpos*) implies anthropology. This is not mere optional, theoretical speculation; it springs from the deepest necessity of a being that must shape itself and therefore needs an orientational model or *Leitbild* to go by. Man's incompletion is compensated for by self-understanding, which tells him how he can perfect himself. His interpretation of himself does not stand separate from an immutable reality; rather, although intending merely to interpret, it has a formative effect on that reality.[13]

Śaiva Siddhānta offers precisely such a *Leitbild* and the task of this study is to attempt to extract from this theological system of thought those features which fall specifically within the section dealing with man. It may be noted here that whilst Śaiva Siddhānta anthropology is inextricably connected with Śaiva Siddhānta theology, special attention is given to the former, as the title of this study explicitly states. Apart from brief references to place the task at hand within the context of the entire Śaiva Siddhānta tradition, the theological aspect will be dealt with summarily at the end of the study to show specifically how the anthropology forms part of the theology.[14]

Despite the fact that, especially since the turn of the century, philosophical anthropology encompasses a vast scope absorbing elements of different disciplines,[15] what Max Scheler wrote before the First World War in his essay 'On the Idea of Man' is no less profound today: 'In a certain sense all central problems of philosophy can be traced back to the question of what man is.'[16] Although this is a wide conception of what philosophical anthropology attempts to deal with, it still refers to what constitutes its distinctive feature and original meaning, namely, to describe 'the basic knowledge of human nature and of the human condition.'[17] This point cannot be taken to mean that philosophical anthropology furnishes final answers to the problem of man without concern for what is a truism in any philosophical activity, viz., without taking into account the variables in all facets concerning man:

> Anthropology, far from ignoring variability, supports it by revealing the conditions that cause it. Its relationship to human variability is like that of structural linguistics to the variety of the languages.[18]

Transferred to the Indian context, this means that whilst a description is attempted of what constitutes the essential nature of man, the description also attempts to account for the evident multifaceted and multidimensional nature of man in the world. Śaiva Siddhānta is one *Leitbild* in this context.

In the light of what has been said above, the implicit answer to the question concerning whether there is at all a concern in

Indian thought of what comes under the theme of philosophical anthropology, is obviously in the positive.

## 1.2 *Philosophical anthropology in Indian thought*

Insofar as the classical systems of Indian thought generally agree that liberation (*mokṣa* or *mukti*) is the highest aim to be achieved, it is man who is directly addressed as the one supremely capable of realizing this goal.[19] This implicit anthropology, or focus on man, serves a soteriological function in the philosophical systems whose ultimate aim is *mokṣa.* It is significant to note that for each of the four traditionally accepted objects of human pursuits (*puruṣārthas*)[20] not only does the word for 'man' have its equivalent in Sanskrit (*puruṣa*), but that among these, liberation is the highest goal man can strive for. The significance of this lies in the fact that liberation is to be pursued by man, that it is an endeavour intrinsically human, and that it is a goal which is identical with the realization of man's essential nature which, by comparison, is inadequately presented in the other pursuits.[21]

Further, there is no single perspective in the Indian tradition which can claim the monopoly for furnishing universally accepted solutions to the problem of man. It is a noteworthy fact that there has been a considerable 'interplay among the viewpoints'[22] evident in the elaborate philosophical argumentation of the literature of practically all the systems in India, even though the 'opponent', or the opposite viewpoint, may not be explicitly stated. What this signifies is that though the other views are criticized, there is, nonetheless, an awareness of the various perspectives or standpoints of the other schools, albeit unacceptable. And insofar as the subject of the debate on the theme of *mokṣa* is man, each school implicitly develops its own anthropology.

Whilst the views on *mokṣa* as an object of human pursuit (*puruṣārtha*) represent the soteriological aspect of each viewpoint, they permeate, nonetheless, the other branches of philosophical activity, namely, epistemology, ethics, and even logic.[23] Although the description of *mokṣa* contains elements which by definition have to be ineffable, a glimpse into its essential nature can be meaningful, in the final analysis, only in terms of the categories of our understanding, limited though they may be ultimately. The emphasis here is on experience (*anubhava* or *bhoga*) and not on description (*lakṣaṇa*).[24] The pursuit of *mokṣa* culminating in the experience of *mokṣa*, is explicitly and by definition, a human experience because *mokṣa* is a *puruṣārtha*, a goal pursued by man. The condition of the possibility of the experience of *mokṣa* is presupposed in the description of it, and both experience and description imply a fundamental philosophical anthropology.

Indian schools of philosophy are notoriously divided on the issue of what constitutes the essential nature of man, evident in their descriptions of *mokṣa*. This is the case even where certain elements are common to many schools as, for example, the view that a description of the role of consciousness (*cit*) features prominently, if not chiefly, in a discussion on man's essential nature, and the view that epistemological issues are crucial to any philosophical anthropology. This situation makes evident the fertile ground around the problem concerning man where ideas and concepts are discussed with greater clarity and precision in the ongoing debates of the various schools.[25] Chronologically, the later schools would seem to have been at an advantage insofar as an opportunity for a different perspective was provided in the face of constant criticism and debate. There was scope for an interpretation, or reinterpretation, of the traditional views in the light of perspectives hitherto accepted. Śaiva Siddhānta is one such school which makes no apologies for drawing from, and building on, the 'pool' of ideas and concepts, whilst at the same time making evident its own unique position.[26]

In putting forward the Śaiva Siddhānta standpoint, the 'upholders' or 'protectors' (*ācāryas*) of the tradition follow the classical scholastic tradition of first assessing the viability of the 'other view' (*pūrva-pakṣa*)—be it an identifiable view of a particular school, or a hypothetical (albeit unacceptable) one which needs to be considered for clarity's sake—before arriving at their own established conclusion (*siddhānta*).[27] Whilst this dialogic or dialectic approach is elaborately followed by upholders of the tradition, it features evidently in the Āgama texts which are regarded as the infallible and authoritative works of the Śaiva Siddhānta tradition.[28] Thus, the method of arriving at the Siddhānta position presupposes an acquaintance with the basic standpoints of the 'other' views, through which the original contribution of the Siddhāntin becomes more striking.[29]

## 1.3 *The terminological framework supporting Śaiva Siddhānta philosophical anthropology*

Śaiva Siddhānta has an intricately worked out doctrine of categories with a detailed description of their nature and functions. The word for 'category' or 'principle' as the tradition uses it is *tattva*. It is derived from the neuter pronominal base *tad* with the suffix *-tva*, added to any noun base, to form the neuter abstract substantive *tattva* (the rules for euphonic changes require the 'd' of *tad* to be replaced by 't'). *Tattva* means: 'true or real state', 'truth', 'reality', 'a true principle'. The synonym that is often used is *padārtha*, which literally means 'the meaning' (*artha*) 'of a word' (*pada*), or 'that which corresponds to the meaning of a word' and, therefore, 'a thing' or 'material object'. It is from these meanings that the term is used to denote 'a category' or 'predicament'. The theory of *tattvas* or *padārthas* serves as a framework, or catalogue, classifying in a broad way what constitutes the basic vocabulary of any system's philosophical perspective.[30]

### 1.3 (a) *The ontological categories*

Siddhānta talks of *tattvas* at two levels which, for convenience' sake, may be referred to as the ontological and cosmological levels. At one level the *tattvas* refer to what stand for ultimate reality, where the *tattvas* signify what has an ontological status, in the sense of being concerned with the 'essence' of things or 'being' in the abstract, but no less *real*. At this level, three *tattvas* are spoken of: *śivam, ātman* and *malam*. Referring to Pāṇini's *Uṇādisūtra*, i, 153, Monier Williams gives the derivation of *Śiva* from the verbal root *śī* which, together with an affix called *kṛit* in Sanskrit used to form a noun, means 'in whom [or what] all things lie'.[31] *Śivam* thus stands for a 'receptacle' or the substrate of ultimate reality constituted of the three *tattvas*. The implication of this meaning, from the Siddhāntin's point of view, is that without *śivam* the status of the other two *tattvas* has no basis. In other words, a discussion of ultimate reality as Śaiva Siddhānta postulates it, necessitates, in the final analysis, a consideration of all three *tattvas* for a proper understanding of the Śaiva Siddhānta perspective.[32]

Without entering into the proofs for the existence of *śivam*—which ultimately are a vindication of the authority of Śaiva Siddhānta scripture—an attempt may be made to give an idea of this complicated concept by citing a few descriptions of it:[33]

> The reality is free from differentiation; it is knowledge, bliss and non-dual. There are neither names nor forms for Śiva, the supreme self.[34]
>
> It is not known by perception, nor is it known by inference, nor is Śaṅkara's [*śivam's*] nature the object of verbal testimony.[35]
>
> ...but *śivam* is declared as being difficult to be known [even] by these and other means of cognition.[36]
>
> *Śiva-tattva* [*śivam*], the peak of all paths, is spoken of thus: unknowable, indescribable, incomparable, stainless, subtle, omnipresent, eternal, firm, indestructible, majestic.[37]
>
> In the Śaiva-Āgamas, Śiva is to be known as: [one] devoid of a beginning, a middle and an end; naturally devoid of *mala*; sovereign, omniscient and perfect.[38]

Whilst the essential nature of *śivam* is inscrutable, ineffable and uncognizable—as evinced in the above quotations—it is nonetheless what can be *known* or, rather, experienced (as explicitly constituting the fact of *mokṣa*). This is evident in verse six of the *Śivajñāna-bodham* which arrives at this conclusion arguing in the following way:

> If it is not seen it is non-existent (*asat*), if it is seen it is insentient (*jaḍa*). The wise ones declare that the nature (*rūpam*) of Śambhu [*śivam*] is to be known differently from [knowing] these two [*asat* and *jaḍa*].[39]

In his commentary on this verse Śivāgrayogin[40] says: "... the wise ones who have the vision, experience [it],"[41] and 'experience' here has the deliberate overtones, for example, of 'the experience of joy'.

An inherent component of the concept of *śivam*, and one that is often used interchangeably with it, is *śakti* or *śiva-śakti*. This feminine gender word literally means things like 'power', 'strength', 'ability' and 'energy'. *Śakti* is the *means* by which *śivam* is manifest and whilst, in one sense, the one can be distinguished from the other, the two together constitute one *tattva* at the ontological level. *Śakti* is thus coexistent with and part of the nature of *śivam*. With regard to *śakti* being the means by which *śivam* is manifest, *śakti* is said to be an 'instrument' (*karaṇa*). This significant qualification serves as the basis for the view in Śaiva Siddhānta theology that the cosmological functions of creation, preservation and destruction, attributed in the final analysis to *śivam*, are possible through *śakti* as the instrument:

> This instrument can be none other than *śakti* itself; it cannot be unintelligent because it must be intelligent; though one, it appears as manifold in perception and activity, on account of the variety of objects.[42]

The description of *śivam* as pure consciousness (*cit*) is useful for describing *śakti* as an abbreviation for *cit-śakti*, the power of consciousness which is inherent to consciousness itself. In this way consciousness can be seen as becoming manifest through a power which coexists with it: 'Verily, the *cit-śakti* which is inherent to *śivam* is only one;'[43] and further: 'This pure *śakti* of *śivam* is inherent to it; on account of its [*śakti's*] differentiated activity, it is said to be the body of Sādākhya'.[44] The significance and indispensability of *cit-śakti* are seen in the fact, as the Siddhāntin sees it, that: 'The entire universe is maintained by it [*cit-śakti*] which, though one, has many forms.'[45]

*Śakti* plays a crucial role in Śaiva Siddhānta, especially since it is indispensable not only for its soteriological function, but for all activity as such. In this sense it constitutes the essential feature of the *ātman* (and, therefore, that of man), also described as being characterized by consciousness and, thereby, inherently possessing the power of consciousness. The discussion on the relationship between the power of consciousness of *śivam* (*śiva-śakti*) and that of the *ātman* (*ātma-cit-śakti*) will be dealt with later. Suffice it to say for the moment that in both the cases consciousness expresses itself through a power which, as already seen, is one power but which is spoken of as being of three kinds: that of volition (*icchā-śakti*), of knowledge (*jñāna-śakti*), and of action or activity (*kriyā-śakti*). One can hardly over-emphasize the unique slant of the Śaiva Siddhānta perspective of considering the means or power of expression of consciousness within the definition of consciousness itself, especially since this position is a significant deviation from that of the Sāṅkhya, Yoga and Advaita Vedānta views.

The concern with the categories of *ātman* and *malam* is the special subject-matter of this study noting, of course, that *śivam*, via *śakti*, permeates every aspect of Siddhānta thought. *Ātman* and *malam* are the chief categories for the understanding of man in Śaiva Siddhānta. For reasons which should become clear in the course of the study, these categories go together, up to a point. Their separation marks the liberation of the *ātman* at which point *malam*, having become impotent, loses its influence over the *ātman*. A few descriptions of these two categories may be cited at this stage for a basic understanding of the framework of Śaiva Siddhānta vocabulary.

The word *ātman* is variously translated as: 'essence', 'nature', 'character', 'the self' or 'the individual soul'. In all cases it constitutes the animating principle in man, identical with the reference to man as a sentient being, one endowed with the principle of consciousness. In this respect *ātman* shares with *śivam* the essential nature of consciousness—together with the powers of consciousness manifest in volition, knowledge, and action—common to both. Whilst the essential nature of both is, therefore, identical, the tradition regards the relationship between them as one of an identity-in-difference (*bheda-abheda*).[46]

Insofar as the *ātman* is characterized by consciousness, a description of its essential nature is bound to include elements as difficult to grasp as that of *śivam's*:

> The supreme *ātman* is celebrated as: all-knowing, all-pervading, tranquil, the essence of all [beings], facing all directions, be-

> yond the sense organs, self-supporting, very subtle, eternal, unchanging, entirely without parts, impossible to be made known adequately, all-pervasive, constant, incomparable. When there is the manifestation of this light, the one abiding in it would obtain the state of *śivam*.[47]

And further:

> One should contemplate the *ātman* through the *ātman*; the abode of the *ātman* is verily in the *ātman*.[48]

The significance for man, whose essential nature constitutes that of the *ātman*, is clear: 'There exists no greater knowledge than that of the *ātman*. One should be intent on this knowledge of *ātman*; what the *ātman* is is the supreme.'[49]

If the *ātman* is regarded as the essence of man, then the above descriptions of it as all-knowing, all-pervasive, etc., defy the need, as Śaiva Siddhānta sees it, for the realization of its eternal nature. This is a crucial problem and it may be said to be the basic issue in Siddhānta philosophical anthropology. Suffice it to say at this stage that the *ātman* is *unable* to manifest itself, and when it does so in man, its manifestation is a limited or fettered one. Moreover, since by definition—as the cited descriptions show—it cannot intrinsically limit or fetter itself, the cause for this state of the *ātman* must be said to be extrinsic to it. This point leads to a consideration of the third category of ultimate reality at the ontological level, viz., *malam*.

The word *malam* literally means: 'dirt', 'filth' 'dust or impurity' in both the physical and metaphysical senses. The arguments for the existence of *malam*[50] as a constituent of ultimate reality—consisting of three irreducible, distinct and eternal categories—fall specifically within the problem of man in Śaiva Siddhānta. *Malam* is associated only with *ātman,* which means that it is related to the essence of man. The Siddhāntin is careful not to consider *śivam* with even the semblance of a trace of *malam*. These two categories are mutually exclusive in their essential natures—although both are parts of the three-fold ontological structure of ultimate reality—with the former being characterized as light (*prakāśa*) and consciousness (*cit*), and the latter as darkness (*tamas*) and insentient (*acit* or *jaḍa*).[51]

*Malam* is a restrictive agent which fetters the expression of *ātman's* powers, evident in the limited knowledge that man possesses, though intrinsically all-knowing. The *Pauṣkara Āgama* argues this point in the following way:

> The *ātman* is covered by *malam*, therefore, it has limited knowledge, although omniscient [intrinsically]; whoever is not one who has limited knowledge, is not restricted by *malam*—like Śiva; therefore, not being such a one, *ātman* is covered by *malam*.[52]

Whereas Śaiva Siddhānta scripture is the final authority as regards the view of the three-fold structure of ultimate reality, there can be no contradiction in arguing, particularly with reference to *malam*, that its existence is derived from the analysis of the human predicament. It is man's finitude, limitedness, and involvement in the throes of the oscillation between experiences of joy and suffering—alien to man's essential nature when it can manifest itself fully, once it is liberated from these factors—that point to a cause for this predicament. For the Siddhāntin this cause is *malam* and, ironically, it is this condition—that of the subjection to its influence—which should lead to the need to overcome it, culminating in the expression of *ātman's* essential nature. A more detailed discussion of these points will have to be postponed until the constitution of man, as seen from the Śaiva Siddhānta perspective, is more closely analysed. What is being attempted for the moment, is to provide the framework indispensable for the treatment of man in Śaiva Siddhānta and the place of *malam* in this framework.

Siddhānta speaks of three kinds of *malam*, viz., *āṇava, karman* and *māyā*. When only the word *malam* is used, it usually refers to the first of these, *āṇava-malam*. The adjective *āṇava* is derived from the word *aṇu* which means: 'fine', 'minute', 'atomic'. It is spoken of as the primordial or original *malam* because *ātman* is 'born with' it (*sahaja*). It is an adjunct which confines the all-knowing and all-pervasiveness of *ātman*. It is what makes the *ātman* 'minute', it makes it an *aṇu*, which means that the *ātman* becomes limited, restricted and fettered. *Āṇava-malam* is said to completely enshroud the *ātman*, offering it no scope at all for the manifestation and expression of its powers of volition, knowledge and action. The *ātman* is thus isolated. Iṭ is at this point that *karma-malam* and *māyā-malam*—said to be adventitious or consequential (*āgantuka*)—offer the *ātman's* powers a modicum of manifestation and limited operation. These two kinds of *malam* will be dealt with later in greater detail. What is to be noted is that without them, the *ātman*, and, therefore, man, is in a forlorn and helpless state.

What has been attempted thus far is an introduction to Śaiva Siddhānta vocabulary as a background to the discussion on man. In dealing with the categories (*tattvas*), the ontological level at which they may be referred to was first considered, viz., as *śivam*, *ātman* and *malam*. Within this level, three more categories have to be referred to. One way to derive them would be to bear in mind the role of *malam*. It was said that it shrouds the *ātman* and thereby fetters it. In other words, *malam* is a bond, a shackle, which holds the *ātman* captive, as it were, restraining and confining it. It is in this context that *malam* is referred to as *pāśam* which literally means: a 'noose', 'chain', or 'fetter'. With its limiting effect on the *ātman*, the *ātman* becomes a *paśu*, a bound entity. It is not incidental that the literal meaning of *paśu* as a 'tethered animal' refers to the plight or predicament of the *ātman*. Extending the metaphor of the *ātman* having become a *paśu* or animal, one can speak of a lord or *pati*—which would be an abbreviation for *paśu-pati*, the lord of animals. Thus the status of a lord is attributed to *pati* who is said to 'take care' of the *paśus*. It is in this role as *pati* that *śivam* operates—through *śakti*—as the agent (*kartṛi*) of the cosmological functions of creation, preservation and destruction. It is *pati* who takes pity over the plight of *paśu* under the spell of *āṇava-malam* and aids the *ātman* in breaking the shackles of *malam* which is done, ironically, by *pati* instigating the operation of *karma-malam* and *māyā-malam*—with which or through which, the *ātman* is given the opportunity to wreak its liberation.

### 1.3 (b) *The cosmological categories*

The second level at which Śaiva Siddhānta categories (*tattvas*) may be discussed is what was referred to as the cosmological level, which applies with specific reference to the 36 categories derived from *māyā* (*-malam*). It may be repeated that *māyā* is one of the three kinds of *malam*—the other two being *āṇava* and *karman*—and that it is from this aspect of the ontological category of *malam* that the 36 categories, beginning with pure sound (*nāda*) and ending with the category 'earth' (*pṛithivī*), are derived at what may be called the cosmological level. At this level the gross manifestation of 'matter' as earth, is ultimately derived from the abstract category of pure sound, which in turn is derived from 'pure matter' (*śuddha-māyā*) which is an aspect of what constitutes a fetter (*pāśa*) and which, further, is ultimately a pseudonym for the ontologically limiting adjunct, viz., *malam*. The crucial point with reference to the 36 categories, as will be seen, is that each one is prescribed a specific role or function and it is with such categories as the intellect, the ego and the sense organs, that their relevance for man is vital. Indeed, whilst these specific categories pertain especially to man, their significance has to be seen in the framework of the ontological categories of ultimate reality, in which the essence of man, the *ātman*, occupies a central position.

Before dealing with the 36 principles or categories (*tattvas*) which are derived from, and said to be the 'evolutes' of *māyā*, a few preliminary remarks may be made in attempting to unravel the intricate and complicated doctrine of Śaiva Siddhānta categories. *Māyā* is the basic stuff which constitutes the sphere in which, and through which, man's experiences in the world take place. *Māyā*, it must be remembered, is one kind of *malam* and is, therefore, insentient. In simple terms, it may be referred to as 'matter' which, of its own accord, is unable to cause any effect. It needs a motivating sentient agent which instigates and sets into motion an evolutionary process by instilling or infusing it with a dynamism intrinsically alien to it.[53] This agent is *śakti*, the power of consciousness inherent to *śivam* and is itself characterized essentially as consciousness. As pure matter, *māyā* is an abstract category arrived at, in the final analysis, through a reflection on man's empirical experience of it. The 'ascent' to pure matter from the experience of the world and the 'descent' from pure matter to the concrete world constitute a reflective analysis which, on the one hand, represents the condition of the possibility of realizing the essential natures of the three ontological categories of ultimate reality, viz., *śivam*, *ātman* and *malam* and, on the other hand, accounts for man's common, everyday experiences.

It is to be noted that it is only the *ātman*—the essential nature of man—which is in the unique position of being able to distinguish the difference between the other two categories of ultimate reality. This special feature should emerge in greater detail and with a stronger impact at each stage of this study. What is to be noted at present is the implication of the Siddhānta view that the *ātman* is in the unique position of 'directing its attention' both on *śivam* and *malam*. In one sense this is a logical conclusion. It was already stated that *śivam* and *malam* are exclusive categories with absolutely no relation between them. Therefore, it can only be the *ātman* which can experience both, chiefly (as will be further explained) on account of 'sharing' the natures of both: as a sentient being, the essence of the *ātman* is characterized by consciousness, which it shares with *śivam*; and as a being involved in worldly experience, it partakes of the objects of experience which are of the insentient nature of *malam*. In dealing with the categories, we are concerned precisely with the latter. The doctrine of the 36 categories constitutes the universe of our experience, the 'theatre' of man's life in the world, the indispensable sphere in which not only does man's nature have a scope for expression but also one which can bring about the awareness of its (*ātman*'s) unique position which, as will be seen, constitutes self-knowledge, i.e., *ātman*'s knowledge of itself.

*Māyā* alone is insufficient to account for the varied experiences of life in the world which the *ātman* undergoes. The involvement in experiences is more intricate for the Siddhāntin than a mere account of the principles which make up human experience. Life in the world is fraught with inconsistencies and apparently absurd situations. This reality too has to be taken into account and so a complementary principle needs to be acknowledged. Thus, *māyā* and *karman* operate together and make possible man's life in the world. The definition of *māyā*, therefore, is:

> It is one, it is inauspicious, it is the seed of the universe, and is possessed of diverse powers. It is indestructible, all-pervasive,

> and one which is a hindrance until the cessation of the authority of its cooperator [*karman*].[54]

This quotation brings out the restrictive power that *māyā*, as a kind of *malam*, has over the *ātman*. It also points out the efficacy of its power as being dependent on the operation of *karman*. Whilst *māyā* (with *karman*, which will be dealt with in the next section) is a restrictive power—which means that it hinders the full expression of the *ātman's* nature—this power turns out to be beneficent in relation to the overwhelming capacity of *āṇava-malam* which offers the *ātman* no scope at all for expression and manifestation. The eternal status of *māyā* referred to in the last quotation is described in the following way:

> At the time of the destruction of the universe the products which have it [*māyā*] as the substratum are in the form of [latent] power. At the time of [*māyā*'s] transformation the manifested forms are employed for the fulfilment (*siddhaye*) of [their] purposes.[55]

The inferential argument which establishes the existence of the category of *māyā* is similar to that which accounts for the category of *śivam*. Just as the existence of the universe as a created product points to an agent responsible for it, so too the objects of the universe point to some basic stuff out of which they evolve. The argument runs thus:

> For the same reason that an agent is inferred through the nature of the universe [viz., that it is a product and, hence, requires an agent responsible for it], there is also a material cause [of the universe]; without threads there can be no piece of cloth.[56]

One more significant description of *māyā* may be cited here by way of justifying the need to postulate such a category which offers man a scope for experience in the world (through which a limited expression and manifestation of the *ātman* becomes evident). The following quotation, in the form of rhetorical questions, refers to the description of it, already given above, as being indestructible and ubiquitous:

> If it were non-eternal whence is produced this product [universe] again? If it were not all-pervasive how would it be everywhere amongst all?[57]

This description of *māyā* obviates the problem of accounting for the material cause of the universe in each phase of the recurrent cycle of creation, preservation and destruction. It also describes the Śaiva Siddhānta position as a realist one. *Māyā* is a category that has a *real* status and man's experience of it as the substrate of the things in the world is not illusive, as is the case with the objects of dream experience. As the material cause of the universe it has an eternal status which it retains even in the so-called phase of destruction where it exists in a potential form:

> That wherein the universe is contained at the time of sleep [destruction] and having been created proceeds forth, is that by which it is called, *māyā*; it is said to be that by the great preceptors.[58]

In postulating this category at the very outset of its systematic account of what constitutes human experience, Śaiva Siddhānta avoids an infinite regress as regards the material cause of the universe. If *māyā* were not ultimately real and thus annihilated at the time of destruction, some material cause would have to be postulated when creation takes place again. In other words, if there were an origin of *māyā* an explanation would have to be given to account for this origin. Then an explanation for the source of this origin would be necessary, and so on. This problem is obviated by saying that *māyā* is unoriginated and, thus, can have no end, or that it has an origin that is beginningless (*anādi*). This is a euphemistic way of saying that it is beyond human capacity to conceive of the ultimate status of *māyā*, not only because all the categories of our understanding and experience are limited through the very evolutes of *māyā*, but also because–at least theoretically–one would have to step out of the framework of *māyā* in order to grasp its reality.

By saying that the knowledge of the ultimate status of *māyā* is beyond human capacity to have such knowledge, what is implied is that such a knowledge is impossible through *māyā* itself. Insofar as the condition of the possibility of liberation from all fetters, including that of *māyā*, is presupposed in the theory of *mokṣa*, a knowledge of ultimate reality is in fact tacitly accepted. For man in the world, this condition is possible, finally, only through *māyā*. That is to say that *māyā* is the fetter through which the *ātman* finally becomes fetterless. *Māyā* is a ladder, as it were, which has to be discarded when its purpose is served. The hierarchy of the 36 categories of *māyā* are the rungs which, step by step through a transcendental reflection on them, forge the rift between what constitutes the essence of *māyā* as a kind of *malam*, and the essence of man (i.e., the *ātman*) which is the animate factor in all human experience—albeit limited by the strictures of *māyā*. It will be seen that *māyā* cannot provide the authentic means of what constitutes knowledge. It undoubtedly constitutes the medium through which man undergoes experience in the world and through which, among other things, cognition takes place. However, knowledge as such, i.e., knowledge of what is ultimately real, is through a means other than that of *māyā*, viz., *cit-śakti*.

In the light of what has been said above, one can speak of the soteriological function of the doctrine of the 36 *tattvas*. This will be dealt with in more detail at a later stage. What is being attempted here is an explanation of the constituents of human experience, in which context it has to be constantly borne in mind that these constituents are insentient by nature. They are the *tattvas* which are derived from *māyā*, a kind of *malam*, and they share naturally the basic insentience characteristic of *malam*. *Māyā appears* as if it bears manifold powers but power as such (*śakti*) is, firstly, an inextricable component of *śivam*—which is the instrument responsible for creation, preservation, and destruction on *śivam*'s behalf—and, secondly, *śakti* is a component also of the *ātman*. In other words, *śivam* and *ātman* are the only sentient categories of the three-fold structure of the ultimate reality and any manifestation of consciousness is possible, in the final analysis, only through either of these two principles. In the present context we are concerned with the essence of man, the *ātman*, in its relation to *māyā* which makes up the features of human experience. It is the *ātman*, characterized by consciousness, which has at its disposal the convenience of the categories which constitute man's experience in the world, and not vice versa. In the reflective analysis of the significance and functions of the 36 *tattvas*, the *tattvas* are to be seen as intended chiefly for providing a scope for *ātman*'s experiences through which (experiences) it comes to realize its own nature.[59]

The way in which man's essential nature—the *ātman* characterized as consciousness—can be realized is by coming to grips with what constitutes man's experiences in the world. This process is identical, firstly, with the analysis of the categories through which an understanding of the role of *māyā* is provided and, secondly, with the reflective analysis which leads to a knowledge, or experience, of the difference between the natures of both *māyā*—as a kind of *malam*—and the *ātman*. At this stage we are concerned with the former which pertains more specifically to man's state in the world. It is not necessary to enter into a detailed description of each category of *māyā* individually since their specific significance for man would be lost without seeing them in the context, e.g., of the states of consciousness—the states which the *ātman* undergoes (*ātma-avasthās*) —and the role of the *ātman* as it features in man as a knowing, cognizing being, i.e., the epistemological role of the categories in making possible man's experience in the world. (It is in this context, further, that the soteriological function of the categories would become more meaningful with reference to man.) Suffice it for the present to give a broad and general classification of the 36 categories. Several of these categories are not adequately translatable into English by a single word and so the Sanskrit original is retained.

It was said that *māyā* is (together with *karman*, to be considered in the next section) one of the two adventitious or consequential (*āgantuka*) *malam* and as a *malam* it is said to have a beginningless origin—and in this sense it can be spoken of as being unoriginated. Its function and role (together with *karman*) are necessitated as a kind of antidote to counteract the overwhelming influence of *āṇava-malam* on the *ātman*'s powers of expression and manifestation. *Māyā* is an unconscious entity and is the stuff out of which the objects of man's experiences come to be and through which man experiences them. This means that *māyā* cannot act on its own but that it has to be 'acted upon' by a conscious principle. The *ātman* is incapable of doing this because of the 'power' of *āṇava-malam* over it and, hence, it is only *śivam*, the conscious principle par excellence, which can 'act on' *māyā*—through which (together with *karman*) the *ātman* is given the possibility to express its powers of volition, knowledge and action. *Śivam* does not perform this gracious act 'directly' but *wills* it through the intrinsic power (*śakti*) for the sake of the *ātman*. In this context, *śivam* may be referred to as *pati* who 'takes pity' over the *ātman* which has become an *aṇu* or a *paśu* on account of *āṇava-malam*. Thus, *śivam* condescends, as it were, to 'rescue' the *ātman* through *śakti* and every role of *śivam* has to be put in the hands of *śakti* as the instrument of *śivam*. Therefore, the operation of *māyā* is possible only through the power of instigation provided by the *śakti* of *śivam*.

Whilst it is usual to speak of the evolutes of *māyā*—the 36 categories—as evolving out of itself, such a description is a contradiction in terms because, as is evident from what has just been said, *māyā* is incapable of evolving without *śakti*. One could attempt to understand the origin of the categories instigated by *śakti* in the following way: firstly, *śakti* initiates what may be described as a chain reaction, with the result that those categories which initially evolve out of *māyā* show evidence of *śakti*'s role more directly by being 'closer' to the original stuff out of which they emerge, at the incitation of *śakti*; secondly, and consequently, the evidence of *śakti* can be said to be progressively 'blurred' in the evolution of the grosser categories which evidently constitute the stuff of man's everyday experience in the world. Thus, the categories have a dynamism which is not their own intrinsically, and to this may be added the point that in the order of the discovery and knowledge of the categories in the Śaiva Siddhānta scheme, man proceeds from the latter to the former, i.e., from the gross manifestations of *māyā*, such as the objects of the world, to the subtle ones such as pure sound.[60] In this process man's essential, conscious nature, characterized as the *ātman*, becomes evident by contrast with the stuff which makes possible its limited expression and for whose dispensation it is ultimately intended.[61]

Śaiva Siddhānta speaks of the evolutes or categories of *māyā* in three groups or levels corresponding to the degrees to which *śakti* becomes evident. These are called: the 'pure' or 'unmixed' (*śuddha*) *māyā*; *māyā* as both 'pure' and 'impure', or mixed, (*śuddha-aśuddha-māyā*); and the realm of 'impure' (*aśuddha*) *māyā*. They correspond respectively to: the inciting, instigating or directing group (*prerakakhaṇḍa*); the group which generates human experience (*bhojayatṛi-khaṇḍa*); and the group which constitutes the objects to be experienced by the *ātman* (*bhogya-khaṇḍa*).[62] This grouping also corresponds to the classification of the categories of *māyā* respectively as the five *śiva-tattvas*, the seven *vidyā-tattvas*, and the twenty-four *ātma-tattvas*. It will be seen how this grouping refers more directly to the functions and roles of the categories within each group.

The five *śiva-tattvas* which make up the first group emerge, at the instigation of *śakti*, out of pure (*śuddha*) *māyā*, which is also called *bindu* and *kuṇḍalinī*.[63] These are called: *nāda* (sound) or *śiva-tattva*[64]; *bindu* or *śakti-tattva*; *sādākhya*; *maheśvara*; and *śuddha-vidyā* (pure knowledge).[65] What is to be noted about the *śiva-tattvas* which constitute the initial transition towards creation as such, is that the evolution of these five categories 'must be understood as evolution not in the sense of transformation (*pariṇāma*) but in the sense only of changes of states (*vṛitti*) of one self-identical material cause'.[66] A detailed assessment of this transcendental realm is not of immediate significance regarding the concern with man in the world. The function of this realm is crucial for those *ātmans* which have reached this stage having surpassed the limitations of time and the effects of *karman*. Time is a category that emerges via *nāda* and it falls within the next realm of categories; and *karman*, the mechanics of which are inoperative without the factor of time (as will be seen), is closely related or mixed with the realm in which time is manifest.

The modification (*vṛitti*) of sound (*nāda*) constitutes the material cause of all the succeeding categories. The initial modification is given a general name and is called both pure and impure or mixed (*śuddha-aśuddha*) *māyā*, or simply mixed or impure *māyā*. It is referred to as both pure and mixed because it evolves out of the pure realm and at the same time cooperates, or is mixed, with *karman* in this 'lower' realm; and it is simply called impure or mixed because it is more directly related to the 'grosser' categories. Its synonym, *mohinī*, which literally means 'deluding', 'confusing', 'perplexing', and 'illusive', conveys the manner in which it functions, and contrasts it with the pure realm from which it emerges. The difference in the nomenclature brings out the difference in the functions of the two realms: *śuddha-māyā* is the pure or unmixed realm in which are grouped the activating, inciting, or directing (*preraka*) *tattvas*; *aśuddha-māyā* is the substratum of the categories which fall within the impure or mixed realm and which are the directed (*prerya*) *tattvas*. By definition, then, the relation between the two 'is of one-sided dependence pointing to the nature of the distinction between the two as one of the levels.'[67] Further, it would seem that the pure realm must function with 'all the purity' characteristic of its nature and it is perplexing that it should be responsible for what deludes or confuses. In principle it has to be granted that the pure realm can function only in a 'pure way' and in accordance with its nature. However, the realm which it controls is under the influence of other factors which have an apparently contradictory consequence. In this realm, the factor of *karman* (and *āṇava-malam* which always lingers in the background of the *ātman*'s expression in the world) has a decisive role which functions with reference to a specific *ātman* and is thus a variable factor, but nonetheless common to all *ātmans* in the world, as will be seen. It is due chiefly to the adjunct of *karman* that this realm is called a mixed or impure realm.

It must be remembered that *māyā* (and also *karman*) is intended for the *ātman* which is possessed by, and under the spell of *āṇava-malam*. With its powers of consciousness—expressed in volition, knowledge and action—under captivity, as it were, the *ātman* is incapable of undergoing any experience at all and, thereby, manifesting its nature. With the introduction of *māyā* (and *karman*) an opportunity for even a partial expression of its powers is provided. Put in metaphorical language, the stage is being gradually set to offer a modicum of scope for the *ātman* to undergo experience. With the *vidyā-tattvas* of *māyā*, the basic ingredients of experience emerge and the *ātman* is invested or conjoined with them. There are five factors which constitute the props of *ātman*'s experience in the world, in all its different states of consciousness, and which are retained by the *ātman* throughout its transmigratory existences—which occur as a consequence of the operation of *karman*. They are called the five *kañcukas* which make up the 'dress', 'vesture' or 'covering' which make the *ātman* 'ready' or 'set' for existence in the world. These are: *kāla* (time); *niyati* (the principle of determination, destiny or necessity which operates particularly in collusion with *karman*); *kalā* (literally 'particle' and stands for the important category out of which evolve the rest of the categories in the entire scheme); *vidyā* (the category responsible for knowledge) and *rāga* (the category responsible for attraction, feeling or passion pertaining to the objects of experience). With these rigid supports—which structurally do not form part of the essential, intrinsic nature of what they support, viz., the *ātman*—the *ātman* is prepared to partake of life in the world, through which, in fact, the intended realization of its own nature should take place.

From the aggregation of the above five categories emerges the *puruṣa-tattva* (also called *puṁs-tattva*) which permits the designation of the *ātman* literally as 'man' (*puruṣa* or *puṁs*), the agent of experience in the world, which functions with the aid of the other categories which constitute the instruments of experience. Identical with the emergence of the *puruṣa-tattva* is the factor of life-breath (*prāṇa*)—in this context the word '*jīva*', which means 'living', is a synonym for *puruṣa* because of the principle of *prāṇa*—which is not given a place in the scheme of the 36 categories but which is assumed and, as will be seen, is a decisive factor in distinguishing the fourth state of consciousness (*turīya*) from that beyond it (*turīyātīta*). This needs to be mentioned here in anticipation since the term is presupposed in the discussion concerning the states of wakefulness, dream, etc. With the *puruṣa-tattva* the *ātman* is now prepared for the objects of experience which, in the scheme of the categories, belong to the next realm.

The first category in the group known as the *ātmatattvas* is *aśuddha-māyā* which, for different reasons, is variously called *mūla-prakṛiti* (or simply *prakṛiti-tattva*, the material cause of the empirical world), *guṇa-tattva*, or *citta-tattva*.[68] This category is a modification of the *kalā-tattva* mentioned above which emerges out of *mohinī* which, in turn, is a modification of *bindu* (*śuddha-māyā*) via *nāda*. It is called *aśuddha* (impure or mixed) by extension of the similar terminology used for *mohinī* (i.e., *śuddha-aśuddha-māyā,* which is also referred to simply as *aśuddha-māyā*)[69] and also because it is more directly responsible for the 'grosser' manifestations of matter. It is in this sense that it is known as *prakṛiti-tattva*, the primitive, material category which is responsible for the evolutes, which become the objects of the *ātman*'s experience in the world. The modification of *prakṛiti-tattva* is *guṇa-tattva* and although this category is not given a separate status in the scheme (as is the case with *prāṇa*). For all practical purposes it has to be seen as an evolute of *prakṛititattva* when the *guṇas* are 'in unmanifest balance.'[70] The *guṇa-tattva* is a compound category which is responsible for the evolution of the three *guṇas*. The word '*guṇa*' means 'quality', 'attribute' or 'property' and *guṇas* are of the three kinds adopted from the Sāṅkhya school, viz., *sattva, rajas* and *tamas*. They are representatives of the physical and the psychological qualities respectively of: calmness or tranquility; of activity or agitation; and of lethargy or dullness. Insofar as the *guṇa-tattva* is the collective term for these qualities and insofar as, in the order of its functions, it is related specifically to man's psychological make up, *guṇa-tattva* can be understood as *citta*, the psyche of man.[71] The *guṇa-tattva* occupies a crucial position in providing the transition from the group of *vidyātattvas* (via the *kalā-tattva* and the *prakṛiti-tattva*) to that of the *ātmà-tattvas*—just as the category called *śuddha-aśuddha-māyā* provides the crucial transition from the *śiva-tattvas* to the *vidyā-tattvas*.

When the *guṇas* are in a state of equilibrium they are unmanifest. The process of the evolution of the categories is possible only when the balance is upset, and it is here particularly that the role of directing or instigating (*preraka*) *tattvas* is indispensable. When the *sattva-guṇa* is incited to take predominance, the sequence of the evolutes continues with the 'origin' of the *buddhi-tattva*, the principle of 'intellect' which plays the role of the judge, the determinator, or decision maker with regard to the nature of the object of experience. This principle will be dealt with in more detail since it permeates all facets of experience in the dream and wakeful states. What is to be noted especially is its nature, which it shares with all the other categories, as a material and insentient entity (*jaḍa* or *acit*), but which is nonetheless, indispensable for man's empirical experience. Closely associated with it, and operating in collusion with it, is its evolute called *ahaṅkāra* which literally means the 'I-maker' but usually is translated as the ego. It is the outcome of the predominance of *rajas* over the other two *guṇas*, viz., *sattva* and *tamas*. This category is a logical outcome of the function of determination attributed to the intellect by pointing to a subject which in fact determines and which is evident in the role of the 'I' or the ego tacit in all human attributes. It is, therefore, the factor of subjectiveness, and it is not surprising that the operation of life-breath itself (*prāṇa* or *vāyu*) is dependent on the *ahaṅkāra-tattva*.[72]

The predominance of one or the other *guṇa* which gives rise to, or is responsible for, a particular category—for example, the intellect arising through the predominance of the *sattva-guṇa* and the ego out of *rajas*—means that the remaining two *guṇas* (including *tamas* as the third) are not absent, but only that they are subordinate to it. This is particularly evident in the sequence of the categories evolving from the *ahaṅkāra-tattva*, differentiated into its three aspects or qualities (*guṇas*) as *sattva*, *rajas* and *tamas*. For the purposes of the functions and types of products evolving from these qualities, the following description applies: *sattva* is called *taijasa* because of its illuminating capacity; *rajas* is called *vaikārika* because of its ability to change and thereby being responsible for activity; and *tamas* is called *bhūtādi* because it is the principle from which the elements (*bhūtas*) such as earth, etc., evolve.[73]

From the *sattva* quality distinguished as *taijasa*, evolves the *manas-tattva*, the category generally translated as the mind. Together with *ahaṅkāra* and *buddhi*, *manas* constitutes what are called the internal organs (*antaḥkaraṇas*) all of which together may be referred to as what make up the *citta* or psyche of man. *Manas* is the mediating factor between *buddhi* and both the motor and sense organs which are stimulated by the objects of experience. It is *manas* which, in fact, directs these organs towards worldly experience. In this context, it will be seen how the *manas* is responsible for, or the cause both of certitude (*saṅkalpa*) and doubt (*vikalpa*), and also that it operates in conjunction with only one sense organ at a time.[74]

From the *sattva* (or *taijasa*) quality of *ahaṅkāra* evolve, in addition to the *manas-tattva*, the five organs or faculties of sense (*jñānendriyas*), viz., those of hearing (*śrotra*), touch (*tvak*), sight (*cakṣus*), taste (*rasana*) and smell (*ghrāṇa*). From the *rajas* (or *vaikārika*) aspect of *ahaṅkāra* emerge the five motor organs (*karmendriyas*), viz., the mouth for speech (*vāc*), hands (*pāṇi*), feet (*pāda*), anus (*pāyu*) and the genitals (*upastha*). From the *tamas* (or *bhūtādi*) quality of the *ahaṅkāra-tattva* evolve two sets of categories distinguished as subtle elements (*tanmātras*) and gross elements (*bhūtas*). Each group consists of five categories each. The subtle elements are the relative counterparts of the five sense organs enumerated above, and are related to particular things which possess certain elements, viz., those of sound (*śabda*), touchability (*sparśa*), form (*rūpa*, which makes sight possible), tastability (*rasa*) and smell (*gandha*). These subtle elements are the features of the five gross elements (*bhūtas*), which are characterized by a particular subtle element. Thus, sound is the characteristic feature of the element called ether (*ākāśa*), touchability of air (*vāyu*), form of fire (*tejas*), tastability of water (*apa*) and smell of the element earth (*prithivī*).

This concludes the brief survey of the 36 categories in Śaiva Siddhānta, which constitute the terminological framework supporting the philosophical anthropology of the school. Reference will be made to these categories frequently in this study and their survey is intended to provide the basic orientation toward the understanding of man in Śaiva Siddhānta. This orientation will not be complete without some remarks concerning the intriguing theory of *karman* which is woven into the philosophical perspective of Śaiva Siddhānta, as is the case with several schools of Indian thought.

### 1.4 *Karman in Śaiva Siddhānta*

From what has been said so far some aspects of the theory of *karman* which are basic to Śaiva Siddhānta have already been alluded to: that *karman*, like *māyā*, is a kind of *malam* and, as such and by definition, operates as a fetter (*pāśa*); that it shares with *māyā* the status of being a consequential or adventitious (*āgantuka*) *malam*; that it also shares with *māyā* the nature of what is insentient or non-conscious (*jaḍa* or *acit*); that whatever 'power' (*śakti*) may be ascribed to *karman*—as with *māyā*—must ultimately have its source in the *śakti*, which is inalienably that of *śivam*; and that, consequently, the ultimate purpose of *karman*—together with *māyā*—is a beneficent one, relative to the malevolent *āṇava-malam* associated with the *ātman*. These features and several others to be dealt with presently in their application to the human situation, constitute a systematic attempt toward an understanding of man in Śaiva Siddhānta.

It was said that Śaiva Siddhānta philosophical anthropology is not a mere classification of the ingredients of human experience, but that it included other dimensions for which the theory of *māyā* alone can offer no reasonable answers. *Māyā* and its evolutes have specific, fixed functions which prevail in every case of their operations. According to the theory they do not deviate from their prescribed roles and whilst, as already pointed out, they constitute the principles of human experience, they cannot be said to be responsible for the obvious variety, change and multi-dimensionality of life in the world. By definition, *māyā* and its evolutes are not open to these facets, which are a fact of experience. The Śaiva Siddhānta account, which accommodates this variety and change of life in the world, involves the operation of the principle of *karman*.

The theory of *karman* in Śaiva Siddhānta is a highly sophisticated and intricately worked out doctrine built into the metaphysical presuppositions of the school. Although there are several features which are common to all schools, which accept the theory—*karman* being part of the 'pool of ideas' that practically all schools in India draw from (with the notable exception of the Cārvāka school)—there is, as will be seen, a peculiarly Siddhānta stamp to this school's version of the theory.[75] Its unique interpretation and contribution will be evident bearing in mind the significant position that *karman* occupies in the system as a whole, and particularly insofar as it is directly concerned with the human situation.

Etymologically the word is derived from the root *kṛi*, which means among other things, 'to do', 'to make', 'to perform', 'to accomplish', 'to cause', 'to effect', 'to prepare' and 'to undertake'. The neuter word *karman* thus means 'an act' or 'action', also in the sense of referring to a religious act or rite, such as a sacrifice or oblation 'especially as originating in the hope of future recompense.'[76] The general significance of these meanings for the theory, as it has survived in Indian thought, may be said to be based on the meaning of the root from which the word is derived, viz., to cause or to effect. By extension, therefore, *karman* signifies that everything in the world, both physical and moral, presupposes a cause, or that a cause is in fact an effect, or that every cause must produce an evident effect at some time. The theory may be intelligible, if not adequate, to explain physical phenomena, but may be questionable in the sphere of ethics or morality, as can be applicable only to man. For the Indian thinkers, the question seems to present no problems on the basic principle, that every act, decision, attitude or behaviour must lead to some result or effect. The ramifications of this point will be dealt with shortly. What is to be noted at the very outset is that whilst this view can lead to a trivialization of the theory of *karman*, apart from providing scope for fatalism, it has a more significant dimension, which has made it a philosophical issue—insofar as it pertains to the nature of man as expressed in the world. In this sense *karman* is a theory that attempts to furnish a descriptive, rational explanation of the variety, change and apparent inconsistencies of life in the world.

The origins of the theory are not very clear and, although the theory 'is not distinctly mentioned before the age of the Upanishads... all are agreed that it had come to form an integral part of Indian thought, before the close of the Vedic period.'[77] The earliest and very remote reference to anything resembling the rudiments of *karman* may, therefore, be said to be found in the *Ṛigveda* itself (4, 27, 1) as quoted in the *Aitareya-upaniṣad* (2, 4).[78] It is beyond the scope of this study to deal with an analysis of the *karman* theory and its development in the literary history of India. Suffice it to say that it is traceable to the earliest recorded literature from which it has been moulded in diverse facets including views on transmigration, morality and the effects of deeds performed by man—all of which point to *karman* being a principle of causation. It is a notable feature of the theory that it has been closely woven into the fabric of philosophical thinking in India for centuries, so much so that it appears to be taken for granted by many schools as being a fact of life and inextricably associated particularly with the human situation, and in this context more specifically as a principle or law of moral causation.

Put simply, the *karman* theory, as it has survived through the ages, is based on the view that the present state of man in the world derives from previous causes and that, consequently, what happens or is done now determines future events and situations. Whilst this theory applies universally, the special interest in it for the purposes of this study is its application and relevance to man especially insofar as it relates to the problem of 'freedom' and 'determination'. What *karman* refers to in this context is that every deed or action leaves behind its traces (*saṁskāras*), which are like the seeds that 'bear fruit' at the appropriate time and place. The two senses in which the word *karman* is used here are not only man's deeds or actions but also the accumulation in seminal form of their impressions—as a seminal principle *karman* in the second sense is thus pregnant with consequences, i.e., it is generative of conditions which lead to the maturation or fruition of certain effects caused by, and as a consequence of, past actions. The agricultural metaphor is the one most commonly employed to explain the mechanics or operation of the theory of *karman*. Just as the natural law is responsible for a seed to bear fruit when the necessary environmental conditions are satisfied, so too the law of *karman* is responsible for the situation, in which the 'fruits' of man's deeds are reaped under the appropriate conditions—the appropriate conditions being determined by the previous deeds.

The question of the perspective from which a theory such as that of *karman* is to be approached is philosophically relevant. To begin with a mere abstract necessity of a theory, or to merely follow a tradition of its application, and then to justify its relevance and applicability to the human situation could lead, philosophically speaking, to questions regarding the very postulation of the theory in the first place. On the other hand, to arrive at a theory—such as that of *karman*—on the basis of a reflection on the phenomena of experience is to attempt a credible and intelligible account of the need to postulate such a theory. In other words, to say on the basis of a reflective analysis of the diversity, variety, and apparent absurdity in the world, that some causal principle needs to be acknowledged—even if only theoretically at the outset—since every effect or product has a cause, is to approach the theory realistically.[79] Rejecting from this perspective the view that the principle of causation can be one of chance or fortuitous coincidence, Śaiva Siddhānta adopts within the framework of its own metaphysical presuppositions, the generally accepted principle of *karman*, which plays a crucial role in this school's systematic account of the categories of experience.

Just as *māyā* was seen to be a category arrived at through a reflection on the nature of man's experience, *karman* too is to be seen as being based on a reflection of man's status in the world and a search for its causal factor. The fact of being in a world where man's experience is reducible to the recurrent oscillation between the polarities of joy and suffering, or pleasure and pain, or happiness and unhappiness, points to a cause for which, in the final analysis, man has to be held responsible.[80] This responsibility brings out the dialectical relation between the 'freedom' and 'determination' mentioned above: the freedom is entailed in the choice to do one thing or another, and the determination entails the fact of being in a condition to have to choose—put in contemporary terminology, this entails 'the being condemned to choose' (even if one chooses not to choose). Just as the merit of discussions about man's choice situations can be trivialized by reducing them to trite truisms, so too can the merit of the descriptive theory of *karman* as a causal factor of the human situation be underestimated and undermined. The implications of the freedom-determination dialectic have to be postponed until other features of the understanding of man in Śaiva Siddhānta are dealt with. What is to be noted is that the theory is an integral part of the philosophical anthropology of the school and one which, together with *māyā*, plays a significant role in Śaiva Siddhānta soteriology.

A clear statement about the position, nature and function of *karman* in Śaiva Siddhanta is:

> Thus, operating between [*śuddha-aśuddha*] *māyā* and *kāla* [*tattvas*] *karman* has no beginning; though manifesting [*ātman*'s powers], it is an obstructing [factor]—as long as it is present there is no [progress to] liberation.[81]

This description of *karman* shows that it shares not only the beginningless nature of *māyā*, but also its beneficent role in offering the *ātman* a scope for expression and manifestation of its powers of consciousness. Whilst this role is indispensable both, nonetheless, operate as fetters (*pāśam*) to the *ātman*'s essential nature expressed and manifested fully only in the state of *mokṣa* or *mukti*. In other words, *karman* too—as with *māyā*—has to be 'discarded' no sooner its role has been played. In a sense, the nature and role of *karman* are more complicated than those of *māyā*: the nature of *māyā* as insentient and the role it plays through its various evolutes are clearly defined and related to man's concrete experience; *karman*, on the other hand, though insentient as well, does not evolve (but is of three kinds, as will be seen) and its role in relation to man has to be inferred on the basis of a reflective analysis of the human condition. In other words, *karman* cannot be 'seen' as is the case with some evolutes of *māyā* (e.g., earth and water). *Karman* is an 'unseen' (*adṛiṣṭa*) principle[82] no less 'real' than *māyā*, insofar as *karman* is the principle of causation. This is to say that whilst *karman* itself is humanly imperceivable—as indeed many subtle forms of *māyā* are—its effects are within human experience as, e.g., with the variety of experiences that may be termed pleasant or unpleasant in life with *karman* as its cause. Further, precisely when and under what conditions the effects of deeds would be realized are not clearly defined, nor can they be verified.

In the attempt to rationalize the cause of the human situation embodied in the *karman* theory, *karman* pertains to acts or deeds performed by man which not only perpetuate the human condition, but also pertains to these very acts which are described as being advantageous, beneficial or favourable (*hitam*) and their opposites (*ahitam*). These acts in turn are described as being responsible respectively for merit (*puṇyam*) and demerit (*pāpam*). At least two points are underscored here. Firstly, the point that *karman* perpetuates the human condition implies its efficacy in all the three dimensions of time, i.e., the present state of man has its cause in the past, and what is done now logically points to some effect in the future. What these effects will be, and what causes are due to the present state, and when precisely the effects of present deeds and acts will manifest themselves or bear fruit, are beyond the limited scope of man to grasp. What is possible, however, is the understanding of the principle of *karman* which rests on the theory of cause and effect, and that *karman* operates as a law. It is to be remembered that *karman* is an insentient principle and its operation, therefore, presupposes a conscious agent which has to set it in 'motion'—as seen also in the case of *māyā*. This agent is *śakti*, inalienably a part of *śivam* and acting as an instrument of *śivam*. Thus, as seen with *māyā*, *śakti* instills a dynamism intrinsically alien to the nature of *karman*, and together *māyā* and *karman* become associated with man for all times. Secondly, and associated with the first point, is the view that man's deeds and actions carry with them a code of conduct, or moral behaviour which, according to the law of *karman*, necessarily points to an accumulation or a 'stock' of meritorious and unmeritorious *karman* which has to be 'spent' in order to step out of the cycle of the law. The conscious effort on the part of man to attempt to use the fetter of *karman* ultimately to be free of its bondage, constitutes the first step towards exploiting the soteriological role of the principle of *karman*.

That it is indeed possible to spend *karman* is clearly expressed in the following verse. (It is to be noted that whilst the principle itself can never be destroyed—being eternal, as seen in the previous quotation—its dissociation from a particular *ātman* only is possible).

> At the time of [cosmic] sleep, it [*karman*] approaches maturity, at the time of creation it is used, and in the end [at the time of cosmic destruction] it remains in *māyā*; it does not come to rest without being made use of.[83]

What this description implies is that experience, which means the 'using up' of *karman*, is the means by which *karman* is brought to rest or made inoperative. In terms of the theory, however, this seems impossible insofar as the very process of using up the stock of *karman* itself involves further accumulation of *karman*, without an end in sight of its neutralization.[84] This problem has a direct bearing on the three kinds of *karman* which Śaiva Siddhānta adopts in the form generally accepted by many other schools, and which need mention here.

The three types of *karman* or effects (even in seminal form) of deeds and actions are: the accumulated stock of *karman* which is always associated with the *ātman*'s recurrent births and called *sañcita-karman*; the *karman* already in progress which is responsible for the *ātman*'s present condition and called *prārabdha-karman*; and the *karman* to be incurred in the future and called *āgāmi-karman*.[85] Whilst these three kinds of *karman* are self-explanatory, the concept of *sañcita-karman* is particularly interesting for Śaiva Siddhānta philosophical anthropology. The perplexing problem associated with it concerns the original, intrinsic nature of the *ātman*, already seen as all-knowing, all-pervasive, constant, and of the nature of consciousness which it shares with *śivam*. The question that arises is: how does the *ātman* become associated with a stock of *karman* in the first place? In other words: given the above description of the *ātman*'s own nature, how does it accumulate *karman* at the outset? These are crucial questions for the philosophical anthropology of the school insofar as the *ātman*'s nature constitutes the essence of man. The answers concern the very validity of such questions. For the Siddhāntin, these questions would not only be inadmissible[86] but an attempt to answer them would involve a circular argument: the accumulated *karman* is the cause for the *ātman*'s present condition; the present condition is due to the accumulated *karman* associated with the *ātman*. The questions are inadmissible for two main reasons. Firstly, it is beyond the scope of human ability to grasp the origin of the operation of *karman* which involves a 'stepping out' of the framework not only of *karman*, but also of *māyā* and *āṇava-malam*.[87] The solution of the problem is contained only in the condition of the possibility of *mokṣa*, when the *ātman*'s powers of volition, knowledge, and action manifest themselves in an unfettered state. Secondly, the questions themselves presuppose an inadmissible perspective to the *karman* theory: the problems may be said to arise because the questions are from the perspective of what in fact is logically concluded, i.e., from the perspective of the accumulated *karman* which is acknowledged on the basis of a reflective analysis of man's present condition. In other words, it is on the basis of the attempt to rationally arrive at a cause for the present effect, or man's state in the world, that the theory of *karman* is postulated in the first place. It is *prārabdha-karman* whose operation is in progress —on the principle that the present effect has a cause—that points to *sañcita* and *āgāmi-karman*.[88] Therefore, the concern with the present condition constitutes the admissible starting point and appropriate perspective toward an understanding of the theory of *karman* and of man who is said to be a victim of its inexorable operation.

In the three-fold classification of *karman*, two principles are indispensable for its operation, viz., *kāla-tattva* (the category of time) and *niyati-tattva* (the category responsible for *karman* to be associated with a particular *ātman*). It was seen how time is practically woven into the *karman* theory itself with reference to the three-dimensional view of *karman* in its relation to the past, the present and the future. Further, if the law of *karman* is to operate systematically then it presupposes a principle which should 'allocate' to a particular *ātman* the consequences, or effects, of its own involvement in experiences. In other words, the *karman* incurred by one *ātman* should not be visited upon another. The principle which operates in collusion with *karman* to guarantee its proper operation in this regard is *niyati-tattva*. An awareness that the *ātman* is itself responsible for all the *karman* incurred and that the effects rebound on that very *ātman* itself, places full responsibility on man as the agent (*kartṛi*) of *karman*. What is presupposed in this Śaiva Siddhānta teaching which bears on the philosophical anthropology of the system, is man's responsibility to 'control' *karman* by operating within the law itself. This responsibility reflects itself in man's behaviour and, thus, enters the realm of ethics and morality. Whatever man does can be classified either as what yields merit (*puṇyam*) or demerit (*pāpam*). It is not the case that the meritorious acts are weighed against the unmeritorious ones and that some balance is naturally struck. In terms of the law of *karman*, the fruit of every kind of act, meritorious or otherwise, must necessarily be reaped. In other words, there is no escape on the part of man from the responsibility of the 'ownership' of all deeds and from the inexorability of the law of *karman* requiring the necessary 'experience' of the effects of actions.

The impossibility of meritorious acts outweighing the unmeritorious ones and the impossibility of man escaping the clutches of the law of *karman*, point to questions regarding the precise means by which the shackles of *karman* are broken—which is indispensable for *mokṣa*. This point concerns, as already seen, the exploitation of the soteriological function of *karman*—together with that of *māyā*—which will be dealt with after developing further the Śaiva Siddhānta philosophical anthropology. What is to be noted in anticipation, however, is that the 'moral act of man is evidence of the immanent freedom in his empirical life.'[89] Further:

> Factually [the] law of *karma* taken by itself implies nothing more than pure succession and a dependent or relative origination. A consciousness of the inalienability of the means and the end is, only negatively, a search for freedom and implicitly a demand for transcendent freedom.[90]

What has been attempted in this section is a brief survey of some of the main features of the *karman* theory. *Karman* is an indispensable term that forms an inextricable part of the basic framework of Śaiva Siddhānta vocabulary, evident in the system of categories developed by the school. The Siddhānta treatment of man would be impossible without recourse to it. The entire framework of the vocabulary outlined above is intended to facilitate the discussion of the subject-matter in the chapters to follow.

### 1.5 *Summary*

It would be useful to attempt to state briefly the Śaiva Siddhānta perspective to philosophical anthropology, in the light of what has already been presented. The essence of man constitutes what has been described as the *ātman* and defined as the principle of consciousness intrinsic to man. In the concern with what constitutes the essence of man, the *ātman* is initially considered in terms of its association with *āṇava-malam* which fetters, shackles, or renders impossible any expression or manifestation of the *ātman*'s powers of consciousness, evident in volition, knowledge and action. *Āṇava-malam* is described as *sahaja-malam* for it is 'born with' or 'arises with' the *ātman*. As a fetter which completely binds the *ātman*, cutting it off from itself, so to speak, it is called literally *pratibandham*. It is responsible for isolating the *ātman*, excluding it and making it exist alone (*kevalin*). It is in a forlorn state (*avasthā*) called *kevala-avasthā*.

At the instigation of *pati*, the 'lord' of the *ātman* that 'becomes' a fettered entity (*paśu*) on account of the *āṇava-malam*, a modicum of scope for the expression of the *ātman*'s powers is provided by *māyā* and *karman*. Although these two categories share the nature of a bond or fetter (*pāśam*) characteristic of *malam* as such, they are, however, consequential or adventitious (*āgantuka*) fetters. They are provided as a consequence of the plight of the *ātman*. They serve as an antidote counteracting, as it were, the overwhelming capacity of *āṇava-malam*. The acquisition of these two fetters signifies the transition from the isolated *kevala* state to a state called *sakala-avasthā*, in which the *ātman* is gradually furnished with the means and objects of experience. Since *māyā* is what the *ātman* is in relation to, as regards being associated with the constituents of experience, it is called *sambandham*; and *karman* is called *anubandham* because it is what 'accompanies' the *ātman* as long as it is involved in the world. It is the *sakala* state which appropriately constitutes the Śaiva Siddhānta philosophical anthropology. In other words, the *sakala-paśu*, the fettered being in the world—fettered by *āṇava*, *karman*, and *māyā-malam* —is man. Man, who is essentially the *ātman*, therefore, is to be seen as 'arising' as a consequence of a transition from being a *kevala-paśu* to being a *sakala-paśu*.

While a modicum of freedom and differentiation is provided to the *sakala-paśu*, i.e., to man, this situation in fact intensifies man's predicament of being in a state of bondage. The 'journey' of the *ātman* has been from one kind of bound state to another, from *kevala* to *sakala*. The description of man's condition presupposes a means by which bondage is overcome through bondage itself. Paradoxically stated, this involves becoming fetterless through the very fetters themselves. The conscious attempt on the part of man to come to grips with a fettered existence and to strive for the realization of the essential nature of the *ātman*—the conscious principle which is man's defining and characteristic feature—is to progressively continue the journey from the *sakala* state to the state of pristine purity called *śuddha-avasthā*. Man transcends man by being man, i.e., by realizing the essential, inalienable nature of man. In this state, *malam* is at rest, and the *ātman* completely one with itself. It will be seen how at the end of this journey, the *ātman* is said to 'regain' its original nature in which the intrinsic powers of consciousness have an unfettered expression and manifestation. That it is possible to achieve this state is expressed in the condition of the possibility of *mokṣa*, where it is no longer appropriate to distinguish Śaiva Siddhānta philosophical anthropology from Śaiva Siddhānta theology. Further, it will be seen how the philosophical anthropology has to be re-read in the background of the theology where the *ātman*, the essential nature of man, is to be considered in its relation to the godhead, *śivam*—a relation in which to regard the expression of consciousness (*cit*) either as that of *śivam* or that of the *ātman* is inapplicable at this transcendental level.

The three states, *kevala*, *sakala* and *śuddha*, are grouped together in what are called the causal states of consciousness (*kāraṇa-avasthās*) insofar as they are the causes of effect-states of consciousness (*kārya-avasthās*) and from which they are to be distinguished. The effect-states are five in number: the wakeful state (*jāgrat*); the dream state of sleep (*svapna*); the dreamless state of sleep, or deep sleep (*suṣupti*); the 'fourth' state of consciousness (*turīya*); and the state 'beyond the fourth' (*turīyātīta*). Although technically the five effect states apply to each of the three causal states, special attention will be given to the five states as they feature particularly in the *sakala* state. It is in this realm that they specifically fall within the Śaiva Siddhānta understanding of man, as is clear from their terminologies.

## 1.6 *The texts on which the study is based*

In the chapters to follow, an attempt is made to deal in detail with specific issues toward the Śaiva Siddhānta understanding of man. These issues cover three broad areas: an analysis and investigation of man's various states of consciousness (*avasthās*) and how the system employs them in accounting for both empirical and transcendental experience (*bhoga*); an exploration of man as a cognizer and verifier of valid knowledge, which is the concern with epistemology (*prāmāṇyavāda*) including within it the concern with man as a linguistic being; and, finally, a consideration of the nature of the transition involved through a life of *yoga* and gnosis (*jñāna*) when *paśu* (man) regains its unconditioned nature as the *ātman* (*ātmalābha*)—which is evident in the fact that the tradition accepts that there indeed exists a condition of the possibility of a freedom (*mokṣa*) from fettered existence. In dealing with these issues this study draws heavily from a voluminous (untranslated) commentary by Śivāgrayogin (sixteenth century) on one of the most basic texts of the Śaiva Siddhānta tradition, the *Śivajñānabodham*. One of the most remarkable features of this text—apart from inspiring several voluminous commentaries on it—is that it contains only twelve verses, in twenty-four lines, which in the Sanskrit is set to a metre called *anuṣṭubh*.[91]

There is an ongoing debate as regards the origin of this text, viz., whether the text is originally in Sanskrit and part of the *Raurava Āgama*[92] or whether it is an independent work originally in the Tamil language.[93] The question of the origin of the text is undoubtedly of immense significance especially in the light of the authoritative status it has in the tradition. The relevance of determining its origin pertains particularly to the historical development of Śaiva Siddhānta in association with the emergence of the school's philosophical literature. The lack of any conclusive evidence to settle the issue, however, does not preclude a study of the content of the text.[94] It is beyond the scope of this study to discuss the historical development of the tradition and the literature associated with it in each significant phase.[95] The text, nonetheless, is extant in both Sanskrit and Tamil with several commentaries on them. This study, as already stated, is based on the Sanskrit commentary by Śivāgrayogin on the Sanskrit version of the *Śivajñānabodham*.[96] In view of the importance of this basic text, which may be said to be as fundamental to Śaiva Siddhānta as the *Brahmasūtra* is to Advaita Vedānta[97], the text with a translation is given in an appendix—the verses are taken from Śivāgrayogin's commentary on them.[98]

Biographical details about Śivāgrayogin are scanty but it seems clear that he flourished in the sixteenth century[99] and, according to tradition, that he belonged to the tradition of teachers called the *Skanda-paramparā*. Two of his works in Sanskrit, which complement each other, represent his brand of Siddhānta.[100] One is explicitly a commentary on the *Śivajñānabodham* called simply *Śivāgrabhāṣya* which states each verse of the *Śivajñānabodham* followed by an elaborate commentary on it. The only publication of this work, not now available, is in the Grantha script.[101] The other work is called *Śaivaparibhāṣā*[102] which closely resembles the concise, scholastic and systematic approach of the former.[103] This study draws chiefly from the former, untranslated work, following the text closely in attempting to grasp its intricate arguments.[104]

The Siddhāntin's standpoint is derived pre-eminently from a critical assessment of the opponents' views, rejecting or incorporating them on the grounds of an argumentation consistent with the school's own philosophical assumptions, and, thereby, arriving at what it calls the conclusive, final, or established position (*siddhānta*). It is from this very process that the name of the school may be derived, viz., as being the established, final position concerning all matters relating to or belonging to, derived or coming from, Śiva, i.e., Śaiva Siddhānta. The proper understanding of the Siddhānta perspective, therefore, involves an analysis of the arguments which establish a particular point. As already pointed out, the issues to be dealt with as outlined above are concerned with the philosophical anthropology of the school entailed in the concept of *paśu-ātman*, and constitute the established view concerning the Śaiva Siddhānta understanding of man.

## NOTES

1. "Among those standard themes of Western philosophical thought which are conspicuously absent in Indian (specifically Hindu) philosophy, *man* seems to be one of the most conspicuous ones. Wilhelm Halbfass, "Anthropological Problems in Classical Indian Philosophy" in *Beiträge zur Indienforschung, Ernst Waldschmidt zum* 80. *Geburtstag gewidmet*

(Berlin: Museum für Indische Kunst, 1977), p. 225. He goes on to add: "To be sure, there are images of man in the Indian tradition, there are challenging ideas and perspectives relating to what we call man; there may even be an elaborate implicit anthropology. But there is no tradition of thematic and explicit thought about man, of trying to define and explicate the nature of man and to distinguish it from other forms of life and existence; there is no tradition of explicit philosophical anthropology, comparable to that tradition in the West.." *ibid.*

2. Lambert Schmithausen, ed., *Paul Hacker Kleine Schriften* (Wiesbaden: Franz Steiner Verlag GMBH, 1978), "Śaṅkara's Conception of Man", p. 243. The article is reprinted from *Studia Missionalia* (Rome: Gregorian University Press, 1970), vol. 19, pp. 123-131. Also in *German Scholars on India*, edited by the Cultural Department of the Federal Republic of Germany, New Delhi, vol. 1, pp. 99-106, published by Chowkhamba, Varanasi, India, under the title "A Note on Śaṅkara's Conception of man", 1973.
3. Ernst Cassirer, *An Essay on Man* (New Haven and London: Yale University Press, 1944), p. 5.
4. *Ibid.*, p. 11.
5. This point is made by H.O. Pappé in the article "Philosophical Anthropology," *The Encyclopedia of Philosophy*, 1972 Reprint ed. See also Michael Landmann, *Philosophical Anthropology*, trans. David A. Parent, (Philadelphia: The Westminster Press, 1971), p. 53 where these questions are summed up in the one question: "What is man?"
6. *Ibid.*
7. *Ibid.*, p. 160.
8. H.O. Pappé, "On Philosophical Anthropology", *Australasian Journal oj Philosophy*, vol. 39 (1961): 49. Cf. also the point that "the task of a critical anthropology will be to determine, from the point of view of reflection on the self, the limits of all knowledge". Berhard Groethuysen, "Towards an Anthropological Philosophy" in Raymond Klibansky and H.J. Paton (eds.) *Philosophy and History, Essays Presented to Ernst Cassirer* (Oxford: Oxford Clarendon Press, 1936), p. 84.
9. Śaiva Siddhānta differs significantly from the Sāṅkhya, Yoga, and Advaita Vedānta views in attributing to consciousness (*cit*) the powers (*śaktis*) of volition (*icchā*), knowledge (*jñāna*), and action (*kriyā*), so that consciousness and its powers can be spoken of as comprising a single unit.
10. *Ibid.*, p. 59.
11. Michael Landmann, *op.cit.*, p. 19.
12. The title of the section, *ibid.*
13. *Ibid.*, p. 23.
14. Practically all the standard works on Śaiva Siddhānta seem to emphasize the theology more strongly, than—and even at the expense of—the anthropology. For Śaiva Siddhānta theology see especially: M. Dhavamony, *Love of God* (Oxford: Oxford Clarendon Press, 1971); A. Rohan Dunuwila, *Śaiva Siddhānta Theology* (Delhi: Motilal Banarsidass, 1985); H. W.

Schomerus, *Der Caiva-Siddhānta, eine Mystik Indiens* (Leipzing: J.C. Hinrichs'sche Buchhandlung, 1912).

15. Thus, one can speak of several branches of philosophical anthropology such as: cultural philosophical anthropology, biological philosophical anthropology, psychological philosophical anthropology, and theological philosophical anthropology. See *The Encyclopedia of Philosophy*, s.v. 'Philosophical Anthropology', by H.O. Pappé.
16. Quoted by Michael Landmann, *op.cit.*, p. 55. He also quotes in the same place what Max Scheler noteworthily wrote towards the end of his life: "If there is a philosophical task whose solution our age needs with singular desperation it is that of a philosophical anthropology. I mean a basic science on the nature and constitution of man."
17. H.O. Pappé, "On Philosophical Anthropology", *Australasian Journal of Philosophy*, vol. 39 (1961): 47.
18. Michael Landmann, *op.cit.*, p. 66.
19. This idea is part of the 'pool of ideas' that Indian systems of thought draw from (including, e.g., *karma, saṁsāra,* and *duḥkha*). Even the heterodox schools of Buddhism and Jainism regard *mokṣa* as the goal to be attained by man. The reactionary Cārvāka school, whilst not accepting the 'traditional' view of *mokṣa,* has its own hedonistic conception of what liberation means for man. In any case, only man has the capability and privilege for realising *mokṣa*; gods, animals and other beings are excluded. Cf., also, Karl H. Potter, *Presuppositions of India's Philosophies* (Englewood Cliffs: Prentice-Hall, Inc., 1963), p. 255: "...the aims of classical Indian thought are such as to guarantee the relevance of philosophy to a human predicament and longing which does not change through the ages."
20. The four are: the gratification of desire (*kāma*); the acquirement of wealth (*artha*); the discharge of duty (*dharma*); and final emancipation (*mokṣa*).
21. Cf. Potter, *Presuppositions*, p. 6; "...*mokṣa* or complete freedom, is a state, but the sense in which this is so is one which makes it inappropriate to apply the same description to the other three. There is no state of *artha,* of *kāma*, or of *dharma* which a man may come to realize or rest in."
22. *The Encyclopedia of Philosophy*, s.v. "Indian Philosophy" by Ninian Smart.
23. In the case of Śaiva Siddhānta, for example, the views on consciousness (*cit*) and its powers (*śaktis*) constitute the crucial issue in the metaphysics of the school. *Cit-śakti* features prominently in epistemology as the only ultimately valid means (*pramāṇa*) of knowledge. This conclusion is arrived at logically in the discussion of what constitutes a *pramāṇa,* on the one hand, and *karaṇa*, or *sādhana* ('instrument' of knowledge) on the other, Insofar as *cit-śakti* is expressed in all human behaviour, where 'values' are expressed in man's actions and deeds, it enters the field of ethics—thus, one can speak of an 'Indian conception of values' (on this see the posthumously published book which bears this title, by M. Hiriyanna [Mysore: Kavyalaya Publishers, 1975], which critically discusses logical value, ethical value, absolute value, and aesthetic value).
24. Cf. the point that 'Śaṅkara refuses to discuss the issue of whether the *jīvanmukta* continues to live or not' because the state of the liberated one

corresponds to what is called "inner experience", J. L. Masson and M. V. Patwardhan, *Aesthetic Rapture*, 2 vols. (Poona: Deccan College, 1970), 2:38. In support of this point Śaṅkara's *Brahma-sūtrabhāṣya* IV. 1. 15 is quoted: *kathaṃ hy ekasya sva-hṛdayapratyayam brahmavedanaṃ* (*brahma-jñānam*, or *brahmānubhāvaḥ*) *dehadhāraṇaṃ cāpareṇa pratikṣeptum śakyeta*. (The words in parenthesis are as they appear in the source cited.)

25. The situation is analogous to the one in which the contribution, though not readily accepted as such, particularly of the Cārvāka school—with its unorthodox and reactionary views—was that it provided a greater need for the emphasis on and concern with epistemology. The Cārvāka is usually caricatured as a philosophical villain and in the absence of any complete original work of the school, an attempt has been made to reconstruct the virtues of the school from available references to it—ignoring the traditional prejudice against the school which leads to an understandable misrepresentation of it. See Keval Krishnan Mittal, *Materialism in Indian Thought* (Delhi: Munshiram Manoharlal Publishers, 1974), pp. 22-60.

26. The obvious cases in point are: accepting the 25 categories of the Sāṅkhya system in addition to 11 of its own (apart from those of *śivam/pati*, *ātman/paśu*, and *malam/pāśa*); the description of the 'states of consciousness' which, in addition to the four of Advaita Vedānta, includes a fifth state, literally called 'beyond the fourth; and the ascription to the nature of consciousness of powers (*śaktis*) which are intrinsic to it and to which they are constitutive—this is a crucial deviation from the Sāṅkhya, Yoga, and Advaita Vedānta views on consciousness. (There seems to be no doubt that the Sāṅkhya system—traditionally considered to be the oldest in India—provides the basic framework for Śaiva Siddhānta, especially as far as the doctrine of *tattvas*, or categories, is concerned. See H.W. Schomerus, *Der Caiva-Siddhānta*, p. 17; "Dass z.B. die Tattva-Lehre, wie wir, sie in dem auf den Āgama auf-gebauten Caiva-Siddhānta vorfinden, jüngeren Datums ist als die Tattva-Lehre des Sāṃkhya-Systems, steht wohl ausser Frage"; and p. 170 : "Es ist...möglich, dass der Siddhānta die Lehre von der Ewigkeit der potentiellen Materie von der Sāṃkhya-Schule übernommen hat".)

27. See above note. Also, although the term *pūrva-pakṣa* literally means 'the first objection to an assertion in any discussion' or 'the prima facie view or argument in any question', the term applies to the opponent's view or the 'other' view.

28. See, e.g., *Mṛigendra Āgama* (*Mṛigendram*), Devakoṭṭai, p. 90 1928, ch. 2, 10: "There is a discussion of liberation, together with the means for it, in the Vedānta, Sāṅkhya, Jaina, Vaiśeṣika, and other views. What is the merit in the Śiva Āgamas?" (vedānta-sāṅkhya-sad-asat-pādārthika-matādiṣu sa-sādhanā muktir-asti ko-viśeṣaś-śiva-āgame.) It may be noted also that the heading of this chapter is '*paramokṣa-nirāsa-prakaraṇam*', the chapter on the refutation of final emancipation [in other schools]. For more details about the Āgama literature see the section on *śabda pramāṇa* below, Chapter 3, p. 132.

29. Thus, in his commentary on the *Śivajñānabodham*, a work as basic to

Śaiva Siddhānta as the *Brahmasūtras* to Vedānta, Aruṇanti divides his work into two parts, dealing with the 'own view' (*svapakṣa*) and with the 'other view' (*parapakṣa*). See the German translation from the Tamil original, D.H.W. Schomerus, *Aruṇantis Śivajñānasiddhiyār*, 2 vols. (Wiesbaden: Franz Steiner Verlag, 1981).

30. The Vaiśeṣika system has 7 *padārthas*, Sāṅkhya 25, Vedānta 7, and Śaiva Siddhānta 36. It may be noted here that the meaning of *tattva* corresponds to the German word *Tatsächlichkeit*. Also, the great saying (*mahā-vākya*) 'you (*tvam*) are that (*tat*)' is represented in Vedānta by the word *tattva* and is interpreted to express the identity of existence as such with the one eternal *brahman*.
31. M. Monier-Williams, *A Sanskrit-English Dictionary*, Motilal Banarsidass ed., s.v. "śiva". The stem *śiva* is the form for deriving the neuter *śivam*, the masculine *śivaḥ* and the feminine *śivā*. In Śaiva Siddhānta, the masculine and neuter forms are often used interchangeably and the feminine form denotes the power (*śakti*) inherent in the masculine and neuter forms.
32. The metaphor that is commonly used in the tradition is that of the ocean. *Śivam* represents the area enclosing the ocean, water represents the *ātman*, and salt *malam*. Whilst this analogy is a fair one, it will become evident that it is unsatisfactory in describing the state of liberation when the *ātman* is liberated from the 'influence' of *malam*.
33. For a detailed discussion of the arguments establishing the existence and reality of *śivam* see: K. Sivaraman, *Śaivism in Philosophical Perspective* (Delhi: Motilal Banarsidass, 1973), pp. 43-201; V.A. Devasenapathi, *Śaiva Siddhānta* (Madras: University of Madras, 1974), pp. 69-137.
34. Vikalpa-rahitaṁ tattvaṃ jñānam-ānandam-avyayam/na ca nāmāni rūpāṇi śivasya paramātmanaḥ. Sūtasaṁhitā of the *Skāndapurāṇa*, quoted by Śivāgrayogin in H.R. Rangaswamy Iyengar and R. Ramasastri, eds. *Śaivaparibhāṣā* (Mysore: Government Press, 1950), p. 29.
35. Na-adhyakṣaṁ na-api tal-laiṅgaṁ na śābdam-api śāṅkaram, *Acintya Āgama*, quoted ibid., p. 30. Cf. also: na-adhyakṣaṁ na-api tal-laiṅgam na śābdam-api śāṅkaram/jñānam-ābhāti vimalaṁ sarvadā sarva-vastuṣu (The knowledge pertaining to *śaṅkaram*, i.e., *śivam*, is not [obtained through] either perception, or inference, or verbal authority. It shines forth purely at all times in all things), *Mṛigendra Āgama*, *op. cit.*, 5:16, p. 172.
36. Evam-ādi-pramāṇais-tu durlakṣyaṁ tac-chivaṁ smṛitam, *Suprabheda Āgama*, jñānapāda, 1:18a, quoted in Bruno Dagens, ed. and trans., *Śaivāgamaparibhāṣāmañjarī* (Pondichérry: Institut Francais D'Indologie, 1979), p. 255 (trans. my own).
37. Aprameyam-anirdeśyam-anaupamyam-anāmayam / sūkṣmaṁ sarvagataṁ nityaṁ dhruvam-avyayam-īśvaram // śiva-tattvam-iti proktaṁ sarva-adhvopari saṁsthitam /, *Svāyaṁbhuva Āgama*, vidyāpāda, 4 : 3 and 4 : 6b, quoted *ibid.*, p. 57. The explanation of the descriptions is given thus: 'Unknowable on account of being infinite; indescribable on account of being invisible, incomparable on account of there being no similarity

[to anything]; stainless on account of being without an impurity; subtle on account of being imperceptible; omnipresent on account of pervasiveness; eternal on account of having no cause; firm on account of immovability; indestructible on account of fulness; and majestic on account of ownership.' (Aprameyam-anantatvādanirdeśyam-alakṣyataḥ / anaupamyam-asādṛiśyād-vimalatvādanāmayam // sūkṣmaṁ ca-anupalabhyatvād-vyāpakatvāc-ca sarvagam / nityaṁ kāraṇa-śūnyatvād-acalavāc-ca tad-dhruvam / avyayaṁ pari-pūrṇatvāt svāṃi-bhāvāt-tatheśvaram //), from the same Āgama, quoted in *Śaivaparibhāṣā, op.cit.*, p. 29.

38. Ādi-madhya-anta-nirmuktaḥ svabhāva-vimalaḥ prabhuḥ / sarvajñaḥ paripūrṇaś-ca śivo jñeyaḥ śiva-āgame //, *Ajita Āgama*, 2, 2618: lb-2*o*, quoted in *Śaivāgamaparibhāṣāmañjarī, op.cit.*, p. 57.
39. *Śivajñānabodham*, verse 6. See Appendix 2 for the Sanskrit.
40. On this sixteenth-century thinker see details, p. 38.
41. ...dṛiṣṭaya viduḥ bhuñjate, in Krishan Sastri, ed., *Śivāgrabhāṣya* (Madras: Suryanar Koil Adinam, 1920) p. 339. In the same place it is said also: ...tasya muktabhogyatvam, '...[there is] an experience of it [*śivam*] by the liberated one where the liberated one is the wise one, the one who knows, the one who has had the experience of *śivam*.
42. Karaṇaṁ ca na śakty-anyat śaktir-na-acetanā citaḥ / viṣayāniyamād-ekaṁ bodhe kṛitye ca tat-tathā //, *Mṛigendra Āgama, op.cit.*, 3:4, p. 123-124.
43. Ekaiva khalu cic-chaktiś-śivasya samavāyinī, *Ratnatrayam*, Devakoṭṭai, 1925, verse 180, p. 66.
44. Yā tasya vimalā śaktiḥ śivasya samavāyinī/ sā-eva mūrtiḥ kriyā-bhedāt-sādākhyā tanur-ucyate, *ibid.*, verse 270, p. 92. In his commentary on this verse Aghoraśiva says that *Sādākhya* means *Sadāśiva* (cf. *Śaivāgamaparibhāṣāmañjarī, op.cit.*, 1:4a, p. 57, which uses the second word). There are five *Sādākhyās* which are forms of *Sadāśiva* which are involved in the cosmological functions of creation, etc.: for details on these forms see Hélène Brunner-Lachaux, *Somaśambhupaddhati*, 3 vols. (Pondichérry: Institut Francais D'Indologie, 1963), Introduction, 1:X.
45. Tayā dhṛitaṁ jagat-sarvam-ekayā-aneka-rūpayā, *Sarvajñānottara*, quoted in *Śaivāgamparibhāṣāmañjarī, op.cit.*, 1:4b, p. 57.
46. This point will be dealt with when the relation of both is considered towards the end of this study.
47. Sarvajñas-sarvagaś-śāntas-sarvātmā sarvatomukhaḥ// atīndriyo nirālambas-susūkṣmaḥ śāśvato 'vyayaḥ / suniṣkalo nirālambo na-ākhyeyo vyāpako dhruvaḥ// niraupamyo' prameyaś-ca paramātmā prakīrtitaḥ/ parasmin-tejasi vyakte tatra-sthaś-śivatām vrajet // *Śivayogaratna* 1113b-115 in Tara Michael, ed., and trans., *Śivayogaratna* (Pondichérry: Institut Francais D'Indologie, 1975), p. 60. The translation is my own. Compare a similar verse in *Mṛigendra Āgama, op.cit.*, 6:7, p. 191: 'The *ātman* is not non-pervasive, not momentary, not single, not inanimate, not a non-agent, and is one possessing consciousness uninterruptedly since it is heard that [it attains] the state of *śivam* at the destruction of the

bonds' (na-avyāpako na-kṣaṇiko na-eko na-api jaḍātmakaḥ/ na-akartā-abhinna-cid-yogī pāśa-ante śivatā-śruteḥ//) .

48. Bhāvayed-ātmanā-ātmānam-ātmanyeva-ātmanaḥ sthitiḥ, *Śivayogaratna*, *op.cit.*, 119a, p. 60.
49. Ātma-lābhāt-paro lābhaḥ kvacid-anyo na vidyate/ tad-ātmānam-upāsīta yo'yam-ātmā paras-tu saḥ//, *ibid.*, 121, p. 60.
50. See below, Chapter 2, p. 80 for these arguments.
51. Cf. verse 7 of the *Śivajñānabodham*, line 1: na-acit-cit-sannidhau kintu na vittas-te ubhe mithaḥ'in the presence of *cit* there is no *acit* and, further, these mutually do not experience each other.' See Appendix 2 for the entire text.
52. Ātmā mala-āvṛitaḥ sarvajñatve kiñcij-jñatā yataḥ / na kiñcij-jñas-tu yaḥ so 'yam malena-api na saṁvṛitaḥ // yathā śivas-tathā na-ayam malenaiva samāvṛtaḥ/, *Pauṣkara Āgama*, paśu-paṭalaḥ, 125-126a.
53. This is a significant point of departure from the Sāṅkhya school where dynamism constitutes the essential feature of matter as such, viz., *prakṛiti*, which is in a state of perpetual movement or dynamism.
54. Tad-ekam-aśivam bījaṁ jagataś-citra-śaktimat / sahakāry-adhikāra-anta-saṁrodhi vyāpy-anaśvaram // *Mṛigendra Āgama*, *op. cit.*, 9:2, p. 228.
55. Tad-ādhārāṇi kāryāṇi śakti-rūpāṇi saṁhṛitau / vikṛtau vyakti-rūpāṇi vyāpriyante'rtha-siddhaye //, *ibid.*, 9:13, p. 241.
56. Kartā'numīyate yena jagad-dharmena hetunā / tenopādānam-apy-asti na paṭas-tantubhir-vinā//, *ibid.*, 9:3, p. 230.
57. Yady-anityam-idaṁ kāryaṁ kasmād-utpadyate punaḥ / avyāpi cet kutas-tat-syāt-sarveṣāṁ sarvato-mukham // *ibid.*, 9:5, p. 231.
58. Māti yatra jagat-suptau sṛiṣṭvā vā yāti sā tataḥ / māyā tena samākhyātā tat-tvam-uktaṁ guru-uttamaiḥ //, quoted in the *Śaivaparibhāṣā* of Śivāgra-yogin, *op.cit.*, p. 87.
59. This position is similar to the Sāṅkhya view of *prakṛiti* operating for the sake of the *puruṣa*. There are at least three clear statements validating this point in the *Sāṅkhyakārikā of Īśvarakṛiṣṇa*, ed. and tr. S.S. Suryanarayana Sastri (Madras: University of Madras, 1935), verses 56-58, pp. 103-107. Verse 57 only may be quoted here to substantiate: 'As non-intelligent milk functions for the nourishment of the calf, even so does Primal Nature function for the liberation of the Spirit.' (Vatsa-vivṛddhi-nimittam kṣīra-sya yathā pravṛttir ajñasya / puruṣa-vimokṣa-nimittam tathā pravṛttiḥ pradhānasya //, *ibid.*, pp. 104-105.) The important difference, however, between the two schools is that whereas *prakṛiti* in Sāṅkhya is endowed with power (*śakti*) or activity, for the Siddhāntin *śakti* is the special feature of consciousness (*cit*). Besides, the Sāṅkhya category of *prakṛiti* occupies a 'lower' position in the Siddhānta scheme of categories. A reason one can furnish for this difference is that for the Siddhāntin the Sāṅkhya category of *prakṛiti* is inadequate insofar as it does not account for the other dimensions of reality, or the role of *māyā*, which the Siddhāntin furnishes in the doctrine of the 36 categories. The differences in the role or function of the material cause of the universe is evident in the

number of categories derived from *māyā* in Śaiva Siddhānta which is numerically higher than the 24 of *prakṛiti* in the Sāṅkhya system.

60. It may be noted that insofar as *māyā* is dependent ultimately on *śakti* for any kind of dynamism, *māyā* and *śakti* (the instrument of *śivam* responsible for evolution) are both causes of the universe. Further, whilst the relation between the two obtains at the transcendental level where distinctions are not readily discernible—except conceptually—the one is regarded as the material cause (*māyā*) operating only through the impulsion of the other which is the instrumental cause (*śakti*).
61. For the descriptive survey of the categories which follows, see also the table of categories in Appendix 1. The survey is a summary of Śivāgrayogin's *Śivāgrabhāṣya*, pp. 143-158; also his *Śaivaparibhāṣā*, pp. 79-131; and the *Mṛigendra Āgama*, pp. 251-312.
62. See also K. Sivaraman, *Śaivism*, p. 231, and the section dealing with the 36 categories, pp. 220-247.
63. That *bindu* is a synonym for *śuddha-māyā* is evident from *Ratnatraya* (Devakoṭṭai: 1925) verse 22, p. 11: 'That is called *bindu*—also known as supreme sound—which is the cause of sound, *bindu*, and letter, from which is produced the pure path where it exists and where it merges.' (Jāyate'dhvā yataś-śuddho vartate yatra līyate / sa binduḥ para-nāda-ākhyaḥ nāda-bindv-arṇa-kāraṇam //). The second term *bindu*, which is an evolute, is not to be confused with the original *bindu* as the material cause synonymous with *śuddha-māyā*. The other synonym referred to, viz., *kuṇḍalinī*, stands for *śakti* and represents the latent power which awaits manifestation in the form of sound, etc., emerging from the supreme sound (*para-nāda*), the term identical with *śuddha-māyā*, the material principle which forms the basis of creation.
64. Not to be confused with *śivam* as one of the three *tattvas* (*tattva-traya*) constituting ultimate reality.
65. For particular details about which of the three (*icchā, jñāna, kriyā*) *śaktis* is specifically responsible for these categories, see K. Sivaraman, *Śaivism*, p. 232.
66. *Ibid.*, p. 233.
67. *Ibid.*, p. 235.
68. See also Śivāgrayogin's *Śaivaparibhāṣā*, pp. 103-104.
69. The point at which each is derived in the scheme is to be noted so as not to confuse the use of these terms.
70. K. Sivaraman, *Śaivism*, p. 242.
71. Although in some contexts the word *citta* may be rendered as memory, intelligence or even reason, in the context here it refers to the principle which is responsible for all these faculties which may be said to belong to the psyche.
72. 'From another manifestation of the intellect is produced the ego (*garva*) which is an instrument of knowledge [and] by whose function the five bodily airs move.' (Atha vyakta-antarād-buddheḥ garvo'bhūt-karaṇaṁ citaḥ / vyāpārād-yasya ceṣṭante śārīrāḥ pañca vāyavaḥ //). *Mṛigendra Āgama*, *op.cit.*, 11-20, p. 307.

73. 'It [*ahaṅkāra-tattva*] is manifested in a three-fold way: the first is *taijasa*, the second is *vaikārika*, and the next is *bhūtādika*. The part that is dominated by *sattva* is called *taijasa* here, what is dominated by *rajas* is *vaikṛita*, and what has an excess of *tamas* is *bhūtādi*.' (Sa ca trividha uddriṣṭaḥ prathamas-tatra taijasaḥ / vaikāriko dvitīyaḥ syāt-tathā bhūtādika para // Sattvenotkṛiṣṭa-bhāgo yaḥ sa taijasa ihocyate / vaikṛito rajasotkṛiṣṭo bhūtādistamasa-adhikaḥ //). *Pauṣkara Āgama*, *puṁs-tattva paṭalaḥ*, 140-141, quoted in Sivāgrayogin's *Śaivaparibhāṣā*, *op. cit.*, p. 116. This three-fold differentiation of the *ahaṅkāra-tattva* is taken over from the Sāṅkhya school with a significant and noteworthy difference: for Sāṅkhya *sattva* is called *vaikārika* and *rajas* is called *taijasa*. This is stated in *Sāṅkhyakārikā*, S.S. Suryanarayana Sastri, ed. and tr. (Madras: University of Madras, 1935), v. 25, pp. 58-59: 'From that form of individuation (which is known as) Vaikṛta (and is) characterised by Sattva (goodness) the elevenfold aggregate proceeds; the subtle elements from (that form known as) Bhūtādi; it is of the nature of Tamas (darkness); both (proceed) from (that form of individuation known as) Taijasa.' (sāttvika ekādaśakaḥ pravartate vaikṛtād ahaṅkārāt / bhūtādes tanmātraḥ, so tāmasaḥ, taijasād ubhayam //). It is to be noted also that, unlike Siddhānta, Sāṅkhya does not attribute to *rajas* the responsibility of evolving any of the remaining categories which are an outcome only of the predominance either of the *sattva* or *tamas* quality of the *ahaṅkāra-tattva*. It may be argued that even for Sāṅkhya no activity is possible without the *rajas* element in the quality of things and, therefore, while its function is not given a separate status, it is presupposed in the roles of *sattva* and *tamas*: "If Sattva and Tamas are the material cause of these evolutes, Rajas is their efficient cause." (Note to the above verse, *ibid.*) Accepting, in principle, the predominance of one particular quality (*guṇa*) over the other two, Śaiva Siddhānta distinguishes categorically the consequence of the domination of each quality and, hence, the threefold classification of the three qualities (*guṇas*) of *ahaṅkāra-tattva*. See *ibid.*, p. xxxii and p. xxxiii for the tables schematically distinguishing the Sāṅkhya and Śaiva Siddhānta evolution of categories. Cf., also, the scheme given in Appendix 1.

74. For example, when it operates together with the organ of sight it is detached from the other sense organs. Further, the quickness and speed evident in perception is attributed to the function of *manas*.

75. There can be no doubt that one can speak of different versions or interpretations of the theory of *karman*: the Jainas, for example, view *karman* as 'particles' which adhere to the *jīva* and weigh it down, thereby perpetuating *saṁsāra*, or a life of suffering in the world; the Mīmāṁsakas view *karman* chiefly as ceremonial rites or rituals to be performed because they are the injunction of the Veda, and the rites are said to generate an unseen factor (*adṛiṣṭa*) helpful in bringing about *mokṣa*; for the Buddhists the theory of *karman* is allied to desire and thirst (*tṛiṣṇā*) which are the cause for suffering (*duḥkha*) in the world, the elimination of which (*tṛiṣṇā*) makes *karman*, the factor responsible for *saṁsāra*, inoperative; further, for the Śūnyavādin *karman* would be ultimately non-existent, as is the so-called agent of

*karman*; for the Śaiva Siddhāntin, as will be seen, *karman* is a principle as 'real' as *māyā* intended not only to explain man's predicament, but also to serve as a means by which man's essential nature is given an opportunity for expression and manifestation.

76. M. Monier-Williams, *A Sanskrit-English Dictionary*, s.v. "*karman.*"
77. M. Hiriyanna, *Values*, p. 169. He says in the same place: "There is a difference of opinion as regards the origin of this doctrine. Some have stated that it was borrowed by the Aryans from the primitive people of their new home, among whom a belief in the passing of the soul after death into trees, etc., was found. But the explanation ignores that that belief is a superstition and, therefore, essentially irrational, while the doctrine of karma aims at satisfying man's logical as well as moral consciousness. On account of this important difference, the doctrine should be regarded not as connected with any primitive belief, but as independently evolved by the Indians themselves." It may be noted that some clarification about the term "primitive people" would have been useful.
78. The reference is taken from the footnote, *ibid.* The exact passage in the *Aitareyopaniṣad* is: "Then, this, his other self, having done his duty in full and having attained old age, departs, and departing hence is born again. . Referring to the Highest Reality there is the following Vedic verse (Rg IV. 27. 1) declared by the sage Vāmadeva: 'Ah! Dwelling inside the womb I understood all the births of all the gods. A hundred bodies as strong as steel restrained me, but like a hawk I broke them by force and came out swiftly.' (Atha-asya-ayam-itara ātmā kṛita-kṛityo vayogataḥ praiti sa itaḥ prayanneva punar-jāyate ...tad-uktam ṛiṣiṇā garbhe nu sann-anv-eṣām-avedam-ahaṁ devānāṁ janimāni śatam mā pura āyasīr-arakṣann-adhaḥ śyeno javasā niradīyam-iti), Swami Sharvananda, tr. and ed., *Aitareyopaniṣad* (Madras: Sri Ramakrishna Math, 1959), pp. 63 and 67. Although this quotation refers only to rebirth, it is relevant insofar as the theory of *karman* includes transmigration, in addition to morality and ethics.
79. This point may be seen in the light of the question one can ask as to why Śaṅkara begins his commentary on a text concerning the ultimate, transscendent nature of *brahman* with an exegesis on the theory of superimposition, which is traditionally referred to as his famous *adhyāsabhāṣya.* This is his prelude to the *Brahmasūtrabhāṣya* which not only lays the foundation of his views, but also furnishes the one, single clue to the understanding of his philosophy of *advaita.* It may be suggested that insofar as his theory of superimposition is based on a reflection of the human situation—evident in his analysis of dream experience in relation to experiences in the wakeful state, and of cases of erroneous knowledge based on ignorance (e.g., the rope-snake analogy)—that Śaṅkara attempts to make credible the ultimate reality of the transcendent *brahman* on the basis of empirical observation and a reflection on it. In other words, just as the theory of *brahman* as the ground of all knowledge is established through an analysis of man's concrete experience, so too should the theory of *karman* be made credible by its reference to empirical experience, i.e., to arrive at the validity of the

*karman* theory on the basis of an analysis of and reflection on the human situation. It is to be noted, however, that *karman* does not share the status attributed to *brahman*.

80. The point that *śakti* is the (instrumental) cause which sets in motion the dynamics and mechanics of *karman* will be dealt with in another context. What is to be noted here is that the principle or law of *karman* is to be distinguished from man's own responsibility to incur *karman* and thereby, to be a victim of the law.
81. Iti māyā-ādi-kāla-anta-pravartakam-anādimat / karma vyañjakam-apy-etat rodhi sad-yan-na muktaye //, *Mṛigendra Āgama, op.cit.*, 8:6, p. 224.
82. Cf. *Mṛigendra Āgama, op.cit.*, 8-3, p. 220: 'Being subtle, *karman* is unseen since it is generated by activity.' (Karma-vyāpāra-janyatva-adṛiṣṭaṁ sūkṣma-bhāvataḥ).
83. *Ibid.*, 8:5. Svāpe vipākam-abhyeti tat-sṛiṣṭāv-upayujyate māyāyām vartate ca-ante na-abhuktaṁ layameti ca //
84. Cf. also what Schomerus, *op.cit.*, pp. 128-129 says: 'Activity as well as the feeling of pleasure or displeasure when experiencing prārabdhakarma creates new deeds which, like the previous deeds, strive towards maturity and consumption and, thus in turn, become prārabdha or saṃcitakarma. Since prārabdhakarma gives rise to new āgāmikarma and since a total consumption of the previous karma is not expected due to the stored saṃcitakarma, it is understandable that the doctrine of karmamala practically ends up in the doctrine of a never-ending transmigration.' (Sowohl die Betätigung als auch das Lust–oder Unlust-Gefühl bei dem Geniessen des Prārabdhakarma stellen wieder neue Taten dar, die ebenso wie die früheren Taten zur Reife und zum Verzehrtwerden drängen, sich also wieder auswachsen zum Prārabdha- bezw. Saṃcitakarma. Da das Prārabdhakarma also neues Āgāmikarma gebiert, und da wegen des aufgespeicherten Saṃcitakarma ein restloses Verzehren des früheren Karma nicht zu erwarten ist, ist es begreiflich, dass die Lehre von dem Karmamala praktisch endigt in der Lehre von der nie sich endenwollenden Seelenwanderung).
85. Cf. also an unidentified line in the *Śaivāgamaparibhāṣāmañjarī, op.cit.*, p. 105 which clearly states: prārabdham sañcitaṁ karma āgāmi ca tridhā bhavet.
86. Compare also what Schomerus says, *op.cit.*, p. 117, emphasis mine: "How does karma arise? Or, what is the same, how does it step into activity? Strictly speaking, there cannot be a *first* appearance since it is beginningless, but one can certainly talk about a reappearance." (Wie tritt nun das Karma in Erscheinung, oder was dasselbe ist, in Aktivitat? Von einem erstmaligen in Erscheinung Treten kann streng genommen keine Rede sein, da es anfangslos ist, wohl aber von einem wieder in Erscheinung Treten).
87. Compare also the point made by K. Sivaraman in his unpublished paper 'Treatment of Karma in Śaiva Siddhānta', McMaster University, Canada, p. 6: 'Like in the general case of 'bondage' itself, the essence of karma discloses itself but in retrospect, from the perspective of dissolution of Karma.'

88. One has to bear in mind, nonetheless, that the mechanics of ***karman*** operate in recurrent cycles, see also Schomerus, *op.cit.*, p. 121.
89. K. Sivaraman, *Śaivism in Philosophical Perspective*, p. 164.
90. *Ibid.*, p. 165.
91. A verse in this commonly used metre is made up of 32 syllables, divided into 8 units (*pādas*) with each unit consisting of 4 syllables.
92. It explains the so-called *Śivajñānabodham* which is taught in the *Raurava Āgama:* bodhitam raurava-tantra-antargataṁ śivajñānbodhākhyam upadiśati, quoted by K. Sivaraman in 'The Role of the Śaivāgama in the Emergence of Śaivasiddhānta: A Philosophical Interpretation', P. Slater and D. Wiebe eds., *Traditions in Contact and Change* (Waterloo: Wilfred Laurier University Press, 1983), p. 55 (translation my own). Cf. the following:

> 'There exists a work of 12 *ślokas*, the *Śivajñānabodham*. This is the fundamental text which is the most important authority in the actual system of the Śivaite philosophy which is called Śaivasiddhānta. Two commentators of these sūtras, Śivāgrayogin and Sadāśiva Śivācārya, claim that these 12 *ślokas* are taken from the *Rauravāgama*. Certain Tamil commentators even claim that it belongs to the 12th *adhyāya* of the 73rd *paṭala*, called *pāśavimocana-paṭala*, of the *Rauravāgama*... These twelve *sūtras* do not appear in the abridged version which we are publishing. There is no indication that they could have belonged to this *Āgama* nor have we yet found a *paṭala* called *pāśavimocanapaṭala*. Further, it is not usual to find a *paṭala* divided into *adhyāyas*. Finally, the last half-*śloka* which concludes the *Śivajñānabodham* declares: '*evaṁ vidyāc chivajñānabodhe śaivārthanirṇayam*' (thus should one know the decision regarding Śivaism in the *Śivajñānabodham*). From this it seems that it is an independent work. However, it is not possible to have a definite opinion on this point since we do not possess a complete manuscript'.

(Il existe une oeuvre de 12 *śloka*, *Śivajñānabodham*. C'est le texte fondamental qui fait le plus autorité dans le systémeactuel de philosophie śivaite appelé *śaivasiddhānta*. Or les deux commentateurs de ces *sūtra*, Śivāgrayogin et Sadāśiva Śivācārya, prétendent que ces 12 *śloka* sont tirés du *Rauravāgama*. Certains commentateurs tamouls prétendent meme que cette portion appartient au 12éme *adhyāya* du 73 éme *paṭala*, appelé *pāśavimocana-paṭala* du *Rauravāgama*. ...Ces douze *sūtra* manguent dans la version abrégée que nous publions. Nulle part il n'est d'indication qu'ils aient pu appartenir à cet āgama et nous n'avons pas davantage trouvé jusqu'ici un *paṭala* intitulé *pāśa-vimocanapaṭala*. Il n'est pas non plus habituel de trouver dans un *paṭala* une division en *adhyāya*. Enfin, le dernier demi-śloka qui achéve le *Śivajñānabodha* déclare: '*evaṃ vidyāc chivajñānabodhe śaivārthanirṇayam*' (qu'ainsi l,on connaisse la décision sur la connaissance relative au Śivaisme dans le *Śivajñānabodha*), Il semble d'aprés cela, qu'il s'agisse d'une oeuvre indépendante. Il n'est cependant pas possible d'avoir sure ce point une opinion définitive tant que nous n'aurons pas un manuscrit complet en notre possession.) Preface to N.R. Bhatt, ed., *Rauravāgama*, 2 vols. (Pondichérry: Institute Francais d'Indologie, 1961-72), 1:ii-iii. I am greatly indebted to Dr. L. Soni for the assistance with the French here and elsewhere in the study.

93. Composed in the thirteenth century by Meykaṇṭhadeva.

94. See also K. Sivaraman's paper 'The role of the Śaivāgama', op.cit., pp. 57-58: 'The question of the relative originality of the Tamil or the Sanskritic versions of the text, ...is not very relevant for this paper. The one point of immediate concern is: What are the formative factors definitive to the structure that is discernibly intrinsic to the text of *Śivajñānabodham*? This question raises a problem in its own right and again of the kind that seems meaningfully resolvable only when perceived as belonging with the question of understanding.' On the basis of the two languages in the Śaiva Siddhānta tradition scholars distinguish Tamil Śaiva Siddhānta from Sanskrit Śaiva Siddhānta. See, for example:

'Like its Sanskrit homonym the Tamil Śaiva Siddhānta is based on the Śaiva Āgamas. It also claims to be based on the Vedas. The rigorously organized doctrines which it teaches are very close to those of the Sanskrit Śaiva Siddhānta. But it is distinguished from it on some fundamental points, since it orients itself toward a unitary conception of the supreme principle and the phenomenal world. It does not lose sight of the difference (*bheda*) which exists between Śiva and the world, but it insists on the absolutely indissoluble character of their union (*abheda*) and thus proposes the theory of *bhedâbheda* ('difference and non-difference') which is opposed, likewise, to the dualism of the Sanskrit authors and the absolute monism of Śaṅkara.' (Comme son homonyme sanscrit, le çaivasiddhânta tamoul se fonde sur les âgama civaites. Il prétend aussi se fonder sur les veda. Les doctrines, rigoureusement organisées, qu'il enseigne sont trés voisines de celles du caivasiddhānta sanscrit. Mais il s'en sépare sur quelques points fondamentaux, quisqu,il s'oriente vers une conception unitaire du principe suprême et du monde phénoménal. Il ne perd pas de vue la différence (*bheda*) qui existe entre Civa et le monde, mais il insiste sur le caractére absolument indissoluble de leur union (*abheda*) et propose ainsi la théorie du *bhedâbheda* ('différence et non-différence'), qui s'oppose également au dualisme des auteurs sanscrits et au monisme absolu de Caṁkara) *Encyclopaedia Universalis*, 1968 ed., s.v. 'Civa et Civaisme', By' P-S. Filliozat.

Also:

'*Śaivadarśana* has doubled itself in the course of its long history. The Sanskrit branch which issued from the *Āgamas* has continued its straight growth, but with fewer and fewer fruits; and a Tamil branch which, apart from being rooted in a different soil, has detached itself from the principal stem and, without establishing any particular ritual, has expressed its doctrine in a powerful and original form, the one which one knows under the name of *Śaiva-Siddhānta* (but which we prefer to call Tamil *Śaiva-Siddhānta*, because the other branch is also a *Śaiva-Siddhānta*...

However, the tie between the Tamil *Śaiva-Siddhānta* and the *Āgamas* has remained very close for a long time. In the sixteenth century the Tamil commentators of the *Siddhiār* knew Sanskrit perfectly well; they draw largely from the *Āgamas* in order to write their treatises and to oppose thier adversaries.' (Le *śaivadarśana* en effet s'est dédoublé au course de sa longue histoire. La branche sanskrite issue des *Āgama* a continué sa croissance droite, mais en donnant des fruits de plus en plus rares; et une branche tamoule, en partie d'ailleurs enracinée dans un humus différent, s'est détachée du tronc principal et, sans instaurer de rituel particulaier, a exprimé sa doctrine sous une forme puissante et originale, celle que l'on connait sous le nom de *Śaiva-Siddhānta* (mais que nous préférons nommer *Śaiva-Siddhānta* tamoul, parce que l'autre branche est aussi un *Śaiva-Siddhānta* ...Cependent, le lien entre le *Śaiva-Siddhānta* tamoul et les *Āgama* est longtemps resté trés étroit. Au XVIéme siécle, les commentateurs tamouls du *Siddhiar* connaissent le sanskrit de facon parfaite; ils puisent largement dans les *Āgama* pour écrire leurs traités et se battre contre leurs adversaires.) Héléne Brunner's article 'Importance de la littérature āgamique' in *Indologica Taurinensia*, vols. III-IV (Official organ of the International Association of Sanskrit Studies), *Proceedings of the Second World Sanskrit Conference* (Torino: Instituo di Indologia), p. 114. The present study does not enter into any discussion over the complex issues related to the originality and differences of the so-called two branches of Śaiva Siddhānta, which presupposes a thorough acquaintance with both Sanskrit and Tamil. The issues entailed therein could well be the subject matter of a complete study in itself. Suffice it for the task at hand to merely indicate an awareness of the ongoing debate represented in the above.

95. The enormous difficulty in conclusively tracing the origins of traditions in India, both Vedic and Āgamic, needs no discussion. The problems entailed here, particularly with Śaivism, which derives its inspiration from the Āgamas, are excellently discussed in Jan Gonda, *A History of Indian Literature*, vol. II, fasc. 1: *Medieval Religious Literature in Sanskrit* (Wiesbaden: Otto Harrassowitz, 1977), "Śivaism:, pp. 153-162; 'The Śivaite Āgama Literature', pp. 163-179; and "The Individual Āgamas", pp. 180-215. A recently published work contains an enlightening introduction and first chapter concerning the point under question by an author from the French Institute of Indology: V. Varadachari, *Āgamas and South Indian Vaiṣṇavism* (Madras: Prof. M. Rangacharya Memorial Trust, 1982), pp. 1-56. For further details about Śaiva Siddhānta literature and the history of the tradition see especially: S. Dasgupta, *A History of Indian Philosophy*, 5 vols. (Cambridge: University Press, 1922), vol. 5; Tribhuvan Prasad Upadhyaya, ed., *Bhaskari*, 3 vols. (Lucknow; New Government Press, 1954), vol. 3; J. Sinha, *Schools of Śaivism*, (Calcutta: Sinha Publishing House, 1970); C.V. Narayana Ayyar, *Origin and Early History of Śaivism*, (Madras: University of Madras, 1974); T.B. Siddalingaiah, *Origin and Development of Śaiva Siddhānta up to fourteenth Century* (Madurai: Madurai Kamaraj University, 1979).

96. Although the content of both the Sanskrit and Tamil versions of the

*Śivajñānabodham* is regarded as being semantically identical, textually there are some differences. Compare the translation of the Sanskrit *sūtras* on pp. 81-82 with the translation of the Tamil text—which comprises the bulk of the book—by Gordon Matthews, *Śiva-Ñāna-Bōdham* (Oxford: University Press, 1948).

97. For a comparison of the *Śivajñānabodham* and the *Brahmasūtra*, see K. Sivaraman, *Śaivism*, pp. 35-36.

98. A few variant readings may be noted, without alteration to the meaning. Compare verses 4, 9 and 11 supplied in the appendix with the versions in J.M. Nallaswami Pillai, *Śivajñāna Siddhiār of Aruṇandi Śivāchārya* (Madras : Meykandan Press, 1913), p. lvi (of the Introduction).

99. See V.A. Devasenapathi, *op.cit.*, p. 9. Sivāgrayogin is perhaps the only Siddhāntin who may be credited with having written in both Sanskrit and Tamil. Although Jñānaprakāśar, his younger contemporary, also wrote in Sanskrit, he is, however, referred to as a Śivasamavādin because of his view 'that souls at release are equal to Śiva in every respect, a view which is interesting and ably argued but totally at variance with the Siddhānta,' *ibid.*, p. 12.

100. What distinguishes him from the others, e.g., Umāpati (fourteenth century) and Śivajñānayogin (eighteenth century) may be reduced to one fundamental difference: whereas for Śivāgrayogin *śivam* is both the material and instrumental cause (*upādāna-nimitta-kāraṇa*), in his sense of the terms, and reflecting a position which seems to be a qualified vindication of the Śivādvaita standpoint of Śrīkaṇṭha (twelfth century), in his commentary of the *Brahmasūtra*, for Umāpati and Śivajñānayogin, on the other hand, *śivam* is only the instrumental cause (*kevala-nimitta-kāraṇa*). See also K. Sivaraman, *Śaivism*, p. 38. It is stated, *ibid.*, that "Umāpati is aware of the closeness of *Śivādvaita* to his position and even says that the distinction between the two is only terminological and not conceptual." In the case of Śivāgrayogin it will be seen in his commentary to *sūtra* 8 of the *Śivajñānabodham* how he justifies his interpretation of the state of non-difference (*ananyatvam*) between the *ātman* and *śivam* as one which permits a 'slight' (*īṣat*) difference (*bheda*): 'therefore, that state is one of non-difference, while there is [still] a slight difference.' (*tasmād-īṣadbhede saty-abheda-eva tattvam*).

101. Krishna Sastri, ed. (Madras: Suryanar Koil Adinam, 1920). Grantha is a script invented by the South Indians in which to write Sanskrit and its similarity to the Tamil script is evident in many letters. The Āgamas, which bear the authoritative status ascribed to the Vedas, have been preserved in the Grantha script. It is only fairly recently, especially through the efforts of the French Institute of Indology in Pondicherry, that access to the vast Āgama literature has been facilitated by the publications in the Devanāgarī script.

102. First published in Devanāgarī, H.R. Rangaswamy Iyengar and R. Ramasastri, eds. (Mysore: Government Press, 1950), Oriental Research Institute Publications, Sanskrit series No. 90. Another edition of the text has also been published, with an English translation by S.S. Suryanarayana

Sastri, in R. Balasubramanian and V.K.S.N. Raghavan, eds. (Madras: University of Madras, 1982), Madras University Philosophical Series—35. In the preface to this edition, p. iii, it is stated: "The *Śaiva-paribhāṣā* which is a valuable manual on Śaiva Siddhānta is comparable to Dharmarāja's *Vedānta-paribhāṣā* of the Advaita school and Śrīnivāsa's *Yatindra-mata-dīpikā* of the Viśiṣṭādvaita school."

103. There is no indication which work was undertaken first. In adition to the two works already mentioned (which this study draws from) Śivāgrayogin's other works in Sanskrit are: *Śivajñānabodha Laghuṭīkā*, Pandit Series, vol. 29 (Banares: E.J. Lazarus and Co., 1907); *Śaiva-sannyāsa-paddhati* (Kumbha Konam, n.p., 1921)—in Grantha.

104. In exegeting the *sūtras* of the *Śivajñānabodham* in this work Śivāgrayogin first provides a concise, 'short' commentary (*saṅgraha-bhāṣya*) immediately followed by an expanded, "detail" commentary (*vistṛita-bhāṣya*), elaborating certain points in greater detail. This method is used for all the twelve *sūtras* of *Śivajñānabodham*, except *sūtras* seven and eleven, where he says detailed commentaries are not necessary. This study draws chiefly from the former, where all his views are succinctly put. Śivāgrayogin's commentary called *Śivāgrabhāṣya* is hereafter cited as *SB*.

CHAPTER 2

# *The definitions of man*

## 2.1 *Man and the states of consciousness*

In what may be called a phenomenological analysis of different levels or states of human experience Indian thinkers contrast firstly the wakeful state from the sleep state.[1] The state of sleep is further considered as comprising two states, namely, the dream state of sleep (*svapna*) and the dreamless state of sleep or deep sleep (*svāpa* or *suṣupti*). On the basis of an investigation into these states a fourth state (*turīya*) is inferred and Śaiva Siddhānta, elaborating on the Yoga[2] and Vedānta scheme, acknowledges a fifth state called 'beyond the fourth' (*turīyātīta*). These states belong to the structure of our active life and constitute the framework of human experience. The phenomenological analysis which leads to the postulation of these five states or levels of experience represents a transcendental reflection of human experience on the basis of which the *ātman*, characterized as consciousness (*cit*), is inferred. Before analysing and discussing these states in greater detail it will be useful to point out broadly what distinguishes and characterizes each state.

When the entire psycho-physical complex of man is in function the state is called the wakeful state (*jāgrat*). It is marked by the manifestation of sense organ (*indriya*) functions together with the functions of the intellect (*buddhi*), of 'memory' (*citta*), and of the life breath (*prāṇa*)—i.e., the function of the *puruṣa-tattva* as it evolves and expresses itself in the functions of the *karmendriyas*, *jñānendriyas* and the *antaḥ-karaṇas*—all of which become vehicles for a partial expression of consciousness (*cit*). The progressive elimination of the function of each of these corresponds to a particular state. Thus, when the functions of all the sense organs are withdrawn and only *buddhi*, *citta* and *prāṇa* serve to manifest consciousness through their functions, the state is called *svapna*, the dream state of sleep. When the function of the *buddhi* is eliminated—in addition to the sense organ functions—and only *citta* and *prāṇa* prevail with consciousness, the state is called *suṣupti*, the dreamless state of sleep or deep sleep. When the function of the *citta* is eliminated or inoperative and only the *prāṇa* manifests consciousness, the state is called *turīya* or the fourth state. When, finally, the *prāṇa* is withdrawn and consciousness manifests itself without any aid—and, perhaps, better described as a 'zero manifestation'—the state beyond the fourth, *turīyātīta*, is attained or, rather, 'descended into'.

In the case of the *sakala-paśu*, this description needs to be qualified. It was already stated that man, the *sakala-paśu*, is a concatenation of *āṇava*, *karma* and *māyā malam*. It is this structure which permits an expression of the *ātman* as manifested in volition, knowledge and action. It was seen how this involved a transition from the *ātman*'s isolated (*kevala*) state enveloped by *āṇava-malam*, to the *sakala* state when the *ātman*, furnished with the instruments and objects of experience, is given a modicum of scope for expression. Further, the transition from the *sakala* to the *śuddha* state for which, as will be seen, *śivam*'s power of compassion or grace (*anugraha-śakti*) is indispensable, is via the *kevala* state itself. In other words, the *ātman*'s 'journey' involves a transition from *kevala* to *sakala*, and from *sakala* to *śuddha* via *kevala*.[3] In the light of what has been said above, the fifth state, *turīyātīta*, would involve a transition or, rather, a return of the *sakala-paśu* to its isolated state as a *kevala-paśu* where it is in need of some kind of 'assistance'—and because only *śivam* can provide it, the assistance is termed grace—on account of the overwhelming power of *malam*. In the journey to *sakala*, *karman* and *māyā* assist in the expression and manifestation of the *ātman*, albeit under the spell of *āṇava-malam*. In the journey to the *śuddha* state the *ātman*, having successfully and completely exploited the use of *karman* and *māyā*, is isolated once again on account of the *āṇava-malam*. In this phase of the journey, which now truly borders on soteriology, the *āṇava-malam* needs to be 'removed'. The *ātman* is no less incapacitated by *āṇava* at this stage than when previously, through *śivam*'s 'veiled' grace, its journey which marked the transition to the *sakala* state was facilitated by *karman* and *māyā*—*śivam*'s 'veiled' grace (*tirodhāna*) is to be distinguished from 'manifest' grace (*anugraha*) which helps effect the transition from the *sakala* to the *śuddha* state. However, the *āṇava-malam* has now matured, so to speak, through experience (*bhoga*) in the world. Its 'ripening' which this process of maturation entails, points to a need for the 'plucking' of *āṇava-malam* which, in the nature of the case, is possible only through *śivam*'s grace (*anugraha*). A further discussion on this soteriological issue will have to be resumed at a later stage. What is to be noted for the present context is that the five states referred to above finally relate progressively to the isolation of consciousness (*cit*) from any limiting adjuncts. In the case of the *sakala-paśu*, however, the states mark a gradual relapse and the fifth state, *turīyātīta*, is to be seen in the context of the *ātman* under the complete spell of *āṇava-malam* once again—albeit in a different or *reverse* 'direction' of the *ātman*'s journey.

For experience in the world the *ātman* or consciousness as such requires the aid of the *indriyas*, *buddhi*, *citta* and *prāṇa*. It is through their role in providing the link between the *ātman* and the objects of experience that life in the world as we know it is possible. The condition of the *ātman*'s relation to the categories necessary for human experience represents a state of limited or fettered expression of its powers. In this fettered state the *ātman*, as already seen, is more appropriately called a *paśu* and a *sakala-paśu* is man in the world of common, everyday experience. The etymological meaning of the word *sakala* furnishes an important sense of the term, as Śaiva Siddhānta uses it. The word is a compound derived from the preposition *sa* (meaning together or along with, accompanied by, having, possessing, containing) and the feminine noun *kalā* (meaning the elements of the gross or material world). The adjective *sakala* thus means 'consisting of parts', 'possessing all its component parts', 'complete or whole', and in the neuter form, the word means 'affected by the elements of the material world'.[4] It is in this context that the significance of the state in which the *sakala-paśu* exists, the *sakala-avasthā*, has the impact of man's state or condition in undergoing worldly experience. In addition to the etymological meaning of the term, is its technical meaning, and one which is unique to the Āgama use of it, viz., as 'along with' the *kalā-tattva*.

## 2.2 *Toward a general definition of man*

In asking what the nature, characteristic and essence of a *sakala-paśu* are, one is in fact asking about a definition of man. What constitutes a definition in the proper sense of the term is a special subject of discussion for Śaiva Siddhānta which has its own slant of defining terms. It is the Āgamas, and particularly the *Śivajñānabodham,* which provide the basis for a need to clarify the concept of definition and its function. In this discussion, the strong influence of Nyāya is evident[5], even if the metaphysical presuppositions of Nyāya realism are not accepted.

In dealing with the question of the definition of the three ultimate categories (*padārthas*) of reality, the *Śivajñānabodham* serves as the basis for a distinction between two related kinds of definition (*lakṣaṇa*), viz., a broad, general definition (*taṭastha-lakṣaṇa*) and a specific, essential definition (*svarūpa-lakṣaṇa*). It may be said that the former is a definition of a property distinct from its essential nature and yet by which the essential nature can indeed be known.[6] The *taṭastha-lakṣaṇa* may be arrived at through an existential reflection on the nature of things in the world as explained in the scheme of *tattvas* and this, in turn, serves as the basis for the *svarūpa-lakṣaṇa* arrived at through a transcendental reflection on what constitutes the essential nature of a category. In the case of what constitutes a complete definition of man, it will be seen in greater detail how, on the one hand, the definition of man generally and broadly is in terms of the being involved in empirical life and how, on the other hand, specifically, intrinsically, and essentially man has to be defined purely in terms of consciousness itself—the latter definition being derived, in fact, from the former.

Śivāgrayogin has no difficulty at all as regards entering into a debate on a definition of man. In verse two of the *Śivajñāna-bodham* it is declared: 'He[7] creates the world for the sake of human beings' (*karoti saṁsṛiṣṭim puṁsām*).[8] Śivāgrayogin inquires into the meaning of this statement and asks: "who are the beings here for whom this world—from *śiva* [*tattva*], etc. to earth—is produced?"[9] This is Śivāgrayogin's preamble to verse three of the *Śivajñānabodham* and it evinces the characteristic continuity and flow of his style displayed throughout his commentary. The preamble anticipates his own discussion on the scheme of *tattvas*, which encompasses man, and says that the answer to the question concerning man is provided in this and in the next verse of the text. The task now, therefore, is to see how verses three and four of the *Śivajñānabodham* furnish a definition of man in the answer that they are said to give.

> Verse three of the text reads:
> There is an *aṇu* in the body on account of: [the cognition of] not-thisness; the excess of mineness; there being consciousness [even] when the senses have ceased [functioning, e.g., in the dream state]; [the recollection of] there being no experience in deep sleep; and on account of there being one [an agent] who perceives when awake.

This verse is in the form of an argument with five reasons to validate the view that there is an element or principle which constitutes man's essence and characteristic feature, and in terms of which, it may be anticipated, the definition of man is to be given. It is in this context that the five reasons given in the verse could well be taken as stages or steps which lead to the idea of the *aṇu*. The word *aṇu* here is to be taken as a synonym for the *ātman* because in the following verse four of the text, the subject is the *ātman* and from the context it is clear that '*aṇu*' in verse three is synonymous with '*ātman*' in verse four. Hence, the *aṇu*, which for all practical purposes is now the *ātman*, is the principle which is constantly aware of, and even makes possible, every physical and psychological experience with which it is invariably connected.

In his commentary to verse three cited above, Śivāgrayogin takes the opportunity to exegete the deliberate use of the third singular form (*asti*) of the verb 'to be' (*as*). This he does especially in view of the fact that Sanskrit grammar permits the omission of certain words, which have to be supplied to facilitate an intelligible, contextual reading of a sentence. This practice is particularly common in the case of various forms of the verb 'to be'. The word '*asti*' in the text is perhaps best rendered here as 'there is' or 'there exists' and Śivāgrayogin says that the word denotes two significant points: 'firstly, [what is] different from the non-existing and, secondly, [what has] an existence undiminished at all times.'[10] Further, it refers to what is always 'abiding' (*sthāyin*). The point of these comments is to draw attention to a characteristic feature or principle in man which experiences the different states of our existence without modifying itself in undergoing these vacillations.

The significance of the phrase 'in the body' in the statement 'there is an *aṇu* in the body' expressed in the verse is to be especially noted insofar as the body cannot be said to constitute the essential feature of man expressed by the term *aṇu* or *ātman*. In addition to the five reasons already alluded to above, this point may be taken to be a sixth reason expressed in the verse to validate the postulation of such a principle. The significance of this principle which exists in the body is evident by contrasting it with the five reasons that account for its existence. It is through a detailed consideration of these reasons that a description and definition of man begin to emerge.

The cognition of not-thisness is the first reason stated in the verse. In his commentary on this point, Śivāgrayogin uses it as the basis from which to launch an attack on the Mādhyamika doctrine of the void (*śūnyavāda*). In essence, the attack is short, direct and precise: 'Since there is a cognition of the void the *aṇu*, which is the cognizer, is not non-existent.'[11] In elaborating this basic refutation of *śūnyavāda* he says:

> If, for you who speak of the voidness of everything, there be no one who cognises "the pot, etc., is void", then this [cognition] becomes invalid. Therefore, it must be said that there is a cognizer of this [cognition] and not that even this [cognizer] is void since there is no evidence to that effect. Through self-recognition...it is not possible to understand voidness in the form of one's own non-existence perceived previously. Moreover, to say "I am not" is a contradiction of activity in oneself.[12]

When the Siddhāntin says that recognition (*pratyabhijñā*) is not a means by which to establish the view that everything is void, the point is that even if one were to grant the cognition or experience of the void it still presupposes a recognizer of the recognition or an experiencer of the experience. This point becomes clearer when the same argument is put in other words:

> Is there a cognition of the void or not? If not, then it [the cognition of the void] becomes unauthentic. Therefore it must be said that in fact there is this [cognition of the void] and not that this [itself] is void since, in this case, the situation of the non-existence of the void would arise. What does not exist cannot prove non-existence, therefore, it has to be said that there is this [cognition of the void]. This is the *ātman* for us.[13]

The strength of this argument is that a cognition of the void cannot itself be the void and if some form of cognition is not acknowledged, then there can be no void to be cognized. The problem entailed in this position is equivalent to what applies in the case of a universal statement in logic, e.g., that 'everything is relative'. This statement itself has to be excluded from the reference to 'everything' for it to have any meaning at all. A similar example is 'everyone is speaking a lie' where the speaker has to be excluded for the sentence to be meaningful. It is in this way that "everything is void" excludes the cognition of everything as void from itself being void. Some status has to be given to the cognition and this is precisely the point of contention with the Śūnyavādin.[14]

As a corollary to the refutation of *śūnyavāda*, the following emerges: "The word 'not-this' [i.e., the cognition of the void] depends on the intellect which is responsible for this statement, therefore, it [the cognition of the void] is the proof for this [intellect]."[15] This point is significant insofar as it points to the 'level' at which the cognition takes place. It is a cognition that is the outcome of the *buddhi-vṛitti*, the modification of the intellect, which takes on the mode of the void and cognizes it as such. It is *cit-śakti*, finally, which makes this possible, albeit delimited by the intellect. The cognition, therefore, does not take place through *cit-śakti* per se but through a fettered *cit-śakti*. What this means is that the cognition of everything being void is but a limited expression of the consciousness which constitutes the essence and characteristic feature of man. To identify a cognition as being that of the void or, in other words, to arrive at a judgement that what was cognized is the void, points to the function of the *buddhi* in the Śaiva Siddhānta scheme of *tattvas*. Thus, the view that everything is void—far from referring to the essence of man—is rather a proof, according to the Siddhāntin, for the category of the intellect.

Further, if the fact of this cognition of the void is not acknowledged, then obviously there cannot be a void to be cognized. This puts into question the validity of the notion of the void itself. The Siddhāntin's conclusion, therefore, is that the essence and defining characteristic of man cannot be in terms of the void.

In exegeting the first reason which establishes the existence of an *aṇu* or *ātman* in the body and in attempting to arrive at a definition of man in a negative way, Śivāgrayogin rejects the position of the Śūnyavādin by arguing that the void can only be intelligible as a cognition of the void. The cognition, further, serves to prove the existence of the intellect which determines the 'object' of cognition which, in the present context, is cognizable as consisting of the absence of any objects. If this void that is cognized were to be taken as constituting man's essence, then the feature of such a cognition would mean that it excludes from its frame of reference a conscious principle which makes such a cognition at all possible. Besides, the fact that the intellect is the instrument of cognition means that one would have to talk of a fettered cognition. In view of these points, it is held that the void cannot constitute the essence of man.

The second reason expressed in the verse which accounts for the view of an essential feature which constitutes the essence of man is: 'on account of the excess of mineness'. The compound used here is made up of 'mineness' (*mamatā*) and 'on account of the excess of' (*udrekāt*). Mineness is defined as "the knowledge of the distinction between the *ātman* and the body in [such statements as] 'this is my body' " and, therefore, the compound together with 'intensity or excess' (*udreka*) means 'on account of the intensity of this [knowledge].'[16] In the light of this comment the syntax which clearly brings out the impact of this part of the verse would, therefore have, to read as follows: 'there is an *aṇu* in the body on account of the intensity of the knowledge about the distinction between the *ātman* and the body.' What this means in short is that 'on account of the intensity of mineness the *aṇu* is not the body.'[17] The phrase 'in the body' expressed in the verse has, therefore, to be construed along with 'the intensity of mineness.' That there is an *aṇu* (or *ātman*) *in* the body means that it is *not* the body and this fact can be realized through the intensity or excess of mineness. Statements such as 'this is my body' which express mineness point to a 'my'. An inquiry into the meaning of this word is in fact an investigation into the view that the essence of man is evidently represented by the body.

The question concerning the body, the consciousness that is manifested in it, and consciousness as such is a matter of considerable debate. The question basically is: is the defining characteristic of man to be given in physical, corporeal terms or in terms of what constitutes the nature of consciousness? Together with others of the same philosophical standpoint on the issue, e.g., the Vedāntins, the Śaiva Siddhāntin launches an attack on the Cārvākas who uphold the view that everything can, and should, be explained only in physical terms. The former who uphold the theory that the essence of man is what is called the *ātman*, characterized chiefly by consciousness, are called ātmavādins and the latter, called dehātmavādins, hold the view that this essence characterized by consciousness is nothing but the outcome of a particular combination of the elements of the body which vanishes when this combination is disturbed with the death of the body.[18]

The following, as Śivāgrayogin puts it, is the chief criticism of the Cārvāka against the ātmavādins:

> What is the proof for the existence of the *ātman* apart from the body? Firstly, it is not perception since there is no perception of it and also since the case of the usage of "my body" is the same as "my *ātman*".[19] Nor even can inference be the proof since there is no indicatory mark[20] and since there is no difference when the body is posited as that [*ātman*]—since it is the locus of consciousness.[21]

Further, the Cārvāka maintains: "Consciousness [occurs only] in a [particular] conglomeration of elements and there is no occurrence of it in the case of a pot, etc. Since things are transformed into the form of a body, etc., having their own manifold natures, there occurs that [consciousness] inherently."[22] Therefore, in the considered opinion of the Cārvāka, no principle beyond the body need be acknowledged "since, as far as consciousness is concerned, there is the propriety in arguing that the body itself is its inherent cause and [also] the 'reasonable cause' ".[23]

The Siddhāntin's answer to the above argument raised by the Cārvāka is: "The body is not the source (*āśraya*) of consciousness since it [the body] is an object of enjoyment, or since it undergoes change, like a pot, etc.; [therefore] something apart from it [the body] must be acknowledged."[24] The point is that the Siddhāntin who insists, on rational grounds, that the notion of consciousness be accepted, regards it as a permanent, unchanging principle which, as such, is not subject to any essential modification. Moreover, an entity that is subject to change, like the body, cannot be said to be the source of an unchanging principle such as consciousness. It is only when consciousness is associated with, and thereby determined by, the body which it *uses* that it appears to share the limitations and impermanence of the body. This refutation is on the authority of the *Mṛigendra Āgama* which Śivāgrayogin quotes:

> If it is said that it [the body] is conscious (*cetana*) then, since it is subject to change and since it is an object of use, it can never [itself] be consciousness (*cit*). The things, like pot, etc., are seen to undergo changes and they are also to be used. Even this [body] is verily [like] that [pot].[25]

This argument is unacceptable to the Cārvāka not only because it has the form of an inference[26] but also because it contains the fallacy called *upādhi*. The exact reason for the Cārvāka's rejection as Śivāgrayogin supposes it to be is: "on account of the [fallacy of] *upādhi* [contained in] 'not being the source (*anāśraya*) of the sense organs [of the body]' ".[27] Although this reason is not elaborated by Śivāgrayogin—since it seems that he adopts the Nyāya position here—it will be useful to see how exactly it may serve the Cārvāka to reject that argument. It is also necessary, thereby, to see how precisely the Siddhāntin justifies the notion of consciousness (*cit*) which is supposed to be indispensable toward an understanding and definition of man.

The fallacy contained in the above argument belongs to the kind[28] the Nyāya calls 'unestablished reasoning' (*asiddha*) and of the three kinds[29] that come under this group, the fallacy in question is termed 'unestablished in respect of its concomitance' (*vyāpyatvāsiddha*). The technical, and somewhat lengthy, logical explanation given by Nyāya of this kind of unestablished reasoning is:

> The reason is said to be *vyāpyatvāsiddha* when it is associated with an adventitious condition (*upādhi*). That is said to be an adventitious condition (*upādhi*), which is pervasive of the *probandum* [*sādhya*] but not pervasive of the *probans* [*sādhana*]. 'To be pervasive of the *probandum* 'means' never to be the counter-correlative (*pratiyogin*) of non-existence (*abhāva*) which co-exists with the *probandum*'. 'Not to be pervasive of the *probans*' means 'being the counter-correlative of non-existence which co-exists with the *probans*'. In the argument—"The mountain has smoke, because it has fire", *contact with wet fuel* is the adventitious condition (*upādhi*). "Where there is smoke, there is contact with wet fuel"—thus it is pervasive of the *probandum*. There is no contact with wet fuel in every place where there is fire; for instance, a red-hot iron ball has no contact with wet fuel; thus the *upādhi* is non-pervasive of the *probans*. In this manner, contact with wet fuel is the *upādhi* in the present instance, because it is pervasive of the *probandum* but not pervasive of the *probans*. And fire, in the argument under reference, is *vyāpyatvāsiddha*, since it is associated with an *adventitious condition* (*upādhi*).[30]

In applying this intricate argument to the context of the discussion at hand, the fallacy pointed out by the Cārvāka would be the following: the *upādhi* 'not being the source of the sense organs of the body' is pervasive of the *sādhya*, viz., 'the body is not the source of consciousness', but not of the *sādhana*, viz., 'the sense organs are not the source of experience'. In other words, just as one can say 'wherever there is smoke there is contact with wet fuel' and not 'wherever there is fire there is contact with wet fuel' (since a red-hot iron ball has no contact with wet fuel), so too one can say 'wherever there is contact with sense organs there is experience' but not 'wherever there is consciousness there is experience' (since consciousness is never without contact with the body and its organs).

Śivāgrayogin says that it is this very objection raised by the Cārvāka that is refuted when the verse under consideration says "on account of the intensity of mineness" (*mamatā-udrekāt*). This is to say that the greater the intensity in everyday life of such feelings as 'this experience is mine' the stronger the impact, by contrast, of its reference to a noncorporeal principle which has such an experience. What is being anticipated here is the Siddhāntin's position that experience is indeed possible through consciousness per se—the so-called experience man has through the body and its organs is but a limited and conditioned experience. The Siddhāntin is philosophically preparing the ground for a case to be made out later, for what is going to be called *śiva-bhoga* (the experience of *śivam* or the experience of the transcendent). The word *bhoga* (experience) without any qualification generally refers to empirical experience that consciousness undergoes using the body and its organs as its instruments. When the word is prefixed by '*śiva*', it points to the experience that consciousness has without the restrictions enforced by corporeality. This point will be considered in more detail later. For the present, it is to be noted that the Siddhāntin rejects the Cārvāka contention that the body is the source of consciousness and that with the dissolution of the body at death, consciousness too, *ipso facto*, is dissolved.

In order to be authoritative in his rejection of the Cārvāka position, and also for the clarity it provides, Śivāgrayogin quotes the *Pauṣkara Āgama* in the section of his commentary under discussion:

> Further, the quality belonging to anything is destroyed with the destruction of the thing, i.e., on account of the presence of the opposite condition. O Twice Born Ones, how can it be otherwise? When the body lies there at death, why is consciousness not ascribed to it? That by the presence or absence of

which the body undergoes either activity or non-activity, is called "consciousness", which is distinct from the body.[31]

What is implicit in this argument is the point that just as the body's destruction is evident at its death, so too should the destroyed consciousness—which the Cārvāka sees as belonging to the body—be also perceived with the dead body. This not being the case, consciousness has to be regarded as being undestroyed with the death of the body. Further, since it is not perceivable in the dead body, consciousness has to be seen essentially as being independent of the body. Its presence in the body, without which the body is inoperative, gives the semblance of an unwarranted identity of the two to the point where the death of the one signifies the destruction of the other.

An argument following from the above is that: 'if the body itself were associated with the quality of consciousness then with its variation it too [consciousness] would grow or diminish, etc.'[32] With this point Śivāgrayogin takes the Cārvāka standpoint to the absurd logical conclusion where not only can there be no recognition of someone seen previously, but the one who recognizes cannot be said to be the same person either, i.e., both would have changed in the course of time—with the unrecognizable differences in the physique of both, there would be a corresponding change, beyond recognition, of the consciousness of each. In view of the fact that the Cārvāka position is inconsistent with common-sense experience, apart from leading to absurd conclusions, the attempt to arrive at a definition of man would have to exclude, in the final analysis, the view which regards consciousness—man's defining, characteristic feature—in terms of what is corporeal or physical which, in fact, are the defining characteristics of insentience (*jaḍatva*).

The third reason expressed in the above verse which makes out a case for consciousness as such is its presence even when the senses have ceased functioning, e.g., in the dream state. The fact that some cognition does indeed occur in the dream state of sleep, is evident in such statements as 'I saw an elephant in my dream'. This means that there is some source (*āśrayatā*) of cognition and that there is an 'I' which had such an experience. On account of this it is necessary to acknowledge that there is an *aṇu* or *ātman* even during the dream state.[33] It is noteworthy that the continuity of consciousness into the dream state from the wakeful state is inferred on the basis of a *post facto* reflection of dream experience. Whereas the analysis of the wakeful state served to refute the contention that the body could be the *ātman*, the analysis of the dream state, on the other hand, demonstrates that the sense organs—which are not indispensable for cognition—can no less be regarded as being the *ātman* because cognition takes place even when they do not function in the dream state. The only difference in the psycho-physical complex of man between these two states is that the operation of the sense organ functions is shut off in the dream state, as also in deep sleep and the other states. The absence of the sense organ functions in the dream state must, therefore, be said to be responsible for the fact that we do not perceive a dream as a dream during the dream experience.

The transition from the wakeful to the dream state is characterized by the cessation of the sense organ functions in the latter. It is the faculty of memory which accounts for the fact of dream experiences, which are recalled in the wakeful state. In other words, one recalls a dream experience because of the 'traces' it leaves behind just as one recalls a previous experience in ordinary, wakeful life because of the impressions left by such an experience (except, of course, that the dream is not seen as a dream in the dream). What permits the recollection of the experiences in both these cases must be assumed to be one and the same feature or principle in man. In view of the fact that the senses do not function in a dream, they cannot be said to constitute the essence of man characterized as the *ātman* 'because one's own destruction can never be known by oneself.'[34] This is to say that if the senses are said to be the *ātman* one would then have to admit that the manifestation of the *ātman* would no longer be possible with the non-functioning of the senses. This would lead to the absurd conclusion of the dream state being identical with death. Therefore, a position which gives any sense of permanency to the sense organs and, thereby, gives to them the status of constituting man's essential, defining characteristic, would have to be rejected.

The fact that a dream is not seen as a dream during the dream experience implies that the object of experience is not experienced *as it is* (*yathārtha*) which, in turn, connotes the operation of 'ignorance' (*avidyā, ajñāna*). This negative phenomenon tacit in the dream experience cannot be supposed to constitute the nature of the *ātman*—which in fact makes possible the recollection of the dream as having been a dream. It is necessary to bear in mind what was said earlier: the transition of the causal states from *sakala* to *śuddha* is via the *kevala* state which completely hinders the *ātman*. The transition from one effect state to the other, as from the wakeful to the dream state, therefore, constitutes a regressive relapse into the state of complete isolation (*kevala*).[35] It is for this reason that the transition from one effect state to the other has to be characterized negatively. It is to be noted in this context that, by contrast, the significance of the wakeful state is crucial. Here the *ātman* has all the instruments of experience in the world at its disposal and the difference between its essential nature and that of the instruments is more strikingly evident. It is to be acknowledged, nonetheless, that the impact of the relevance of the wakeful state is based on a reflective analysis of all the other effect states in the framework of the causal states of consciousness.[36] The exploitation of this insight is a step towards the realization of man's essential nature. This point is concerned more specifically with Śaiva Siddhānta soteriology, which will be taken up in more detail later. What is to be noted in the present context is that in the attempt to arrive at what constitutes a defining, characteristic feature of man's nature, the sense organs and their functions do not qualify. The reason for this was seen in the fact—upon recollection—of dream experiences which take place without the sense organ functions. The verse, therefore, offers scope for a discussion of other possibilities.

The fourth reason stated in the verse under consideration that accounts for the existence of an *ātman* or *aṇu* characterized by consciousness, is the recollection of the lack of any experience in deep sleep (*suṣupti*). The fourth state (*turīya*) and the state beyond the fourth (*turīyātīta*) are also discussed in this context. If, on the basis of the recollection of dream experience, it follows that the sense organs cannot be regarded as constituting the essence of man then, on the basis of the experience of deep sleep (which is later recollected), it follows that the intellect (*buddhi*) cannot be regarded as that either. Although the *buddhi* is absent in deep sleep, as already pointed out, there is still—in retrospect—the experience of having slept very well. The fact that the experience did indeed take place, clearly evident in the memory of it, points to a principle apart from the *buddhi* which is aware of the experience. This principle may be thought to be the *citta* ('memory') or the *prāṇa* (life breath), both of which are said to be present in deep sleep. The fact that there is a memory of the experience of deep sleep shows that the *citta* functioned in that state and the fact that the body did not die proves the function of *prāṇa* as well. However, the *citta* cannot be what constitutes man's essential nature since it is said to be absent in the fourth state (*turīya*) where there is evidence of the function of *prāṇa* alone, as the instrument of consciousness. There is no memory of this state—nor of the fifth—because of the absence of the *citta*, but the fact that there is an experience of *turīya* is stated unequivocally in the revealed texts.[37]

Further, not even *prāṇa* can be substituted for consciousness as such because in the state which reveals the intrinsic, essential nature of man, in *turīyātīta*, *prāṇa* is said to be absent. Consciousness is in itself in this state, with not a single trait of any principle which makes it comparable to any one of the other four states. Consciousness is indeed the single common principle in all the states, except that the complete manifestation of its potency is tarnished, coloured by the other principles with which it comes in contact. In Śivāgrayogin's own words:

> The intellect, memory, and the life breath are not the *aṇu*. This is the meaning ultimately, since it is said that these are absent respectively in the state of deep sleep, in the fourth state, and in the state beyond the fourth. Here too [i.e., as in the case of the dream state] their absence is known through the Smṛiti and Āgama texts.[38]

The *Pauṣkara Āgama* which Śivāgrayogin quotes furnishes the reason why these three principles cannot be regarded as constituting the essence of man:

> The intellect, etc., does not constitute *ātman-ness*—on account of the effects of which there is [in fact] a proof for the *ātman*—

> because their existence is established on the ground that they are responsible for different effects. Here too, if they are responsible [for the *ātman*] everything would be one.[39]

The point here is that each principle such as the *buddhi*, the *citta*, etc., has a specific, limited and clearly defined function which cannot be a substitute for the *ātman* which, in effect, consolidates the data presented by them. Their very limitation is proof of an all-encompassing principle which coordinates and makes their functions possible. Moreover, if any one of these is substituted for the *ātman*, there would be no point in referring to the others insofar as these would be encompassed by the one, substituted principle. They are not indispensable for the existence of the *ātman*, which merely utilizes them for experience in the world. They, on the other hand, would be inoperative without the presence and power of the *ātman*; it is because of their close association with the *ātman* that sentience is erroneously ascribed to them. Further, if any one of these were to be substituted for the *ātman*, then there would be the problem of distinguishing the function, for example, of the sense organs from that of the internal organs. The conclusion, therefore, must be that the essence of man is characterized by a conscious principle which, in fact, defines man and which has at its disposal the functions of the sense organs, the intellect, memory, and the life breath.

The fifth reason that is furnished by the verse for such a conscious principle is the fact of there being a perceiver in the wakeful state. In this state there is a stream of cognitions (*jñānasantati*) evident in the flow of sense perceptions and the awareness of them. It would appear that this very flow is what characterizes the essence of man but, as Śivāgrayogin says, this is precisely what is refuted when the verse speaks of a perceiver in the wakeful state. In his own words:

> [Since] it is said [in the verse] that there is a cognizer when one is awake, the word *aṇu* is connected with the expression for 'existence at all times'. The *aṇu* exists at all times. It is not a stream of momentary cognitions, since immediately after waking up there is an awareness of the things to be done remaining

> from the previous wakeful state. If the view [were accepted] that the *ātman* is a stream of cognitions known as *ālaya*, and which is momentary, then, since the earlier stream is broken in deep sleep and since the stream that arises after waking is a different stream—and on account of these two streams being different —there would be no connection which may be said to be connected to a single stream.[40]

What has to be acknowledged, therefore, is that there is an abiding principle not only in the background of the so-called stream of cognitions which is said to be momentary, but also in the different states of experience such as in dream and deep sleep. Such a principle accounts for the 'continuity' of the life of an individual in the different states of consciousness.

In terms of the two kinds of definition already referred to, viz., the broad, general definition (*taṭastha-lakṣaṇa*) and the essential, specific definition (*svarūpa-lakṣaṇa*), and in view of Śivāgrayogin's statement that verses three and four of the *Śiva-jñānabodham* furnish the definition of man, the above discussion is a general definition of man in Śaiva Siddhānta, as derived from the third verse. Put more precisely, this general definition is to be seen in the context of the five reasons which make up the argument for an *ātman* or *aṇu* which has 'an existence undiminished at all times'. If one takes into consideration the content of the verse alone, then it may be said that the notion of the *ātman* is presupposed in the argument. However, on the basis of Śivāgrayogin's commentary on the elements of the argument in the verse, a conscious principle underlying the different levels of experience can be arrived at rationally, and it is this very principle that is referred to as the *ātman* in man. It is the cognition of nothing, the intensity of the feeling of mineness, an awareness of what goes on in the wakeful state, etc., that point in a general way to the existence of the *ātman*; they are indicators, in a broad way, of a principle which makes these experiences possible. The verse does not deal with the specific issue of the *ātman* itself; it does not provide a definition of its essential nature—which would constitute the essential definition of man. This is left to the next verse to provide, which is considered now in the next section.

## 2.3 *Toward a specific definition of man*

It has already been pointed out that in the case of the *sakala-paśu* the transition from one state of consciousness to the other is finally a regression to the state of isolation (*kevala-avasthā*) when the *ātman* is 'once again' completely under the spell of (*āṇava-*)*malam*. It is at this point in the reflective analysis of the essential nature of man that the efficacy, role, and proof for the existence of *malam* become most striking and crucial to consider. It is especially noteworthy, therefore, that in commenting on the fourth verse of the *Śivajñānabodham*—which is supposed to furnish the specific, essential definition (*svarūpa-lakṣaṇa*) of man characterized as the *ātman*—Śivāgrayogin devotes approximately half his commentary on this verse to a discussion on the proof for the existence of *malam* and the Śaiva Siddhānta justification for the postulation of such a category. The discussion is in fact necessitated by the appearance of the word in the verse itself—it appears in the second half of the verse and the discussion on it makes up much of the second half of the commentary on it.

As is characteristic of his style, Śivāgrayogin provides the link to his commentary on verse four of the *Śivajñānabodham*. In summarizing his discussion on the previous verse he says: "It has been said that the internal organs, etc., are not of the nature of the *ātman*, on account of not continuing in all the states such as deep sleep, etc."[41] This point follows from the discussion on the elimination or non-function of certain principles which determine a particular state of consciousness. The internal organs (*antaḥ-karaṇas*) which Śivāgrayogin refers to here — the word being taken from the fourth verse — represent the intellect (*buddhi*), the mind (*manas*), the ego or I-maker (*ahaṅkāra*), the five sense organs (*jñānendriyas*), and the five motor organs (*karmendriyas*).[42] This means, as already seen, that he is referring to the state when the 'memory' (*citta*) and life breath (*prāṇa*) prevail with consciousness (*cit*). But, it may be suggested by a prospective opponent, 'not even the *ātman* exists then, since there can be no proof [for its existence in deep sleep, etc.]'[43] Śivāgrayogin says that it is in anticipation of this very doubt that the author of the *Śivajñāna-*

*bodham* 'establishes the connection [of the *ātman*] with the five states'[44] in the fourth verse which declares that:

> The *ātman* is different from the internal organs also [i.e., apart from *citta* and *prāṇa*] associated [with them, though] like a king with ministers; therefore, it [*ātman*] exists in the five states having its own knowledge and action restricted by *malam*.[45]

What is implicit in Śivāgrayogin's commentary on this verse is the 'connection' of the *ātman* with the five states represented by the 'continuity' of life from one situation or experience to another. In his own words, with the help of an analogy, the *ātman* undergoing the five states may be understood in the following way:

> There is a continuity of it [*ātman*] with the five states on account of the recognition of a single self (*eka ātman*) connected with the five states in, for example: "That 'I' who yesterday was without money, is the very 'I' who today is with money".[46]

The situation of the change of fortune from one day to the next is intended to represent the change and underlying continuity involved in the passage of the *ātman* through the five states.[47] It is in this way that Śivāgrayogin commences with his attempt to extract out of the verse the reason for the existence of the *ātman* which, in the previous verse, was merely postulated and, thereby, arrives at the essential definition of man.

The question of the *ātman* experiencing the different states prompts, even if for argument's sake, an immediate rejection of such a notion.[48] Śivāgrayogin responds to this by referring to the Āgamas which mention categorically the condition of a possibility of liberation from the fettered state of existence which is represented by the experiences of the five states of life in the world: "It is established in the Āgamas that it [*ātman*] has unbridled [expression of the] powers of knowledge and action in the state of liberation."[49] It follows from this that there is a fettered existence from which the *ātman* can be freed and, therefore, the entire discussion on the essential nature of the *ātman*, of man, rests ultimately on the authority of scripture.[50] Whilst the actual nature of the state of liberation is beyond human comprehension—insofar as it falls beyond the range of the categories of our understanding (by presupposing the inefficacy of *karman, māyā* and *āṇava-malam* in this state)—and an adequate description (*lakṣaṇa*) of it impossible, the certainty of the possibility of its experience (*anubhava*), however, seems to be beyond question. The tradition's contribution toward an understanding of man rests on an appreciation of this basic presupposition.

Śivāgrayogin follows this point with some noteworthy remarks on the power (*śakti*) of the *ātman*, i.e., the consciousness intrinsic to the nature of man. His points here are terse and effectively extract the underlying meaning of the verse. The context is the question of the possibility of *śakti* being unfettered, which arises over the issue (raised in the verse) of the *ātman* undergoing the five states. The argument revolves around the origin of *śakti*. He says:

> It is not proper to regard it [*śakti*] as being produced [afresh] at that time [of liberation], nor does it come from *īśvara* since, in that case, it [unfettered *śakti*]—which has the form of liberation [itself]—would be non-eternal.[51]

What this means is that in either of these two cases, i.e., being produced afresh or being derived from *īśvara* (*pati* or the lord), one would have to acknowledge an 'origin' of the *śakti* in the *aṇu* or *ātman* at the time of liberation. On the fundamental theory that whatever has an origin must have an end, the absurd situation of an end of liberation would arise. The conclusion is: 'And, therefore, it must be said that the *aṇu* has omniscience, etc., [intrinsically].'[52]

Three terms are significant in grasping the full relevance of this conclusion,[53] viz., *śakti, mukti* and *sarvajñatva*. *Śakti*, as stated above, is of the form of liberation (*mukti*). This means that the power of consciousness intrinsic to the *ātman* (*ātma-cit-śakti*)—which has a fettered expression in man—is fully manifest at the time of liberation. In other words, the attainment of freedom from bondage, from the *pāśas* which restrict man, is identical with the unfolding of man's essential nature. It is in this sense that *śakti*, i.e., unfettered (*asaṅkucita*) *śakti*, is of the form of *mukti*—there being no essential difference between the two, except that *mukti* implies a giving up of, or a liberation from, fetters and *śakti* implies the unlimited unfolding and expression of the powers of consciousness. This is to say that the *ātman* is now celebrated as all-knowing, all-pervading, constant, etc.[54] All these points are presupposed in Śivāgrayogin's conclusion above and if these implicit details are to be taken with the seriousness they deserve, for the understanding of man in Śaiva Siddhānta, then the crucial question now is:

> So, since it [*ātman*] is all-knowing, independent and has all its 'desires' fulfilled, how [does it undergo] the five states of dependence[55] or how [does it have] the experience of objects mixed with the suffering already talked of?[56]

The answer to these questions is the solution to the problems concerning the human predicament, to man's situation in a world fraught with experiences of joy and suffering—both of which being couched ultimately in pain because of their apparent eternal recurrence. Śivāgrayogin says that it is in anticipation of these questions and problems, the verse declares that the *ātman* is one 'having its own knowledge and action restricted by *malam*.' Taking into consideration that *śakti* is not produced anew, is not produced afresh, at the time of liberation (*mukti*), the following has to be acceded to: 'Although there is its [*ātman*'s] power of knowledge and action now [in man's fettered existence], still, on account of its [*śakti*'s] restrictedness and its parviscience, there occurs non-independence, unfulfilled desires, and the experience of the five states.'[57] This means that *malam* has the ability to shroud and restrict the intrinsic powers of consciousness. This ability signifies a certain weakness on the part of the *ātman* to succumb to the influence of *malam*. It is this weakness that makes the *ātman* a *paśu* and accounts for man's condition in the world, and it is its status as bound and fettered that points to a *paśu-pati* a lord of bound beings, capable of operating in this condition with grace.

If, for argument's sake, one were to accept *malam*'s ability to fetter the *ātman*, then an interesting problem arises, as an opponent could well point out:

> Now, this being so [the *ātman* fettered by *malam*] there could not, even more so, be its [*ātman*'s] experience of the five states—since it [*ātman*] is like a stone with the power of knowledge and action obscured [by *malam*]. Therefore, it [the argument] is [like one ] fleeing from a scorpion out of fear and fallen in the mouth of a venomous snake.[58]

The tone of the opponent's argument, piercing as it is, has a touch of sarcastic humour about it: on the one hand, the Siddhāntin says that the *ātman* is so shrouded by *malam* that, being like a stone, it is incapable of coming out of this rut; on the other hand, and under these circumstances, it is stated, further, that the *ātman* undergoes or experiences the five states. How can there be any experience if at the very outset the *ātman*'s powers are obstructed? Therefore, in attempting to avoid one difficulty the Siddhāntin gets into another—a case of a philosophical jump from the proverbial pan into the fire. What is implicit in the opponent's retorts is that it would be 'better' for the *ātman* to remain under the complete spell of *malam*, rather than have to undergo the experiences of the five states which entail a life of suffering in the world. In that way the *ātman* would be immune to, or exempted from, a painful existence. It would be like a stone, unaware of everything going on around it—undoubtedly a 'better' condition than a life of suffering. From the opponent's perspective this argument may sound convincing, but it is inadmissible from the Siddhāntin's standpoint. The notion of *malam* is arrived at from an existential analysis of the human predicament (and acknowledges the gracious role of *śivam*); the opponent, on the other hand, seems to view the problem, *prima facie*, only from the point of view of *malam*'s origin. Therefore, according to Śivāgrayogin, there is an anticipatory parry of these issues when the verse says 'associated'.

The word suggests an object—and from the context such an object would be a counter-correlative (*pratiyogin*)—from which the *ātman* is different and to which it is in some kind of relation (*sambandha*). This object, as implied in the verse, can only be the internal organs (and by extension, *citta* and *prāṇā* as well). In commenting on the relevance of this as an account for life in the world, Śivāgrayogin says:

> This is the sense: the *malam* [shrouding the *ātman*] is dispelled little by little, and sometimes, by the internal organs and *kalā* [*tattva*], etc., which are transformed through modification, into the form of this or that pot, etc., and thus it [*ātman*] experiences such and such object; in this way there is the possibility of the wakeful and other states.[59]

This exegesis on the word 'associated' (*anvita*) in the verse may be seen as the origin of the *sakala* state of the *ātman* insofar as it presupposes the categories of experience (the evolutes of *māyā*) which are at the *ātman*'s disposal. The expression of the *ātman*'s powers of knowledge and action (and volition) in the world is commensurate with the degree to which the instruments, such as the internal organs, are able to grasp a particular object. The knowledge of an object is not *complete* insofar as the knowledge is determined by the ability and function of a particular organ of perception. This limitation is no reflection on the nature of the *ātman* which only 'associates' with these organs. The *ātman* is assisted by the organs which serve to dispel the *malam* and thereby, make experience in the world possible. Without this assistance (made available through *śivam*'s grace) the *ātman* would remain in its forlorn and wretched isolated (*kevala*) state. It is when each sense is in contact with its respective object of perception, e.g., the ear with sound, the nose with smell, etc., that experience takes place. The senses provide a channel of contact between the *ātman* and the object and this contact partially removes the obscuration responsible for the *ātman*'s ignorance concerning the nature of things.

The above points should not give the impression that the *ātman*'s knowledge comes into being in the experience of objects. This would be a contradiction of its essential nature, already seen, as all-knowing (besides, the presupposition of an end to what has a beginning also applies here). It has to be repeated in this context that: 'Therefore, it is to be accepted that it [omniscience] is there intrinsically [in the *ātman*] even during transmigratory existence,'[60] and that, as the verse implies, 'there is the occurrence of the five states on account of its own knowledge and action being obscured by *malam*.[61] The way in which this situation is to be understood is analogous to the king associated with ministers, as mentioned in the verse. Stressing the word 'associated' (*anvita*) Śivāgrayogin interprets the compound *mantri-bhūpa* (minister-king) as *mantri-yukto-bhūpo*, 'the king who is joined with ministers'.[62]

The significance of this analogy is that the ministers, whilst representing sovereignty, are no reflection on the individual, essential nature of the king himself. In the same way, the organs of the body which function on the authority and power of the *ātman*, do not intrinsically represent the uniqueness of the *ātman*'s nature. Both the king and the *ātman*, however, are limited to what 'information' is passed on to them—by the ministers and the organs of the body—in their knowledge of the world. Hence the compound is to be construed as the king *and* the ministers, to represent the *ātman* *and* the internal organs, etc.,—the two elements of the conjunction not to be seen as forming a single essential, indivisible unit. The stress on 'associated' (*anvita*) or 'joined with' (*yukta*) brings out this significant semantic difference.

As far as the *ātman* is concerned, the different levels of consciousness, of life in the world—such as what make up dream and deep sleep experiences—are accountable on the theory of the *ātman*'s association and dissociation with the sense organs, the intellect, etc., as already seen. The cause for the necessity to undergo such a predicament is attributed to the efficacy of *malam*, which restricts or fetters the expression of the *ātman*'s powers. The question concerning the origin of *malam* in this context does not satisfactorily explain *how* the *ātman* comes to be in the weak position of succumbing to *malam* in the first place—insofar as *malam* is said to exist with the *ātman* as does verdigris in copper since beginningless time (*anādi*). It becomes intelligible when approached from the perspective of the human condition in which certain issues, such as dependency and limitedness, are realistically rationalized. Śivāgrayogin attempts to do this when he asks, anticipating an opponent's retort: 'Now, what is the proof for the existence of *malam*?'[63]

The answer to this question from the Śaiva Siddhānta perspective is one which presupposes a recognition of the possibility of liberation (*mukti*). This point is implicit in the following quotation which also sanctions Śivāgrayogin's question above:

> When there is an absence of fetters, what the cause was for dependency must be explained; if [this cause were] natural then the word 'liberated' cannot apply with regard to liberated beings.[64]

In other words, an explanation is required for the *ātman*'s dependency or bound state. This is to say: why in the first place it was in a condition from which it had to be liberated, is what should be explained. The reason for the need to make explicit this clarification is obvious: "First, there can be no perception such as 'I am ignorant' since this non-knowledge cannot be an object [of perception]. Nor even can there be an inference [of *malam*] since there is no indicatory mark.'[65] Non-knowledge or ignorance (*ajñāna*) is equated with *malam* here. This implies that since one's ignorance cannot be an object of perception (in which case one would *know* it) *malam*—the root cause of ignorance which is thereby essentially identical with *malam*—cannot be an object of perception either. Further, in the absence of any indicatory mark or sign (*liṅga*)[66] for *malam*, one cannot validly infer its existence the way one can, for example, infer fire on the perception of smoke.

Apart from perception and inference, Śaiva Siddhānta recognizes a third means of valid knowledge, that of scripture (*śabda*), which is put into service here.[67] It is on the strength of this authority that it can be said: 'Now, *paśu*'s dependence must be due to something [else] since it [dependence] is not natural [to *paśu*]...[68] This sentence ends with the analogy 'like a coloured form which has become a pot' (*ghaṭa-gata-rakta-rūpavat*). The compound is a difficult one to interpret. It seems that the following is the point: a pot made out of a coloured substance limits the substance to the form of the pot. Just as the substance clay is limited and determined by an external cause, e.g., the potter, to a particular form of its manifestation, so too does the *ātman* become dependent and limited in the expression of its powers on the external cause of *malam*. Hence, the *ātman* is made into a *paśu* as, *mutatis mutandis*, the substance clay is made into a pot. Śivāgrayogin says that such an argument is not based on 'unestablished reasoning' (*asiddha*)[69] 'since there is a disappearance of dependence in the state of liberation.'[70] It is clear from the above, that Śivāgrayogin's discussion on the proof for the existence of *malam* begins with the view of dependency caused by what is called *malam* which is seen as being alien to the nature of the *ātman* and this position is established ultimately on the authority of scripture.[71]

The perspective from which the discussion is undertaken presupposes a cause for man's life in a transitory world. In this context it can be said without fear of contradiction that:

> Therefore, the involvement in experiences which are impure, closely associated with pain, and lasting for but a moment, is due to something on account of adventitiousness [of the involvement]. Since there must be a cause for the involvement in such experiences, *malaness* is established on the strength of subject-adjunctness.[72]

The argument is an intricate one which presupposes several points. Life in the world as represented in the discussion of the five states of consciousness, mentioned in the verse under consideration, is regarded as a fettered existence. It is couched in suffering because of its seemingly endless recurrence. Since it is assumed that the essential nature of man is limited by and dependent on instruments, such as the organs of the body, for its expression and manifestation, some causative factor needs to be postulated for such a condition. Further, not only is this cause to be seen as being essentially alien to the nature of the *ātman* in man, but it is also something to be seen as adventitious or added on (*āgantuka*).[73]

The term 'subject-adjunctness' (*pakṣa-dharmatā*) is a logical one that is applied to inferences, a favourite topic of discussion in the Nyāya school. Bearing in mind the stock proposition concerning smoke and fire in the Nyāya view of valid inferential statements, the following is the definition of the term:

"Wherever there is smoke there is fire"—This type of invariable concomitance is *vyāpti* (co-extension).

Subject-adjunctness (*pakṣa-dharmatā*) consists in the invariable concomitant (*vyāpya*) [smoke] being present in things like a mountain (denoted by *pakṣa* or the minor term).[74]

It is the association of smoke with the mountain that makes the inference about fire a valid one. The smoke is an incidental object, i.e., an adjunct, that 'accompanies' the mountain, viz., the subject, and it is a non-essential attribute as far as the mountain itself is concerned. In applying this definition of subject-adjunctness to Śivāgrayogin's argument above, the following emerges: the involvement in experience or life in the world must have a cause, which is called *malam*. On the strength of the theory of subject-adjunctness, *malam* has to be seen as an incidental object, i.e., an adjunct, that 'accompanies' the *ātman*, viz., the subject, and it must, therefore, be a non-essential attribute as far as the *ātman* itself is concerned.

In a footnote to the text, the editor of *Śivāgrabhāṣya* supplies a clarification which is a noteworthy extension of the above logical points presupposed by Śivāgrayogin. It is also a scholastic defence of Śivāgrayogin's argument. A paraphrase of the editor's enlightening remarks is: it is true that for the existence of a pot one can speak of the potter's wheel, etc., as general causes for the pot, and our (Siddhāntin's) purpose would be served by a general cause for the *ātman*'s involvement in experiences—viz., by postulating *malam* as such a cause; but just as a wheel cannot be established as a cause for the pot without the *wheelness* of the wheel, so too the involvement in experiences cannot be established without the *malaness* of *malam* as its cause.[75] This lucid note is significant, further, not only in accounting for, and thereby proving, the existence of *malam*, but also for clarifying the sense in which *malam* is regarded as being eternally existent: when a particular *ātman* is liberated from *malam* at the time of liberation (*mukti*) *malam* exists impotently or uselessly with reference to that particular *ātman*. It is not any more efficient than a potter's wheel which does not function.

The basic point in Śivāgrayogin's argument for the existence of *malam* rests on an insight into the nature of man's involvement in the world and the dependence implicit in it. What underlies and is presupposed in the discussion is the unfettered, unlimited expression of the powers of consciousness which, under the present conditions, is given only a modicum of scope for manifestation. On the view that some cause must be seen as responsible for it, the notion of *malam* is postulated. The validity of its proof—apart from citing scripture as the authority—rests on the acceptance of man's bound condition. In terms of the intricately worked out system of Śaiva Siddhānta categories (*tattvas*), and in terms of what further points are considered in the proof for the existence of *malam*, it needs to be shown why the category *malam* itself is the sole cause for man's predicament. Therefore, in continuing his proof for the existence of *malam*, Śivāgrayogin justifies why it alone is this particular cause and not, for example, *rāga-tattva*, nor *mithyā-jñāna* (erroneous knowledge), nor even *karman*.[76]

The possibility of *rāga-tattva* as a substitute for the role of *malam* is rejected on the authority of the *Pauṣkara Āgama* which Śivāgrayogin quotes:

> If this [*ātman*] is not impure how is its involvement in experiences acquired? If it [the involvement] could exist in a virtuous one then it would also be in a liberated *ātman*. If you [in opposition] should say that *rāga* is the cause for the involvement so why [should it be caused] by *malam* then, indeed, *rāga* is responsible for the involvement [in experiences] in a virtuous one. If it [*rāga*] were the cause for the involvement even in a virtuous one, then it would be in a liberated one as well, there being no difference [between these two]; but neither Śiva nor the liberated one is involved in experiences at any time.[77]

The point in quoting this authority is to express the view that, indeed, one cannot deny that *rāga-tattva* is responsible for man's involvement in experiences in the world—in fact, this is the very role assigned to this category in the Śaiva Siddhānta scheme.[78] However, truly virtuous beings are not under its influence, let alone the liberated ones. Conversely, if one were to accept its power over virtuous ones, then its efficacy would be evident in liberated ones as well. But this is not the case, as the authoritative scripture declares. Virtuous and liberated beings are not involved in experiences *in the way in which others are* and, hence, *rāga-tattva* cannot be assigned the function of *malam*.

Thus far, Śivāgrayogin has accounted for the existence of *malam* on two grounds. Firstly, on the grounds of dependency, i.e., since independence is the essential feature of the *ātman*—evident when it is liberated—it means that in the state of bondage dependency obtains and the cause for this must be attributed to *malam*. Secondly, *malam* is established on the grounds of the involvement in transitory, worldly experiences which are tinged with suffering. By way of elaborating these two points and by way of an introduction to his rejection of the view that *mithyā-jñāna* (erroneous knowledge) or *karman* may be substituted for the role of *malam*, the discussion now centres around the terms parviscience or limited knowledge (*kiñcijjñatva*) and omniscience or all-knowingness (*sarvajñatva*). A quotation from the *Pauṣkara Āgama* establishes the existence of *malam* as the decisive factor for the significance and distinction between these two concepts:

> The *ātman* is covered by *malam*, therefore, it has limited knowledge, although omniscient [intrinsically]; whoever is not one who has limited knowledge, is not restricted by *malam*—like Śiva; therefore, not being such a one, the *ātman* is covered by *malam*.[79]

In anticipating an opponent's rebuff, Śivāgrayogin points out that this inference based only on negation or negative data (*kevala-vyatireki-anumāna*)[80] is unacceptable because, it may be argued, to draw the distinction between parviscience and omniscience is useless (*aprayojaka*) as regards proving that the *ātman*'s restriction of powers is due to *malam* (*mala-āvṛitatvaṁ prati*).[81] The conclusion that can be drawn from this argument is that 'the occurrence of limited knowledge is through the restriction [caused] by erroneous knowledge, *karman*, etc.'[82] Śivāgrayogin's task now, therefore, is to consider this objection.

In rejecting erroneous knowledge as a substitute for *malam* Śivāgrayogin says that it "does not arise when there is a manifestation of objects properly"[83] and, therefore, in the case of sight, for example, something has to be supposed as a cause for shrouded vision, such as a cataract in the eye. Further, this has to be supposed, 'because erroneous knowledge is temporary and in its absence the situation arises when there is a clear manifestation of everything..'[84] This justification of the Siddhāntin's standpoint is an argument based on what is declared in the *Pauṣkara Āgama*, which Śivāgrayogin quotes:

> Nor is this [*malam* to be called] erroneous knowledge because it does not arise of its own accord. The cognition of silver in the shell does not arise without a cataract [in the eye]. Moreover, is this erroneous knowledge adventitious or not? If it were adventitious it can never hinder *cit-śakti*; if it were not adventitious then it can never be erroneous knowledge.[85]

The point here is that erroneous knowledge and *malam* are not identical and the function of the one cannot be substituted for by the other because although erroneous knowledge may be overcome, man's involvement in experience and painful, dependent existence persist.

The last sentence of the above quotation attempts, implicitly, to reject the view that there can be an origin of *malam*. It is one of the three categories of ultimate reality and exists eternally. *Malam*, i.e., *āṇava-malam*, is not adventitious (*āgantuka*) as *karman* and *māyā* are. The latter two are necessary consequents of *āṇava-malam*, as already seen. If one were to talk of *āṇava-malam* arising or being born with (*sahaja*) the *ātman* since beginningless time (*anādi*), then there can be no question of it arising and/or disappearing—it exists all the time and *karman* and *māyā* serve the purpose only to give the *ātman* a scope for the expression of its powers, evident in experience. If (*āṇava*) *malam* were adventitious, instead, it cannot suddenly restrict the power of consciousness inherent to the *ātman* (*ātma-cit-śakti*) which previously was unhindered—in this case the possibility of an end to liberation would be a striking paradox and one which is inadmissible from the Siddhānta perspective (as also with others accepting the possibility of *mokṣa*). Further, the adventitious categories, *karman* and *māyā*, do not restrict the *ātman*, as already said, but rather aid it. This means that if erroneous knowledge were adventitious it should cause valid knowledge, which is a contradiction in terms. If it were not adventitious, it would not come and go, as in fact it does—it would prevail all the time and cease to be erroneous knowledge insofar as an occasion would never arise when it would be possible for it to be contrasted with valid knowledge. In other words, (*āṇava*) *malam* alone, and not the erratic and irregular erroneous knowledge, can be the cause for man's predicament.

Śivāgrayogin now rejects the contention that *karman* may be substituted for *malam* as the agent responsible for the *ātman*'s limited knowledge (*kiñcijjñatva*). He begins by making two points: firstly, 'by the fact that even *karman* has a beginning, it is impossible that it can veil the light of the *ātman* which has no beginning' and, secondly, 'even though *karman* is held responsible for experiences—on the grounds that it may be justified as being a beginningless stream—it is impossible that it can veil experiences which have the form of knowledge.'[86] Further, 'because it [*karman*] is regarded [as being instrumental only] with categories derived from [*śuddha-aśuddha*] *māyā* and since it is absent in the higher realms, the situation would arise that these [realms] would be unaffected [by *karman*].'[87] The argument here is that if *karman* were to be accepted as an agent responsible for restricting the powers of the *ātman*, then it would have to operate in all the realms that are encompassed by the Siddhānta scheme of thirty-six *tattvas*. This, however, is not the case with regard to the realm of *śuddha-māyā* and, hence, the effect of *karman* has a limited scope.

This point which argues the view that *karman* cannot be substituted for by *malam* is put more precisely when Śivāgrayogin says: "By bringing about experiences it is accepted that it [*karman*] is responsible for experiences alone; if it were responsible also for veiling [the powers of the *ātman*], effected by something else, the situation of a confusion of category [functions] would arise."[88] Śivāgrayogin quotes five verses from the *Pauṣkara Āgama*, which not only specifically reject *karman* as a substitute for *malam* but are noteworthy as an authoritative, summary statement of several points concerning the proof for the existence of *malam* discussed above:

> Not even *karman* is able to hinder knowledge, O Twice Born Ones, because it has a beginning and it is established that man [is responsible] for the efficacy of *karman*. Moreover, it is the *cause* of experiences alone, so how can it *hinder* experiences? Since there are experiences in the form of knowledge, these cannot be shrouded by this [*karman*]. *Karman* has the natures of merit and demerit which are restricted to the intellect [only]. The higher realm [beyond the intellect] is not pervaded [by these two] so how can they cause any hindrance [there]? Moreover, these two are responsible for experiences, so how could they be engaged in [another] activity [such as hindering]? If they are [accepted as being] responsible for activity in one area, then [now] they would be the cause for activity elsewhere too! There can be no such mixing of a category [function], since there is a distinction of their effects. Therefore, it is established that *karman* cannot cause the hindering of *cit-śakti*.[89]

After establishing in this way (a) that *malam* cannot be substituted for by *karman* as an agent responsible for the *ātman*'s limited knowledge, chiefly because this role would mean that *karman* functions beyond its domain and (b) that erroneous knowledge is due to some extraneous cause and, thus, cannot itself be responsible for what in fact causes erroneous knowledge, Śivāgrayogin now deals with the crucial question of the relationship (*sambandha*) between the *ātman* and *malam*. He says that this relationship cannot be one of inherence (*samavāya*) because if this were accepted, the *ātman* and *malam* would become identical ultimately.[90] 'Nor is the relationship one of veiling because this would depend on another relationship.'[91] By this is meant the following: if the relationship between the *ātman* and *malam* constitutes a veiling (*āvāraka*), then it presupposes a relationship between *malam* and the nature of the object that is veiled from the *ātman*'s ability to experience or have the knowledge of. In terms of the Śaiva Siddhānta categories of ultimate reality, this presupposes a relationship between *malam* and *śivam*, on the one hand, and between *malam* and *itself*, on the other (apart from the one between *malam* and the *ātman*). The first relationship is categorically inadmissible, because as already seen, *malam* and *śivam* are exclusive categories. The second is impossible because *malam* is insentient or unconscious (*jaḍa* or *acit*) and there can be no question of it being in any relationship at all—in this sense, strictly speaking, one would have to talk of the *ātman* being in relationship with *malam* and not vice versa. Further, it may be noted that an infinite regress is implicit in the problem of relationship as implicit in Śivāgrayogin's argument here, with one relationship, at least theoretically, leading to another and so on.

The above arguments do not deny that there is indeed some kind of relationship between the *ātman* and *malam*. The only question is: what kind of relationship can adequately and rationally account for man's condition in the world, within the framework of the Siddhāntin's philosophical presuppositions? A relationship which is one of the inherence or of veiling is rejected for the reasons already pointed out. The rejection is perhaps more striking when seen against the background of the kind of relationship suggested by the Siddhāntin. The conclusion Śivāgrayogin arrives at, therefore, is that the relationship between the *ātman* and *malam* must be one of conjunction (*saṁyoga*).[92] This interpretation of the relationship presupposes a disjunction (*viyoga*). (It may be pointed out here that this view of the relationship between the *ātman* and *malam* prepares the philosophical ground on which the condition of a state of liberation becomes possible.) Further, on account of this conjunction, and bearing in mind that the *ātman* and *malam* are not identical, *malam* has to be seen as a substance (*dravya*).[93] Moreover, by the fact that it veils the *ātman* completely in its state of primordial isolation or bondage (*kevala-avasthā*), and in view of its continued relationship with the *ātman* even in the involvement in experiences of man's life in the world, *malam* has to be regarded as being all-pervasive.[94] It may be repeated in this context that *malam* is one of the categories of ultimate reality and, hence, exists eternally. In the state of liberation—marked by the disjunction of the relationship between it and the *ātman*—*malam* itself is not destroyed. The relationship between them, however, no longer prevails.

The above arguments lead into Śivāgrayogin's next point, viz., that *malaṁ* cannot be regarded as being manifold in number but as a single entity.[95] The reason given for this is that it would be a 'cumbersome view' (*kalpanā-gaurava*) to see *malam* as manifold, even though it is all-pervasive. This reason is not discussed in any detail but it is obvious that the view is a vindication of scripture.[96] He is quick to add, however, that to conceive of *malam* as a single unit does not mean that when, in the state of liberation, a particular *ātman* is liberated from *malam*'s restrictive powers that all *ātmans* are thereby liberated.[97] He anticipates here what is a subject of discussion in his commentary on verse ten of the *Śivajñānabodham* saying that, in fact, 'the liberation of a particular *ātman* is on account of the removal of the conjunction between it and *manas*.'[98] The word '*manas*' here is used as a synonym for *malam*. The commentary on verse ten is mainly about the state of *mukti*, the state of the *ātman's* liberation from the shackles of *malam* and it may be noted here in anticipation, that Śivāgrayogin says in that context that: "since *malam* is removed by a direct realization [of the nature of *śivam*] there is no contact [between the *ātman* and *malam*]."[99]

The question concerning the origin of *malam*—which was seen to be an inadmissible one to ask—can now be modified and put with regard to the origin of the conjunction (*saṁyoga*) between the *ātman* and *malam*. The answer given is that the conjunction is without a beginning (*anādi*) because *karman*, etc., are absent when the contact occurs.[100] It has already been seen that the category of time (*kāla*) operates in close collusion with *karman* and that both time and *karman* function only in the realm of *śuddha-aśuddha-māyā*. When it is said that both of them are absent when the conjunction between the *ātman* and *malam* takes place, the state of complete isolation (*kevala-avasthā*) is referred to. It is this condition which leads to the operation of *karman* and *māya* (with time included) as means through which the *ātman* could manifest itself. Hence, the conjunction takes place 'prior' to the operation of *karman* and *māyā*. To regard the conjunction as being beginningless does not mean that it cannot be destroyed[101]—the conjunction, not *malam* itself, is destroyed—because it can be said that: 'Even though beginningless, there is a destruction through a collection of the apparatus which brings about the destruction [of the conjunction].'[102] In other words, when the means[103] which bring about the unlimited and unfettered expression of the *ātman*'s powers of volition, knowledge and action are effective, *malam*'s tendency to counter this expression is itself checked, hindered and kept at bay. The possibility of this state of liberation (*mukti*), to which scripture ultimately testifies, is the proof, finally, of the existence of *malam*.

## 2.4 *Summary*

In the light of the above discussion on the general and specific features concerning the *ātman*, the following definition of man according to Śaiva Siddhānta may be said to emerge: a bound being (*paśu*) in the world implicitly expressing and manifesting an *ātman* with the aid of the instruments of the body; and a being that is characterized by consciousness as its intrinsic, essential nature. The cause for the bound state was attributed to the efficacy of *malam*. Any discussion on the nature of the *ātman* would have to consider seriously the *ātman*'s association or conjunction with *malam*—a conjunction that is said to have been there since beginningless time (*anādi*), to the point that a definition of man would also encompass a definition of *malam*. The crucial issue here is that *malam* is not to be seen as being innate or intrinsic to the nature of the *ātman*. The question of *malam*'s origin is to be seen, as already pointed out, from the effects that the association causes, namely, man's dependent existence (*pāratantryam*) with the evidence of limited knowledge (*kiñcijjñatva*). It is necessary to emphasize this perspective to the question concerning *malam* in order to appreciate the Siddhāntin's philosophical justification for postulating such a category.

Further, the Śaiva Siddhānta understanding of man may be said to commence with an analysis of the condition in which, endowed with the faculties of volition, cognition and action—all of which are intrinsic to man as powers of consciousness (*cit-śakti*)—man experiences the joys and sufferings of life in the world. Life in the world, which constitutes an involvement (*āsakti*) in experiences, is a limited and fettered expression of man's potential powers of consciousness and, in this sense, life in the world is one which tacitly constitutes suffering (*duḥkha*).

The condition of the possibility of man being a liberated being (*mukta-ātman*) points to the means which make such a state a reality. These means represent, basically, an effort on the part of man to see things 'as they are' (*yathā-artha*), which means the conscious effort to realize the natures of the categories of ultimate reality, namely, *śivam*, *ātman* and *malam*. Thus, man's endowment of the instruments of experience for life in the world involves both negative and positive aspects: the instruments make possible a limited expression of the consciousness which is man's essence and this, by contrast, implies the need to 'overcome' the dependency and limited knowledge effected by *malam*.

By way of elaborating the attempt to arrive toward an understanding of man in Śaiva Siddhānta, it is necessary to consider how the instruments of experience, which are at man's disposal, are employed in life in the world. Perhaps the most striking way in which these instruments are employed, is in the exploration of man's role as the cognizer and verifier of valid knowledge. This involves an analysis of the epistemological aspects of man's involvement in experiences. These have to be considered insofar as they constitute an attempt to gain knowledge of 'things as they are', and are indispensable toward an understanding of man in Śaiva Siddhānta.

## NOTES

1. See, for example, the following three references to sleep in the *Yogasūtras:* "Sources-of-valid-ideas and misconceptions and predicate relations and sleep and memory" (1, 6); "Sleep is a fluctuation [of mind-stuff] supported by the cause (*pratyaya*, that is *tamas*) of the [transient] negation [of the waking and the dreaming fluctuations]" (1, 10); "Or [the mind stuff reaches the stable state] by having as the supporting-object a perception in dream or in sleep" (1, 38). All translations are quoted exactly, including the parentheses, from J.H. Woods, (trans.), *The Yoga-System of Patañjali* (Delhi: Motilal Banarsidass, 1966; reprint ed., Harvard University Press, The Harvard Oriental Series, vol. 17, n.d.), pp. 19, 29 and 76 respectively.
2. Although Patañjali does not use the word *turīya* in any of his *sūtras*, there is a reference to it in Vācaspati Miśra's commentary to Yogasūtra 1:38, see Woods, *op.cit.*, pp. 76-77.
3. Transcendentally, however, the order is different in that the attainment of

the *śuddha* state is seen as the state in which the *ātman regains* its pristine purity.

4. M. Monier-Williams, *op.cit.*, p. 1124 where the derivation of the word is given.
5. For example, in accepting the Nyāya emphasis that a definition should not contain the faults of over-applicability (*ativyāpti*), partial inapplicability (*avyāpti*), and total inapplicability (*asambhava*). The following is a concise clarification of these defects: "A definition, that is too wide and that consists of an attribute which is present in the things sought to be defined as well as those not to be defined, has the defect of *ativyāpti*; while a definition which does not apply to some of the things defined has the defect of *avyāpti*; and one which is wholly inapplicable to any of the things defined has the defect of *asambhava*." S. Kuppuswami Sastri, *A Primer of Indian Logic According to Annambhaṭṭa's Tarkasaṁgraha*, 3rd edn. (Madras: The Kuppuswami Sastri Research Institute, 1961), pp. 10-11.
6. See also K. Sivaraman, *Śaivism*, p. 130: "The *taṭasthalakṣaṇa* may only define the 'that' and not the 'what' of Śiva."
7. The subject refers to "*kartā*" in verse one of the text, i.e., the agent who, having destroyed the world, creates it again.
8. For the entire verse and for any future reference to the *Śivajnānabodham*, see Appendix 2 which contains all the verses. In exegeting the word *puṁsām* Śivāgrayogin says: "by the word *puṁs* only *aṇu* is always meant" (*puṁśabdena cā-aṇu-mātraṁ sarvam-ucyate*). What this means is that the word for 'human being' in the context here would have to be taken as a synonym for all living beings in the world. The particular use of the word *puṁs*, nonetheless, needs to be noted, especially since the word in the masculine form means: "the qualities of man as dependent on the acts done in a previous existence," M. Monier-Williams, *op.cit.*, p. 630.
9. Tatra ko-vā pumān yasya-eṣā śiva-ādy-avani-paryantā saṁsṛitiḥ sambhāva_yeta, *SB*, p. 261.
10. Asti-śabdo 'sad-vyāvṛitti-paro' saṅkucita-sārva-kālika-astitva-paraś-ca, *SB*, p. 262.
11. Śūnya-pratipatteḥ pratipattā 'ṇur-na-asann-iti. *Ibid.*
12. Sarva-śūnya-vādinas-tava ghaṭa-ādi śūnyam-iti yadi kena-cin-na pratipadyate tadā tasya-aprāmāṇikatva-āpattiḥ. Tathā ca tasya pratipattā-vācyaḥ. Na ca so'pi śūnyaḥ tatra pramāṇa-abhāvāt. Na hi svayam ... pratyabhijñayā tadānīm-avagatas-sva-abhāva-rūpaṁ śūnyatvam-avagantum-arhati. Idānīṁ na-aham-asmi-iti sva-ātmani kriyā-virodhaś-ca. *Ibid.*
13. Yadvā śūnya-pratipattir-asti na-vā. Yadi na-asti tadā tasya-aprāmāṇikatva-āpattiḥ. Tathā ca sā asti-iti vācyam. Na ca sā-api-śūnyā tathātve śūnya-asiddhi-prasaṅgāt. Na hy-asatyā'siddhaṁ sādhyata iti sā sati-iti vācyā. Sā-eva-asmākam-ātma-iti. *SB*, p. 262. The editor of the text offers a clarification in a footnote on the word *ātman* here. He begins by asking the question: "Now, can it be said that the cognition of the voidness of everything is the *ātman* for us? If it is said that [it contradicts our view that] the *ātman* is indeed the cognizer [i.e., not the void that is cognized] then it is not so since, from what we have already said, it is possible to

refute your [*śūnya*] doctrine even by adopting the Advaitin's standpoint. For us, too, knowledge (*citti*) is itself of the nature of the *ātman*, since it is acknowledged [by us] that there is a manifestation of the non-existence of everything in deep sleep." (Nanu sarva-śūnyatva-pratipattir-eva-asmākam-ātmeti katham-ucyate. Pratipattaiva khalv-ātmeti cen-na. Tasya prathamam-evoktatvena-advaiti-matam-ādaya-api vādi-nigraha-sambhavāt. Sva-mate'py-ātma-rūpa-cittyaiva suṣuptau sarva-siṣaya-abhāva-prakāśa-abhyupagamāc-oa.) The editor seems to be anticipating the discussion on the meaning of the words "*bodhe bodhṛitvāt*" (on account of being one who perceives when awake) which is the fifth reason arguing for the existence of the *ātman*, expressed in the third verse of the *Śivajñānabodham*. It is only through a close inspection (*anusandhāna*) in the wakeful state that one can say, on recollection, that one slept well and that one did not remember anything at all. This is the only valid means for the view that in deep sleep there is a cognition of nothing, or the void, which is recalled by the cognizer in the wakeful state. The cognition of nothing in deep sleep is comparable to the cognition, for example, of the absence of a pot in the wakeful state, except that in the former there is no immediate awareness that there is indeed a cognition of the absence of any object. It may be noted that whereas for the Advaitin even the cognition of a pot at the empirical level is ultimately unreal insofar as it is a case of superimposition (*adhyāsa*) on the ultimately real *brahman* of what is alien to its nature (cf., e.g., the rope-snake analogy—the perception of the void, too, would be a case in point of being under the influence of *māyā*), for the Siddhāntin, on the other hand, the world is real and what is perceived during the wakeful state does not have an 'illusory' status insofar as both the world and the *ātmans* share the status of being two of the three categories of ultimate reality (the void that is cognized would have the 'real' status as that of the perception of nothing and the Siddhāntin uses this argument, as seen, to justify the existence of a cognizer, namely, the *ātman*).

14. See also K. Sivaraman, *Śaivism*, p. 284: "...selfhood is involved in the very act of the denial of the self."
15. Neti-iti-padaṁ tad-abhilāpa-hetu-bhūtāyāṁ buddhau vartate tatas-tat-siddhiḥ. *SB*, pp. 264-265.
16. Mamatā mamedaṁ śarīram-iti śarīra-ātma-bheda-buddhiḥ tasyā udrekāt. *SB*, p. 261. The impact of the word *udrekāt* is significantly made stronger by the three synonyms used to clarify it, in the same place: *ādhikyāt*, *adhikabalatvāt* and *bhūyastvāt*.
17. Mamatodrekān-na-deho'ṇur-iti sambandhaḥ. *SB*, p. 264. The word *aṇu* here has to be construed as a synonym for the *ātman*.
18. Dehātmavādins are generally considered to be a section of Cārvākas who hold the view that the *ātman* is the body. Other varieties of the Cārvāka brand of Indian materialism include those who regard the sense organs (*indriyas*) as the *ātman*, those who identify life breath (*prāṇa*) with the *ātman*, and those who see no difference between the mind (*manas*) and the *ātman*. For an excellent brief survey of these, see G. Kaviraj, *Aspects of Indian Philosophy* (Burdwan: University of Burdwan, 1966) pp. 62-71.

19. The point here is that, for the Cārvāka, there is no difference between saying 'this is my body' and 'this is my *ātman*'; if any distinction is maintained, then there arises the absurd situation of the *ātman* being different from what is denoted by the word 'my'.
20. According to the strictly logical approach of Nyāya a valid inference must possess an indicatory mark (*liṅga*). Thus, for example, in the proposition 'there is fire because there is smoke' smoke is the *liṅga*, the invariable mark or sign which, on the basis of perception, proves the existence of fire. It is the absence of such a sign for the *ātman* that the Cārvāka is referring to here.
21. Deha-atirikta-ātma-sad-bhāve kiṁ mānam. Na tāvat pratyakṣaṁ tasya-anupalambhāt. Mama-deha iti pratyayasya mama-ātmeti-vad-upapatteḥ. Na-apy-anumānaṁ liṅga-abhāvāt. Caitanya-āśrayatvena tat-kalpane dehena-arthāntaratvāt. *SB*, p. 263.
22. Na ca caitanyasya bhūta-samavāye ghaṭa-ādiṣv-api tat-prasaktiḥ. Vastūnāṁ vicitra-sva-bhāvatayā deha-ādi-rūpeṇa pariṇata eva bhūte tat-samavāyopapatteḥ. *Ibid.*
23. ..caitanyaṁ prati klṛipta-hetu-bhāvasya dehasyaiva samavāyitva-kalpanautcityāc-ca. *Ibid.*
24. Nanu deho na caitanya-āśrayaḥ bhogyatvāt vikāritvād-vā ghaṭa-vad-iti caitanya-āśrayas-tad-anyo'bhyupagantavyaḥ. *SB*, p. 264.
25. Cetanaś-cen-na bhogyatvād-vikāritvāc-ca jātu-cit / Bhogyā-vikāriṇo dṛiṣṭāś-cid-vihinā ghaṭa-ādayaḥ // So'py-evam..// *Mṛigendra Āgama*, 6:4-5, as referred to in *SB*, p. 264.
26. An inference not verifiable concretely by perception, is unacceptable to the Cārvāka, for whom perception is the only ultimately valid means of knowledge. Since consciousness cannot be perceived in a dead body—having been dissolved with the death of the body—it must be regarded as non-existent. For the Cārvāka, consciousness emerges through the mere conglomeration, in a specifically balanced order, of the elements which make up the body. At death this balance is disrupted and consciousness vanishes. See especially, S. Radhakrishnan and C.A. Moore (eds.), *A Source Book in Indian Philosophy* (Princeton: Princeton University Press, 1957), pp. 227-249, and K.K. Mittal, *Materialism in Indian Thought* (New Delhi: Munshiram Manoharlal Publishers, 1974), pp. 22-60.
27. Indriya-anāśrayatvasyopādhitvāt. *SB*. p. 264.
28. There are five kinds of fallacious reasons or 'semblances of reason' (*hetvābhāsāḥ*) according to the Nyāya logician Annambhaṭṭa, in his *Tarkasaṁgraha*, section 36 which deals with inference: "the reason that strays away (*savyabhicāra*), the adverse reason (*viruddha*), the opposable reason (*satpratipakṣa*), the unestablished reason (*asiddha*), and the stultified reason (*bādhita*)." S. Kuppuswami Sastri, *op.cit.*, p. 235.
29. The three kinds of unestablished reason (*asiddha*) are: "unestablished in respect of abode (*āśrayāsiddha*), unestablished in respect of itself (*svarūpāsiddha*), and unestablished in respect of its concomitance (*vyāpyatvāsiddha*)." *Ibid.*, p. 237.
30. *Ibid.*, pp. 238-239.

31. Kiñ-ca yasya-tu-yo-dharmaḥ tan-nāśād-dharma-nāśanam / Virodhi-guṇa-sad-bhāvāt atha-syād-anyathā-dvijāḥ // Dehe saty-api caitanyaṁ mṛite kim-iti neṣyate / Yad-bhāva-yad-abhāvābhyāṁ ceṣṭa-aceṣṭe bhajet-tanuḥ // Tac-caitanyam-iti-proktam vyatiriktaṁ tu dehataḥ // *SB*, p. 265.
32. Dehasyaiva caitanya-guṇa-yogitve tasyopacaya-apacaya-ādinā bhedena... *SB*, p. 265.
33. Asti svapne gajam-ahaṁ paśyāmi-iti jñāna-āśrayatayā'ham-tv-ena ca-anubhavād-aṇuḥ. *SB*, p. 266.
34. Na-hi sva-ātma-vināśaḥ svena jñātuṁ śakyate. *Ibid.*
35. This point accepts the theory, which the tradition accepts, of the extraordinary experience of divine or transcendental communication, be it in a dream or in any other state of consciousness.
36. The importance of the wakeful state can hardly be over-emphasized insofar as the austerities (*sādhana*) that are recommended for the conscious striving towards the understanding of the nature of the *ātman*, have to be practised in the wakeful state. Also, the liberated being still in the world (*jīvanmukta*) is in a level or state that is compared to the wakeful one; see, for example, *Brahmasūtra* IV.iv.14, *bhāve jāgrad-vat* which is translated as: "When the finally released Jīva-Self, is in an embodied condition, it is, as it is, in a waking condition." V.M. Apte (trans.), *Brahma-Sūtra Shānkara-Bhāshya* (Bombay: Popular Book Depot, 1960), p. 868.
37. See below for Śivāgrayogin's explanation based on the *Pauṣkara Āgama* which he quotes.
38. Buddhi-citta-prāṇaḥ na-aṇavaḥ. Suṣupti-turīya-turīyātīteṣu yathā-kramaṁ teṣām-abhāvād-ity-asya paryavasito'rthaḥ. Atra-api tadā teṣām-abhāvaḥ smṛity-āgamābhyām-avagamyate. *SB*, p. 266.
39. Buddhy-ādināṁ na ca-ātmatvam yat-kāryāt siddhir-ātmanaḥ/Tad-anya-kārya-hetutvāt teṣāṃ siddhir-yataḥ sthitā//Atra-api teṣāṃ hetutve viśvaṃ-apy-ekam-iṣyatām//From the *Pauṣkara Āgama* quoted in *SB*, p. 267.
40. Bodhe boddhṛitvād-asty-aṇur-iti sārvakālika-sattā-vacanena-aṇu-śabdasya sambandhaḥ. Aṇur-asti sārvakālikaḥ. Na kṣaṇika-vijñāna-santānaḥ. Prabodha-anantaraṁ pūrva-jāgara-kṛita-karma-śeṣa-boddhṛitvāt. Kṣaṇika-ālaya-vijñāna-santāna-ātma-pakṣe pūrva-santānasya suṣuptau vicchinnatvena prabodha-anantarotpanna-santānasya santāna-antaratvena tayor-bhinna-santānatvāt santānaikya-prayuktam-apy-ukta-anusandhānaṁ na syāt. *Ibid.*
41. Antaḥ-karaṇādīnāṁ svāpa-ādi-sarva-avasthā-ananusyūtatvād-anātmatvam-uktam. *SB*, p. 291.
42. See Chapter 1, p. 26 above and the appendix for their positions in the scheme of *tattvas*.
43. Nanv-ātmā'pi tadānīṁ na-asty-eva pramāṇa-abhāvāt...*SB*, p. 291.
44. ...ity-āśaṅkya-avasthā-pañcaka-anusyūtiṁ pratipādayati. *Ibid.*
45. See the appendix for the Sanskrit.
46. Ya eva-ahaṁ pūrvedyur nirdhana āsaṁ sa eva-aham-adya sadhano bhavāmi-ity-avasthā-pañcaka-anusyūtaika-ātma pratyabhijñānād-avasthā-pañcaka-anusyūtatvaṁ tasyeti bhāvaḥ. *Ibid.*

47. The analogy is inadequate if one compares the state of fortune with the unfortunate, isolated (*kevala*) state that the *sakala-paśu* ultimately experiences.
48. Nanu pañca-avasthā-anubhavas-tasya na saṁbhavati. *SB*, p. 291.
49. ...muktau tasya-asaṅkucita-jñāna-kriyā-śaktir-āgama-siddhā. *Ibid.*
50. For a detailed discussion, see the section on scripture as a valid means of knowledge, chapter 3, p. 132 below.
51. Na ca sā tadānīm-utpadyate īśvarāt-saṁkramati-iti vā kalpayituṁ yuktam. Mokṣa-rūpāyās-tasyā anityatva-prasaṅgāt. *Ibid.*
52. Tathā ca sarvajñatva-ādikam-apy-aṇor-asti-iti vācyam. *Ibid.* In a footnote to the text, the editor gives an alternate reading of this line (apparently from another MS of the text): Tathā ca sedanīm-apy-aṇor-asti-iti paṭhāntaram. "Therefore, it [that power (*sā*)] is there even now [in the bound state]." The second reading makes more explicit the point that there is no *origin* of *śakti* but that it exists as part of the intrinsic nature of the *ātman*.
53. Between the two cases mentioned in note 51 above and the conclusion in the next note is a sentence about a refutation to be made later on concerning the view that *śakti* is produced or comes from some other source. It is noted here only to point out that the discussion is not in any way altered.
54. See chapter 1 p. 11 above with a quotation from the *Śivayogaratna* and the note to it, 47, with a quotation from the *Mṛigendra Āgama.*
55. In explaining this compound, viz., *paratantra-pañca-avasthā* (the five states of dependence), the editor of the text suggests in a footnote that it should be construed as: *paratantrasya yā pañca-avasthā tad-anubhava ity-arthaḥ* ("the one who is dependent is the one who has the five states—the experience of this, is the meaning [of the compound]"). *SB*, p. 292.
56. Itthaṁ ca tasya sarva-jñatvāt svatantratvād-āpta-kāmatvāc-ca kathaṁ paratantra-pañca-avasthā-anubhavaḥ kathaṁ vā pūrvokta duḥkha-vyāmiśra-viṣaya-bhogas-tasya.., *SB*, pp. 291-292.
57. Yadyapi-idānīm-api tasya jñāna-kriyā-śaktir-asty-eva tathā-api tasyā-ruddhatvād-asarva-jñatvāt paratantra-tayā'nāpta-kāmatayā pañca-avasthā -anubhava upapadyate...*SB*, p. 292.
58. Nanv-evam sutarāṁ pañca-avasthā'nubhavas-tasya na syāt ruddha-jñāna-kriyā-śaktitvena pāṣāṇa-tulyatvāt. Tathā ca vṛiścika-bhayāt palāyamān-asya-āśīviṣa-mukha-nipātaḥ...*Ibid.*
59. Tathā ca tat-tat ghaṭa-ādy-ākāra-vṛitti-pariṇata-antaḥ-karaṇena kalā-ādinā ca kadācit kiñcit kiñcid-vidārita-malas-taṁ-tam-artham-anubhavati-iti jāgara-ādy-upapattir-iti bhāvaḥ. *Ibid.*
60. Atas-svābhāvikatayā saṁsāra-daśāyām-apy-asti-ity-abhyupeyam. *SB*, p. 293.
61. Mala-ruddha-sva-dṛik-kriyatvāt avasthā-pañcakopeta-iti. *Ibid.*
62. *Mantri-yukto bhūpo mantri-bhūpa iti. Ibid.* Śivāgrayogin interprets this compound as a *madhyama-pada-lopi-samāsa*, a compound which omits the middle member. The stock example of such a compound it *śāka-pārthiva*, the king of an era, which is an abbreviation for *śāka-priya-pārthiva*, the king dear to the era. The word *śāka* also means "vegetable" and there is no

grammatical difference in the use of the compound to read it as "the king fond of vegetables."

63. Nanu mala-sad-bhāve kiṁ mānam. *SB*, p. 295.
64. Pāśa-abhāve pāratantryaṁ vaktavyaṁ kiṁ nibandhanam / Svābhāvikaṁ cen-mukteṣu mukta-śabdo nivartate // *Mṛgendra Āgama*, 7:2, quoted in *SB*, p. 295.
65. Na tāvad-ajño'smi-ity-ādi pratyakṣaṁ tasya jñāna-abhāva-viṣayatvāt. Na-apy-anumānaṁ liṅga-abhāvāt. *SB*, p. 295. See also note 20 above.
66. See note 20 above.
67. The three means of valid knowledge are discussed in the chapter on *prāmāṇyavāda*.
68. Nanu paśoḥ pāratantryaṁ kiñcid-āyattaṁ asvābhāvikatvāt...*SB*, p. 295.
69. See p. 65 above.
70. Na ca-asiddiḥ. Muktatā-daśāyāṁ pāratantrya-adarśanāt. *Ibid.*
71. Whilst scripture is the final authority, the role of inference is also implicit in it. In this context the sign or indicatory mark (*liṅga*)—without which there can be no valid inferential statements—which, for Śivāgrayogin, is a statement based on scriptural authority, is the following reason (*hetu*) which validates his argument based on inference: "since there is a disappearance of dependence in the state of liberation." See the above note for the Sanskrit and reference.
72. Evaṁ kṣaṇa-vidhvaṁsiṣu duḥkha-anuṣakteṣv-aśuddheṣu bhogeṣu saktiḥ kiñcid-āyattā āgantukatvāt ghaṭa-ādi-vat. Tādriśa-bhoga-āsakti-hetutvena malatvam-api pakṣa-dharmatābalāt sidhyāti. *SB*, p. 295.
73. This term is not to be confused with the same used for *karman* and *māyā* as adventitious (*āgantuka*) *malam*. The *malam* referred to in the context under discussion is *āṇava-malam* which is *sahaja-malam*, because it is "born with" the *ātman*. The term *āgantuka* here refers to the 'association' of *āṇava* with the *ātman*. In this sense, it is "added on" or incidental to the *ātman*.
74. S. Kuppuswami Sastri, *Indian Logic*, p. 189.
75. *Ghaṭa-ādi-hetu-bhūta-cakra-ādi-sādhāraṇyena hetutva-mātreṇa siddhāv-api yathā cakratva-ādikaṁ vinā cakra-āder ghaṭa-ādi-hetutvaṁ na siddhyaty-evaṁ malatvaṁ vinā bhoga-āsakti-hetutvaṁ na siddhyati-iti bhāvaḥ. SB*, p. 295.
76. In his *Śaivaparibhāṣā* he rejects, in addition, the suggestion that *māyā* and the body could be substitutes for the role of *malam*, Iyengar and Ramasastri, eds., (Mysore: Oriental Research Institute, 1950), pp. 76-77. The main point in the rejection of these—viz., that each is responsible for effects different from what *āṇava-malam* is supposed to be responsible for—is implicit in the *Śivāgrabhāṣya* discussion, and need not be dealt with in particular, especially since Śivāgrayogin himself does not consider them here.
77. *Kiñca-ayaṁ malino no cet saktir bhogeṣu kiṁ-kṛitā / Yadi sā nirmale'pi syān-mukta-ātmasv-api sā bhavet // Rāgo'sti kāraṇam sakter-iti-cet kiṁ-malena tu / Satyaṁ rāgo'sti taddhetur na sa kiñcitkaro'male // Amale'pi sa cet-saktyai syān-mukte'py-aviśeṣataḥ / Na hi muktaś-śivo vā'pi bhoga-*

*āsaktaḥ kadācana* // *Pauṣkara Āgama, paśupaṭalaḥ,* 126-128, quoted in *SB*, *p*. 295.

78. See chapter 1, p. 23 above.
79. See *ibid.*, p. 12.
80. The logical explanation and example of such a kind of inference defined by Nyāya, is the syllogism: "Earth is different from the rest (*not-earth*), for it has smell; whichever is not different from the rest (*not-earth*) has no smell, as water; this (earth) is not so—i.e., it does not have the absence of smell or *gandhābhāva*, with which the absence of difference from *not-earth* (*pṛthivītarabhedābhāva*) is invariably concomitant (*vyāpya*); therefore, it is not so—i.e., it is not devoid of difference from *non-earth*." S. Kuppuswami Sastri, *Indian Logic*, p. 233.
81. *SB*, p. 296.
82. Mithyā-jñāna-karma-ādi-niruddhatvena kiñcij-jñatva-upapatteḥ. .*Ibid.*
83. Mithyā-jñānasya yathā-vad-artha-prakāśe'nupattyā...*Ibid.*
84. ...mithyā-jñānasya kādācitkatvena tad-abhāva-daśāyāṁ sarvasya-api prakāśa-prasaṅgāc-ca. *Ibid.*
85. Na-apy-etad-anyathā-jñānaṁ tasya-apy-anudayāt-svataḥ / Śuktikā-rajata jñānaṁ na bhavet-paṭalaṁ vinā // Kiñca-etad-anyathā-jñānam-āgantukam -atha-itarat / Āgantukaṁ cec-cicchakter-bādhakaṁ na kadācana // Yady-anāgantukaṁ tarhi na-anyathā-jñānam-eva tat // Paśupaṭalaḥ, 117-119, quoted in *SB*, p. 296.
86. Karmaṇo'py-ādi-mattvena-anādy-ātma-prakāśa-āvārakatva-ayogāt pravāha-anāditvena tad-upapattāv-api karmaṇo bhoga-hetutve jñāna-ātmaka-bhoga-āvārakatva-ayogāt. *SB*, p. 296. The reference to the beginninglessness of *āṇava-malam* needs to be seen in the context of the isolated (*kevala*) state when the *ātman* is without *karman* and *māyā*.
87. Māyeya-tattva-buddhigatasya tasya tad-ūrdhva-bhuvana-gateṣv-abhāvena teṣām-anāvṛitattva-prasaṅgāc-ca. *Ibid.*
88. Bhoga-hetutvenaiva klṛiptatayā taj-jananena-anyathā-siddhasya-āvaraṇam praty-api hetutve tattva-sāṅkarya-prasaṅgāc-ca. *Ibid.*
89. Karmaṇā'pi na ca jñāna-bādhaḥ sambhavati dvijāḥ / Sādhyatvāt-karmaṇaḥ puṁsaḥ sādhakatvena saṁsthiteḥ // Kiñca bhogaika-hetus-tat-kathaṁ bhogasya bādhakam / Yato jñāna-ātmako bhogo na hi tena tad-āvṛitiḥ // Dharma-adharma-ātmakaṁ karma tau-ca bauddhau vyavasthitau / Vyāpty-abhāvāt-tayor-ūrdhvaṁ bādhakau sarvataḥ katham // Kiñca bhoga-pravṛittau tau vyāpriyete kathaṁ vṛittau / Anyatra-api pravṛittasya yady-anyatra-api hetutā // Anyatra tattva-asaṁsṛiṣṭiḥ kārya-bhedād-vihanyate / Tasmān-na karma-cic-chakter-bādhakam saṁvyavasthitam // Paśupaṭalam, 130-134, quoted in *SB*, pp. 296-297.
90. Tasya ca-ātmanā sambandho na samavāyaḥ tat-sattve tādātmya-prasaṅgāt. *Ibid.*, p. 297.
91. Na ca-āvārakatvam-eva sambandhaḥ tasya sambandha-antara-āyattatvāt. *Ibid.*
92. See next note for the Sanskrit.
93. Ataḥ pariśeṣāt-saṁyoga eva sambandhaḥ. Saṁyogitvāc-ca dravyatvam. *SB*, p. 297.

94. Vyāpaka-ācchādakatayā vyāpakatvam. *Ibid.*
95. Nānātve kalpanā-gauravād-ekatvaṁ ca-abhyupeyam. *Ibid.*
96. See, for example, the following from the *Mṛigendra Āgama*, *op.cit.*, 7:8 and 7:10, p. 202 and p. 204:

    "That [*malam*] is one for all beings, it is beginningless, dense, and great. Residing in each *ātman*, it possesses manifold *śaktis* which perish when their time comes to an end." (Tad-ekaṁ sarva-bhūtānām-anādi-nibiḍaṁ mahat / Praty-ātma-stha-sva-kāla-anta-apāyi-śakti-samūhavat //)

    "That [*malam*] is single; if it were several [these] would be produced like such things [resembling them]. But, since there is no appearance of liberation simultaneously [for all *ātmans*], it has several *śaktis*." (Tad-ekaṁ bahu-saṅkhyaṁ tu tādṛig-utpattimad-yataḥ / Kintu tac-chaktayo naikā yugapan-mukty-adarśanāt //).
97. Na caivam-ekasya muktau sarveṣām muktis-syād-iti vācyam. *SB*, p. 297.
98. Vastu-tas-tu tat-tad-ātma-manas-saṁyoga-nāśāt-tasya tasya muktir-iti daśame vakṣyate. *Ibid.*
99. Tatra malasya tāvat sākṣātkāreṇa-apasāritatvād-asaṁsparśaḥ. *SB*, p. 461.
100. Mala-ātmanoś-ca saṁyogo'nādir-eva. Janakatva-abhimatasya karma-āder-abhāvāt. *SB*, p. 297.
101. Na caivam tasya vināśo na syāt anāditvād-iti vācyam. *Ibid.*
102. Anāditve'pi vināśaka-sāmagrī-samavadhānena vināśa-upapatteḥ. *Ibid.*
103. Śivāgrayogin does not mention here what exactly these means are, but he refers obviously to the religious discipline (*sādhana*) of supreme devotion to Śiva. Refer, for example, to verse ten of the *Śivajñānabodham* in the appendix, the end of which reads: "supreme devotion should be had for this one [Śiva] who is the *ātman's* aid."

CHAPTER 3

# *Man as a cognitive Being*

## 3.1 *Cit-śakti as the only means of valid cognition*

Early in the history of Indian thought consistent attention has been paid to what exactly constitutes cognition, the means of cognition, and the validity of cognition.[1] This epistemological concern—which constitutes logical reasoning (*tarka*)—while attempting to provide the basis for an intelligible discourse on matters of common, everyday experience, served the purpose finally, albeit even indirectly, of distinguishing it from what constitutes the knowledge of ultimate reality, or of indicating how it could yield a knowledge of one's own essential nature. In this sense, the concern with epistemology in Indian thought may be said to represent a philosophy of being and knowing, involving, thereby, the metaphysical concern implicit in epistemology, where the empirical subject-object distinction ceases to be viewed as also reflecting ultimate reality.[2]

In other words, one may speak of a two-fold function in the Indian concern with epistemology: a concern which is closely connected with what comes under the general theme of cognition, and a concern—on the basis of the 'validity' of cognition—with *knowledge* as such. Both these concerns involve an experience (*anubhava*, *bhoga*) as a consequence of man's involvement in the world. In terms of the twofold function of Indian epistemology, a distinction may be drawn between 'cognition-experience' and 'knowledge-experience'. The former may be said to be the contact which takes place between an object and a subject through the means of the senses, leading to such experiences as listening, tasting, touching, etc. Cognition in this sense would encompass inference, verbal testimony and other means of cognition.[3] The latter, on the one hand, may be equated with valid cognition-experience, as when one *knows* the reality of an object through a perception of it (in which case error, illusion, etc., are ruled out[4]) and, on the other hand, it would involve an experience, for example, of one's nature not derived through the usual means of valid cognition. Knowledge in the latter sense, as will be seen, would also preeminently include an experience that can be described as intuitive, transcendental, or religious, without the distinction between a subject and an object which characterizes cognition.[5] At the empirical level, therefore, knowledge may be said to involve cognition but not vice versa—i.e., cognition—insofar as it could be false or erroneous—does not necessarily involve or assume the status of knowledge.

The above distinction is assumed in the discussions concerning the cognition of objects and the knowledge of ultimate reality, and the distinction is implicit in the terms *pramā* and *jñāna.* These terms are often loosely taken to mean 'knowledge' but in the light of what has been said above, *pramā* is more correctly rendered as 'cognition' since it presupposes a means of cognition, i.e., a *pramāṇa.* In the case of *jñāna,* in the sense of the knowledge of ultimate reality, a means is indeed acknowledged, namely, a *sādhana,* but in the context here this represents a special yogic attitude of contemplation or meditation on the nature of reality as such. Several schools of Indian thought (e.g., Śaiva Siddhānta and the schools of Vedānta) agree that the experience which is a knowledge of ultimate reality—referred to as *śivajñāna* or *brahmajñāna*—cannot be had through any means of cognition (*pramāṇa*), though it may indirectly help in bringing this about (as will be seen in more detail shortly).[6]

In the concern with theories of cognition, one can discern two broad trends in Indian philosophy: the theory of intrinsic validity (*svataḥ-prāmāṇyavāda*) and the theory of extrinsic validity (*parataḥ-prāmāṇyavāda*). The adherents of the former are, for example, the Mīmāṁsakas, Vedāntins, and Śaiva Siddhāntins. For them, valid cognition, i.e., empirical knowledge, is true by its very nature and the so-called erroneous nature or invalidity of knowledge is due to some defect in the means or source of cognition (*kāraṇa doṣa*), e.g., defective eyesight. Thus, one cannot speak of 'false knowledge' but rather of an error in the means through which cognition takes place. This view is opposed to the latter theory of extrinsic validity, propounded by the Nyāya school, where an extraneous factor or condition needs to be fulfilled in the origin (*utpattau*) or the ascertainment (*jñaptau*) of cognition to establish its validity.[7]

The fundamental question underlying epistemology (*prāmāṇyavāda*) in both these trends concerns what precisely constitutes the valid means of cognition, i.e., *pramāṇa*. In the epistemological context this term has implicit in it three cognate words, all of which are derived from the root *mā* prefixed by *pra*: *prameya* or the object of cognition, *pramā* or *pramiti* which is the cognition itself, and the *pramātṛi* or the subject, who is the cognizer. The verb *pramā* itself means several things: to measure to mete out, to estimate, to arrange, to form a correct notion of something, to understand or to know.[8] The causative form of the verb, *pramāpayati*, meaning 'to cause correct knowledge, afford proof or authority', brings out the epistemological sense of the means (*pramāṇa*) as the right measure, the standard or authority of the means of *pramā*, the correct notion, true knowledge or valid cognition.[9]

In rationalizing what exactly may be called a *pramāṇa* (a means of valid cognition) the Siddhāntin says:

> That without which there is no valid cognition of any object whatever, that alone is to be acknowledged as the valid means of cognition, and sight, etc., are not such [valid means].[10]

This conclusion is based on the logical assumption that:

> Whatever is an object of cognition is not a means of cognition, since it [the object] is cognized through some means.[11]

This insightful conclusion, which is unique to Śaiva Siddhānta, seems contrary to what is generally accepted as being a possible means of valid cognition, viz., perception, which is acknowledged by all schools which deal with epistemology, and an explanation is necessary for the precise sense in which the Siddhāntin maintains this position. The reason is twofold. Firstly, as stated above, whatever is a means of cognition is not an object of cognition and since the senses can be objects (i.e., of an 'inner' perception, as will be seen further), they cannot strictly be called the means by which cognition really takes place. Secondly, the scope of the senses is limited insofar as each sense has its own specific, and limited, frame of reference. There is no doubt for the Siddhāntin, however, that there is some cognitive element in man which is not restricted as the senses are. This element or principle is responsible for the possibility of the various forms of cognition which should, therefore, be called the *pramāṇa*, in the true sense of the term. In Śivāgrayogin's own words:

> It should be acknowledged that there is some means of cognition which grasps all objects, since it is impossible that the senses such as sight, etc., can grasp objects other than those which are their respective objects.[12]

The authority on the basis of which this argument is made, clarifies the Siddhāntin's point even further:

> In the perception of sound there is no sight and in the perception of colour there is no hearing. It is *saṁvid* (consciousness) which grasps everything and, therefore, it alone is regarded as the valid means of cognition.[13]

Śivāgrayogin identifies *saṁvid* with *cit-śakti* when he says, about the means of cognition which grasps all objects, that 'that, indeed, is *cit-śakti*.'[14] What this means for man as a cognitive being is that:

> The *ātman's cit-śakti*, which is a synonym for [what yields] valid cognition and which is devoid of memory, misapprehension, and doubt, is the general definition of [what constitutes] the valid means of cognition.[15]

Insofar as *cit* is not only indestructible but is in fact also inseparable from its *śakti*—as already seen (Chapter 1, p. 9) with the power of consciousness being inherent to consciousness itself—it follows that there should be an uninterrupted 'knowledge-experience' of itself through its own *śakti*. But, then, this is possible, as already categorically stated above, only with the *cit-śakti* which is devoid of doubt, misapprehension and memory.

These three factors are limiting agents of man's intrinsic power of consciousness (*ātma-cit-śakti*)—on account of the efficacy of its association with *malam*. Each of these is clearly defined as follows. Doubt is "a notion conditioned by two alternatives, on account of perceiving common features, such as [when one wonders] 'is this a pillar or a person?' etc."[16] Misapprehension is 'the notion of something not in the thing as such, as [when one apprehends] silver in the mother-of-pearl, etc.'[17] Memory is 'a notion arising from impressions produced in previous experiences such as a lover's vision of the beloved, etc.'[18] The conclusion, therefore, is that 'the *cit-śakti* which is devoid of these three is, indeed, the valid means of cognition.'[19]

Since man is not devoid of these three factors, which are consequences of the involvement in worldly experiences, it follows that there can be no knowledge of *cit* (consciousness) which its own *śakti* is capable of fully furnishing. The question asked earlier may be repeated in the context here: why is man in a state such that the powers of consciousness (*cit-śakti*) are conditioned and, thereby, hindered by doubt, misapprehension and memory? The question becomes crucial especially in the light of the possibility, as already seen, of *cit-śakti* functioning in an unfettered state. The answer to the question was provided in the discussion concerning the proof for the existence of *malam*, and its efficacy in limiting the expression of the *ātman*'s power of consciousness. The limitation under which *cit-śakti* operates in man does not, however, preclude the Siddhāntin's view that it is in fact the only means of cognition and knowledge as such.

In view of the unique standpoint in accepting *cit-śakti* as the only *pramāṇa*, it is important to see how Śivāgrayogin discusses in detail the validity of such a position—it is important insofar as it furnishes the precise sense in which the Siddhāntin argues his case, especially in view of the thesis that man's essential nature is defined by consciousness (*cit*) and the power (*śakti*) intrinsic to it.

The discussion in this context centres around the synonymous terms *karaṇa* and *sādhana*, which mean 'an instrument, agent, or apparatus' which serves as a 'means' through which anything may be effected or accomplished. The words *avyāpti* and *ativyāpti* also occur frequently in the discussion and are used to express fallacies in any definition of a term. *Avyāpti* is the fallacy of a definition which is too narrow insofar as there can be evidence of instances not encompassed or pervaded (*avyāpti*) by the definition, e.g., the definition that man is a being who eats cooked food does not include those who eat raw food. *Ativyāpti* is the fallacy of a definition which is too wide since its scope extends beyond its intended limits or over-pervades (*ativyāpti*) into instances which cannot strictly be said to be included in the definition, e.g., in the definition that man is a mortal being, mortality applies to elephants and ants, as well.

Before setting forth his own definition Śivāgrayogin first considers what an opponent might have to say. The objection is that *cit-śakti* as a definition of *pramāṇa* cannot be accepted because, firstly, a *pramāṇa*:

> cannot be an instrument (*sādhana*) of valid cognition since it [the definition] is too wide with regard to a lamp, etc., [which would also be included]. This has even been said in the *Pauṣkara* [*Āgama*, 7:11]: "Now, whatever is the instrument (*sādhana*) of valid cognition, why cannot it be a means of cognition (*pramāṇa*)? That cannot be since the situation will arise where the eyes, the lamp, etc., will have the nature of the means of cognition (*pramāṇatva*)".[20]

The method of putting authoritative statements in the mouth of the opponent is stylistically very effective. It is the acquaintance with Śivāgrayogin's own standpoint that facilitates the task of distinguishing his view from that of the opponent.

The fallacy of the definition which the opponent points out here is that an instrument which cannot operate on its own, e.g., a lamp, could be taken as the real means of cognition, and not necessarily *cit-śakti* alone. In the light of this statement the opponent points out further, that if *cit-śakti* were to be considered as the valid cognition itself (*pramiti*)—which the Siddhāntin does, as already seen—then it is impossible that it can also serve as an instrument (*sādhana*) for cognition itself.[21] The objection amounts to saying that if *cit-śakti* is identical with *pramiti* (valid cognition) then *pramiti* would be an eternal feature because *cit-śakti* is eternal. In other words, potentially there would always be a condition of valid cognition if the Siddhāntin's position were tenable, but this is not the case as far as man is concerned.

The next objection that the opponent raises, in anticipation of a possible clarification, is that the Siddhāntin cannot say:

> *Cit-śakti* alone is not the valid cognition (*pramiti*) but *cit-śakti* which is defined (*avacchinnā*) by this or that object and it [*cit-śakti*] is produced through the production of the qualifying object and, thus, it is not impossible for it [*cit-śakti*] to be an instrument (*sādhana*); and there can be no fallacy of over-pervasion concerning things like a lamp, etc., since the word '*sādhana*' is [not different] from the word '*karaṇa*'.

This argument from the opponent's point of view gives the impression that a *pramāṇa*, for the Siddhāntin, could well be a *sādhana* or *karaṇa* and if *cit-śakti*'s relation to objects is the determining factor for what constitutes a definition of a *pramāṇa*, then clearly the senses too would have to be included according to such a definition. The opponent's argument is that if the Siddhāntin accepts this position, then obviously there cannot be the charge of having a definition which is too wide.

The opponent, however, realizes that this is precisely what the Siddhāntin cannot accept because of an evident problem in such a position, under certain conditions:

> It is through the existence of a qualifying object—and as a consequence of such an object alone—that *cit-śakti* is generated, even when there is no contact of the eye, etc., [with an object]; and in such a case [there be no valid cognition] since it is not produced through sight, etc.[22]

It is clear, according to the opponent, that when the eyes are not in contact with an object, the perception of the object is impossible. Conversely, it may be said that when there is no visible object, the function of otherwise proper sight is useless in perceiving objects, for example, at night. If the sense of sight were accepted as being a *pramāṇa*, as shown in the previous argument, then it would mean that the mere possession of good sight is sufficient to yield valid cognition, even when there is no direct contact with an object. Further, and on the other hand, the mere presence of an object should yield cognition even without sight, since the mere presence of the object is said to 'produce' *cit-śakti*. Therefore, as the opponent implies, with *cit-śakti* as the *pramāṇa* cognition, *ipso facto*, should take place. In other words, in neither of these cases is there valid cognition, i.e., neither with *cit-śakti* alone, and without the sense of sight, nor with sight alone which is not capable of seeing in the dark.

The opponent goes on to say that "since even a doubt, an erroneous cognition, etc., would be aspects of *cit-śakti* which is qualified by this or that object, there would be too wide a definition as regards the 'cause' (*karaṇa*) of these."[23] The argument is that if *cit-śakti* is the *pramāṇa*, and if it is said to function as an instrument of cognition, such as sight, then such a definition is far too wide in its scope, since it would be responsible not only for valid cognition (*pramiti*), but for doubts and erroneous cognition as well. In short, this means that it is impossible for the Siddhāntin to have a viable definition of *cit-śakti* as the only means of cognition, since the instruments of perception, such as sight, would have to be included insofar as there is any reference to an object.[24] In such a case there can be no distinction between the causes of valid and invalid cognition, and whatever is said to be the cause of both would have a scope inadmissibly too wide in its application. Hence, the Siddhāntin's notion of *cit-śakti* as the only valid means of cognition is untenable according to the opponent.

The above objections rest on what precisely constitutes the definition of an instrument (*karaṇa*, *sādhana*) of cognition. The Siddhāntin thus has to consider the opponent's views on the matter before arriving at a final definition of *cit-śakti* as a *pramāṇa*.

Śivāgrayogin objects to five different views on the nature of instrumentality (*karaṇatvam*) that the above arguments of the opponent take for granted. He says that a final settlement is impossible as to whether instrumentality is—

1. connected with a result by being distinguished as separate from it (*ayoga-vyavacchedena phala-sambandhittvam*);
2. a possession of a function (*vyāpāravatvam*);

3. a possession of a function connected with a result (*phala-niyata-vyāpāravatvam*);
4. the being set into motion by an agent of action (*kartṛi-preryatvam*); or
5. an assemblage of instruments of valid cognition (*pramā-sāmagrītvam*.

For a proper understanding of the Siddhānta position, it is necessary to see what Śivāgrayogin says about each of these points.

Instrumentality (*karaṇatvam*) cannot be said to be connected with a result, since such a view would contain the fallacies of a definition being both too wide and even too narrow.[25] It would be too wide insofar as it would include *karman*, intended here in the grammatical sense of 'object', which involves pleasure and pain. Such a position is inadmissible because pleasure and pain cannot be regarded as instruments (*karaṇas*) since they are results (*phalas*) of previously performed deeds. Such a definition of instrumentality is, therefore, given too wide a scope. Further, if instrumentality is connected only with a result, then certain instances of perception are excluded from the definition as, for example, when the function of sight is operative but the object is not really seen. That is, the eyes 'function' but there is no result insofar as there is no cognition of any object—a case of seeing without looking. In this way, instrumentality defined as what is connected with a result has to be ruled out.

The second definition of instrumentality, namely, that it is the possession of a function, is also unacceptable for the reason that it is too wide insofar as it would include things like a pot and a lamp.[26] These objects undoubtedly possess certain functions, but these functions do not necessarily make them 'means' of valid cognition, even though a lamp, for example, as an instrument may be an aid to perception. On the other hand, these functions exclude the activity of subsumptive reflection (*parāmarśa*), i.e., the activity which yields the knowledge of the minor term of an inference in its connection with the major term, and which is an 'instrument' of any inference, though itself devoid of any 'function'.[27] It cannot be said, further, that the instrument (*karaṇa*) is the indicatory mark or sign (*liṅga*) which has the function (*vyāpārakam*) of this subsumptive reflection—the argument is that in the inference 'there is fire because of smoke', smoke is the sign (*liṅga*) of fire but it cannot be the instrument (*karaṇa*) of the inference.

The above argument, in other words, is invalid because it is impossible for the *liṅga* to be a special instrument (*karaṇa*) of an inference because it is improper to say that a *liṅga* produces anything 'since it has the nature of the past and the future.'[28] In other words, a sign such as smoke, which leads to the inference about the presence of fire, in principle exists all the time and is manifest at all times whenever there is fire. The sign of fire is smoke and this is always so. It is the *sign* of fire and not the *instrument* which brings about the inference of fire (nor is it the instrument which causes fire) and, hence, a *liṅga* cannot be the *karaṇa* which comes into contact with a particular object at a particular time. The definition of instrumentality as the possession of a function is fraught with the above problems and is, therefore, unacceptable to the Siddhāntin.

The above arguments serve as the basis for a refutation of the third definition of instrumentality, viz., that it is the possession of a function necessarily connected with a definite result. 'When it is dark, etc., the contact of the eye [with an object] does not produce any result, and in the absence of any rule for this [viz., that whenever the function of sight is operative the object must be cognized] the definition excludes sight, etc.'[29] Whilst the previous argument is a refutation of what was taken to be an 'instrument' which is always present, this argument now refutes—on the basis of its being too narrow—the view that the cognition of an object must necessarily take place when the corresponding sense is operative. It cannot be argued to compromise the situation (the Siddhāntin tells the opponent) that indeed there can be no sight in darkness but that, for example, for sight to be possible in the dark—and thereby lead necessarily to the production of a result, viz., the sight of the object—there can be for sight in darkness 'an association with some other cause.'[30]

The objection that the Siddhāntin raises here is that the opponent cannot justify a definition of instrumentality in this context, i.e. as what must necessarily produce a result, by admitting an aid, e.g., a lamp, which makes visibility possible in the dark. If this were the case, that is, if one were to justify arguments in such a way, then every activity in the world could be explained—and explained away—by such conditions. The phrase 'connected with a result' to explain instrumentality, thereby becomes meaningless,[31] apart from the fact that the value of a definition would be lost. In other words, there is no significance attached to the cognition which sight itself is said to provide if an additional factor, on account of which visibility becomes possible in certain instances, were accepted. Such a position would mean an inadmissible inclusion within its scope also of *karman*, action in general, which would immediately produce the necessary result by the various modes of auxiliaries—just as the lamp would produce the desired result of the sight of an object at night.[32]

Further, "if it is said that the difference in the terms 'instrument', 'act', and 'agent' is due only to a difference of designation (*upādhi*), then it is not so." If this were the case, then each term, including the agent of an action, would be absorbed into the other. Moreover, the eyes, for example, would become as good as non-existent in the case of an inference (e.g., of fire), made possible by some instrument involved in the perception of an object (e.g., of smoke). In this way, the term 'instrumentality' is devoid of any significance whatsoever.[33] The Siddhāntin points out here that there is no arbitrariness in the distinction contained in usages such as: an agent (*kartṛi*) performing an act (*karman*) using an instrument (*karaṇa*). In other words, Śivāgrayogin is arguing the point that aids (such as lamps) to instruments (such as eyes, through which sight takes place) are not instruments, strictly speaking, and this applies especially in the epistemological context, where there is a concern with the way in which cognition and knowledge occurs. The following is presupposed in the argument here: just as the lamp is not the instrument of sight in relation to the eyes, the eyes themselves are not, strictly speaking, the means of sight in relation to the conscious power (*cit-śakti*) which makes their operation possible. In the light of this, the conclusion which the Siddhāntin comes to is that instrumentality which is defined as the possession of a function which is necessarily connected with a definite result, is quite unacceptable.

The fourth definition of instrumentality as the being set into motion by an agent of action, is also rejected. Śivāgrayogin's considered opinion is that this is too broad a definition, so as to include even the body, and only partially applies to subsumptive reflection. The body cannot be the means per se of cognition insofar as it is itself set into motion, no less than a lamp has to be turned on for sight at night. That is to say that just as a lamp or light is an auxiliary factor for sight, so too the eye itself is, by extension, an auxiliary factor at the service of the real means of perception (or inference), viz., *cit-śakti*. Whilst subsumptive reflection (*parāmarśa*) is acceptable as an instrument (*karaṇa*), only insofar as it yields a valid conclusion (*anumiti*), and is an indispensable component of an inference (*anumāna*)—as already seen—nonetheless, as far as the definition under consideration is concerned, it cannot be regarded as an independent agent (*svatantra-kartṛi*), responsible for the act of inferring a conclusion. *Parāmarśa* constitutes a 'complex'[34] component of the inferential process as a whole and, apart from this, it is 'not conditioned by the will of an agent (*puruṣa-tantra*) but by the object (*vatsu-tantra*) or by another knowledge which serves as its means (*pramāṇa-tantra*).'[35] In the light of these defects, the view of instrumentality under consideration would also have to be unacceptable.

The fifth definition of instrumentality as an assemblage of the instruments of cognition, would also have to be rejected on the grounds that each sense of perception, individually, would be excluded from the definition. This is the case since:

> ...by [the word] assemblage (*sāmagrī*) [is meant what] has the form of a collection (*samudāya*) of instruments (*karaṇas*) and a collection would mean even sight, etc., which [individually] are not different from what make up the parts of the collection (*samudāyin*); by this, even the cognizer, the object cognized, etc., would be the means of cognition if [each sense were] an assemblage; this would be a case of a transgression of the custom of the distinction [between one and the other].[36]

This refutation by the Siddhāntin has several noteworthy points. Firstly, if instrumentality is defined as a collection of factors then the organ of sight, as a distinct entity, is excluded from being an instrument by itself. Secondly, if the organ of sight were itself seen as a collection of entities then such a definition would include within it the object which it, in fact, cognizes—since the object perceived would have to be included in the collection of causes responsible for cognition. Conversely, and thirdly, there would be no reason why the object perceived could not be regarded as the instrument of perception in the collection of causes. Fourthly, the common practice of distinguishing a subject from an object would have to be abandoned in everyday discourse. Fifthly, a collection of the causes of cognition which does not distinguish the three components of the cognizer, the cognized thing, and the means of cognition, in fact cannot logically be deemed a collection—such a threefold distinction cannot be entertained in terms of the definition of instrumentality under consideration.[37]

The above objections, further, are justified for the following reason: 'because it is improper for a collection of causes to be a means of cognition since it [the collection of causes] is an object cognized.' This argument is based on what *Pauṣkara Āgama* 7:12 says, which Śivāgrayogin repeats in the context here:

> Whatever is an object of cognition cannot be a means of cognition, since it [the object] is cognized by some means.

It is on the basis of all the reasons stated above that the Siddhāntin says conclusively: "Therefore, the general definition of a means (*pramāṇa*) is not proper."

After discussing the impossibility of a means (*pramāṇa*) being an instrument (*sādhana, karaṇa*)—which a lamp and the senses are—Śivāgrayogin now states what precisely is to be regarded as the real means of cognition:

> *Cit-śakti* which is delimited by this or that object is the valid cognition, with regard to such an object, and this [*cit-śakti*] alone is the valid means of cognition.[38]

With this clear statement identifying the means of cognition and the cognition itself, *cit-śakti* is given a unique position by the

Siddhāntin. It is inextricably a part of *cit* (consciousness) and in the epistemological context the two terms *cit* and *śakti* are interchangeable. Therefore, to say that *cit-śakti* is the *pramāṇa* is to say, in effect, that *cit* itself fulfils this function. It is in the light of this identity that *cit-śakti* is both the *pramāṇa* (the means of valid cognition) and the *pramā* (the valid cognition itself). Although Śivāgrayogin does not state it here explicitly, it may be added that *cit-śakti* is also the *pramātṛi* (the cognizing subject), insofar as it constitutes the essential feature or definition of man in the sense in which a quality (*dharma* or *guṇa*) is identical with what possesses the quality (*dharmin* or *guṇin*).

It must be noted that despite the fact that *cit-śakti* is the eternally illuminating factor in man 'it cannot be said that there is the contingency of manifesting an object all the time.' This point is a crucial one because, unlike a lamp, *cit-śakti* is independent and its ability to provide knowledge—which is identical with itself as the means of knowledge—should, by definition, always reveal the objects of cognition in an unhindered and unlimited way. But this is obviously not the case with man in the world and an explanation is necessary so as not to relegate the concept of *cit-śakti* as the *pramāṇa* to a position not different from that of the opponent—where the role of *cit-śakti* as an instrument of cognition would inadmissibly be identified with that, for example, of a lamp.

Although *cit-śakti* is intrinsically independent it *becomes* hindered and fettered through the factor of *malam*, as already seen. This factor which is responsible, further, for *cit-śakti* to bear corporeality—albeit in order to be rid of all fetters finally—makes *cit-śakti* rely on the role of the *buddhi* (intellect) as an instrument to aid it. This situation represents the predicament of man, entailing the striking paradox of being essentially independent while at the same time being conditioned, namely, by the *buddhi*, the indispensable principle for man's experience in the world. *Buddhi* which has a limited scope and function, as will be seen in greater detail below, is the chief aid to *cit-śakti* which comes under its sway in all matters, and especially in cognition. It enables *cit-śakti* to manifest itself in a limited way. In other words, in view of the need—as already seen—for the *ātman* to undergo worldly experience, the power of consciousness intrinsic to it (*ātma-cit-śakti*) consequently, and in the nature of the case, is limited. This means that the *buddhi* allows or makes possible a partial or restricted expression of *cit-śakti*.

It is to be noted that the ability of the *buddhi* to operate is made possible by *cit-śakti* itself and there is, in this context, the paradoxical situation of *cit-śakti* being fettered by the *buddhi* and the *buddhi* itself requiring the power of *cit* for its very operation. It has already been seen that the *buddhi* (intellect) belongs to the category of things which are of the nature of non-consciousness or insentience (*acit*, *jaḍa*) and, hence, requires a conscious motivating factor, namely, *cit-śakti*. Whilst the *buddhi* is useless without *cit-śakti* it is, nonetheless, indispensable for man's life in the world. The limitation which the *buddhi* effects is *temporary* since its potency vanishes with the impotency of *malam*. The manifestation of the *buddhi* occurs, as already seen through its *vṛitti* (mode or modification), which is what makes cognition possible via the different senses. It may be said in this context that just as *cit* manifests itself through its *śakti*, *buddhi* manifests itself through its *vṛitti* (excepting, for the moment, the point that the intellect is intrinsically insentient).

The above points are presupposed when Śivāgrayogin says, in continuing his explanation of *cit-śakti* as the only *pramāṇa*, that *cit-śakti* does not cognize objects all the time. His argument is an intricate one and may be put in his own words before attempting to consider it in detail. The reason why *cit-śakti* does not cognize objects all the time, he says, is:

> Because, when there is no appearance of a *buddhi-vṛitti* which is effected by sight, etc., the contact with the object—by being obscured by *malam*—is as good as non-existent. However, when it [*buddhi-vṛitti*] arises by removing *malam*, and since the contact with the object is unobscured—since this is the occasion for *cit-śakti* to become delimited by that object—there arises the manifestation [of the object] for that period of time.[39]

What this means is that the *vṛitti* of *buddhi* is not only responsible for a meaningful and useful contact between *cit-śakti* and the object of perception, but also for the duration of such a contact. No sooner the *vṛitti* ceases than the obscuring veil of *malam* returns, the contact with the object is broken and, thus, cognition does not occur. In this sense the *vṛitti* is like a lamp which makes visibility possible as long as it operates. The fact that *cit-śakti* is made to rely on the function of the *buddhi-vṛitti* is due to the restrictive potency of *malam* and this situation is no reflection on the intrinsic nature of *cit-śakti* as the all-pervasive, eternal factor of cognition and knowledge as such. It is only the *ātman*'s association with *malam* that necessitates the reliance of *cit-śakti* on the *vṛittis* of the *buddhi* for life in the world.

Śivāgrayogin gives another interpretation of what exactly is meant by the relation between *cit-śakti* and an object:

> The contact of the object with *cit-śakti* is the altered state of the *buddhi-vṛitti* in the form of the experience of the object *as it is*, and because the delimitation of the object is only temporary, there occurs a manifestation [of the object] only temporarily.

The lamp analogy may be applied here as well: just as the light of the lamp may be said to encompass the object according to its shape and size and, thereby, make it cognizable as such, so too a *buddhi-vṛitti* may be said to take on the nature and character of an object and, thereby, make it evidently cognizable as such. Further, just as a lamp can only manifest objects that come within its range, so too cognition takes place to *the extent to which the buddhi-vṛitti is capable of functioning*. Here again, this limitation to, and contingency on, the capacity of the *buddhi-vṛitti* is no reflection on the nature of *cit-śakti.*

From the above description, it would seem that whenever the *buddhi-vṛitti* with the aid, for example, of the senses, is instrumental in forging a link between an object and *cit-śakti*, the resultant cognition must necessarily be valid, in view of the fact that *cit-śakti* is 'the manifesting source or ground of knowledge.'[40] Whilst this must certainly be the case if *cit-śakti*—with its essential nature as the illuminating factor of cognition—is said to be the only *pramāṇa*, it would mean, nonetheless, that the role of doubt, error and memory[41] in empirical cognition would also have to be attributed to *cit-śakti*. In the light of the Siddhāntin's persistent claim that *cit-śakti* is not only the source of truth and validity but is also knowledge itself, this view would involve a striking anomaly if it were responsible for doubt and error as well. It is in order to be precise about the definition of *cit-śakti* as the only *pramāṇa*, that Śivāgrayogin repeats, in this context, the authoritative statement of the *Pauṣkara Āgama* (7:22):

> *Cit-śakti* which is free of doubt, etc., is acknowledged as the valid means of cognition.[42]

This statement in itself is clear, but the question still remains as to how exactly it is to be interpreted. Śivāgrayogin provides an insightful exegesis here, the clarity of which is strikingly evident. He says: "The phrase 'free of doubt, etc.,' means 'the object-conditioned *buddhi-vṛitti* which is free of doubt, etc.,' and only after that, is there a [proper] delimitation by this or that object." Explaining further, he adds:

> By the fact that it is impossible for *cit-śakti* to be identified with a *buddhi-vṛitti* which is ridden with doubt,[43] etc., and since this would give rise to a contradiction in the phrase "[*cit-śakti*] free of that [doubt, etc.]", the meaning is: "only after the conditioned *buddhi-vṛitti* is free of that [doubt, etc.]", because this is the necessary conclusion.[44]

What this typically compact Sanskrit construction means is that it is contradictory to say that *cit-śakti* per se must be free of doubt, misapprehension and the conditions of memory in order to be a *pramāṇa*. The *Pauṣkara Āgama* does seem to mean this, in the quotation above, but this has to be understood—as is implicit in Śivāgrayogin's commentary on it—in the light of the definition of *cit-śakti* as the essentially unerring, undoubting conscious principle constituting the nature of man, vis a vis the role of the *buddhi* as a necessary aid to *cit-śakti* (which has become associated with *malam*, to its own detriment). *Cit* provides the power or ability (*śakti*) necessary for the *buddhi* to function, and illumines, manifests, and cognizes what the *buddhi* presents to *cit*, through its *vṛitti*. Consequently, doubt and error have to be attributed to the *buddhi*. In other words, *cit-śakti* manifests the contents that the *buddhi-vṛitti* acquires 'in the form of the experience of the object *as it is*,' as seen above.

Śivāgrayogin cautions the opponent's impatience at this insistence on *cit-śakti* as the only *pramāṇa*, as a consequence of which it might now be said : 'Away with *cit-śakti*! Let the *buddhi-vṛitti* alone be the light for the [cognition of] objects.'[45] This is unacceptable for the following reason which clinches the argument: 'since the *buddhi* is insentient, as is also its *vṛitti*, and since the illumination of objects can only be on account of *cit-śakti* which is of the form of consciousness (*saṁvid*).'[46] This conclusion is on the authority of the *Pauṣkara Āgama* (7:17) statement which Śivāgrayogin quotes:

> Since it is of the nature of non-consciousness, and since it is not different from the eye, etc., nor from what is derived out of *prakṛiti*, *buddhi* is not the *pramāṇa*.

The word *buddhi* here, as Śivāgrayogin says, is to be construed as *buddhi-vṛitti* 'because its *vṛitti* is not different from it.'[47]

The analysis which establishes *cit-śakti* as both the *pramāṇa* and the *pramiti* is grounded on a transcendental reflection on the nature of man as the cognizer involved in worldly experience. This special status is given to *cit-śakti* because it stands for consciousness (*cit*) and its intrinsic power (*śakti*). *Cit* or consciousness, which is not essentially different from its own power or *śakti*, is eternal, all-pervasive, and constitutes man's essence described as the *ātman*, as already seen. It is the motivating principle of all activity characteristic of sentience (a fundamental position opposed to the Sāṅkhya, Yoga, and Advaita views). As such, it falls outside the realm of what can be referred to in spatial and temporal terms. When *cit-śakti* becomes associated with the limiting and, thereby, fettering adjuncts, there arises the possibility of a mistaken mutual identity between them. *Buddhi*, *manas* and *ahaṅkāra* are three potential candidates for the erroneous identification with *cit-śakti*. Of these the *buddhi* is the most important to consider, as has been done above. In view of its indispensable function in the realm of phenomena, serving as an aid to *cit-śakti*, it appears to perform as *cit-śakti* itself, at whose disposal it in fact is. It is the role of the *buddhi* which forges the link between the empirical realm of phenomena and the transcendental realm where *cit-śakti* is said to reign supreme. At the empirical level *cit-śakti* administers, so to speak, through aids such as the *buddhi*, and becomes coloured by what the *buddhi* presents to it. *Cit-śakti* is thereby brought to the empirical level at the hands of the *buddhi*, guided and misguided by it. It is here, at this level, that whatever can be spoken of in spatial and temporal terms becomes erroneously directed at *cit-śakti*, which essentially transcends it.

When it is said that the *buddhi* forges the link between the phenomena (of which the *buddhi* is itself a part) and consciousness, what is implicit in the epistemological context, is that the *buddhi* operates in close association with the *manas* (mind), the *ahaṅkāra* (ego), and the *indriyas* (organs of sense), which are finally under the control of the *buddhi*. *Cit-śakti* illumines the information they provide, acquired by the instruments of sense perception (*pratyakṣa*), inference (*anumāna*) and verbal testimony or scriptural authority (*śabda* or *śruti*). In the light of what has been said about *cit-śakti* as the only means of cognition (*pramāṇa*), it is to be noted that these three, which are generally regarded as means of cognition, are to be seen merely as instruments (as with the *buddhi*) which are operative only because *cit-śakti* makes possible an expression of their ability. It is only in this sense, namely, that *cit-śakti* alone is the means of cognition and knowledge—which at the empirical level requires the indispensable aid of certain instruments—that *pratyakṣa*, *anumāna*, and *śabda* are also indirectly referred to as *pramāṇas*, or means of cognition. When doubt, error, and memory enter into the fabric of cognition, these are attributed, as already seen, to the *buddhi* which, in turn, acquires them via sense perception, inference and testimony. It is in this context that valid and non-valid cognition applies. As far as *cit-śakti* per se is concerned, it is beyond validity and non-validity and stands for *truth* as such. It is necessary now, therefore, to consider *pratyakṣa*, *anumāna*, and *śabda* as *pramāṇas* in the specific sense in which Śaiva Siddhānta regards them—they are necessary insofar as they broaden the scope toward the Śaiva Siddhānta understanding of man.

Before discussing the so-called three means of cognition, it is to be noted that it is precisely in this context of the concern with the theory of cognition that certain conditions—generally acknowledged by all systems of Indian thought, including Śaiva Siddhānta—need to be fulfilled, in order that the accepted means of cognition retain their unique roles and natures. These conditions may be summarized as follows:

1. The cognition that each means furnishes must be *new* and not attainable by any other means.
2. One means may aid another in making the cognition possible—e.g., perception may aid the cognition arrived at through an inference—but the means in question should *not be reducible to another.*
3. The cognition arrived at through a particular means should not be contradicted (*abādhita*) by another means.
4. The accepted means of cognition should *appeal to reason* and in the case of scriptural authority (*śruti, śabda*), for example, (as will be seen), the revealed truth must appear *probable* and be made intelligible in terms of human experience (otherwise *śruti* would fail in its purpose).

It is in the light of a serious consideration of these factors that the Siddhāntin accepts only three 'means' of cognition[48] which may now be dealt with, as Śivāgrayogin considers them.

### 3.2 *Sense perception* (*pratyakṣa*)

Sense perception is man's most basic and most important instrument of cognition. Its significance for epistemology can hardly be over-emphasized, especially since it is also the ground for the validity of all other instruments of cognition. Its importance is recognized by all systems of Indian philosophy and its significance is evident in the fact that it is usually the first described. What this means is that if the validity of sense perception as a means of cognition is first established, then the validity, for example, of inference could have credibility—providing, of course, that the inferential process itself is sound.

In following the generally accepted definition of sense perception as a means of valid cognition[49] in Indian thought, the Siddhāntin also acknowledges that perception has to be defined as 'immediate cognition'.[50] It is the only type of cognition which is completely unmediated, i.e., the contact between the object perceived and the sense of perception is a direct one. Further, 'the immediacy is a special quality [of perception] which is not fragmentary.'[51] By this is meant that the immediacy or directness involved between the object and the sense which perceives it, is not partial but whole. A subtle distinction is implicit here between the immediacy of an object to a particular sense, and the judgement about the object arrived at on the basis of the evident object.

The Śaiva Siddhānta realism involved in this point is noteworthy. The object exists really, it is not something which has the status of a dream object. When an object comes within the range of the 'proper' function of a particular sense, its immediacy is evident completely, i.e., the immediacy is not partial or fragmentary. In other words, if the object comes within the range of the function of a sense, then perception takes place. On this principle, namely, that the objects really exist and that the senses have the ability to perceive them, the validity or invalidity of the cognition that results is a secondary issue. In either case, some object is in question, the immediacy of which, as far as the perception of it is concerned, cannot be partial (*khaṇḍa*), which the judgement concerning the object might indeed be.

Whilst the immediacy entailed in perception is unfragmentary, the 'process' of perception itself, according to the Siddhāntin, is broadly said to be of two kinds: an indeterminate perception (*nirvikalpaka-pratyakṣa*) and a determinate perception (*savikalpaka-pratyakṣa*). What these are exactly is defined by the *Pauṣkara Āgama* (7:28):

> The perception of the bare nature of a thing is indeterminate and [the perception] together with a relation to a name, class, etc., is determinate.[52]

This broad twofold division of perception is based on the functions of two indispensable categories for cognition, viz., the *buddhi* (intellect) and the *manas* (mind). It is the *buddhi-vṛitti*, as already seen, that forges the link between the object and *cit-śakti* and in this process the *buddhi-vṛitti* is assisted by the *manas*, which is in 'closer' contact with the sense organ that perceives the object. The sense organ feeds the sense data to the *manas* in a general way, and the *buddhi* specifies the object or passes judgement concerning it. At the level of the *manas*, the perception is indeterminate and, as a consequence of the function of the *buddhi*, the perception becomes determinate. What this means is that the perception of the one and the same object undergoes these two phases, before cognition may be said to have arisen.

These phases are not open to verification and are descriptive postulates that attempt to describe the phenomenon of perception. These phases, further, are related directly to the specific roles assigned to the categories of the *buddhi* (intellect) and the *manas* (mind). The following may be mentioned by way of an example to attempt a further clarification of this distinction in perception which is purely psychological. When one perceives an object at a distance, the fact of the object there results in the cognition of something, the nature of which cannot be determined. At a closer examination, it is decided that the bare, indeterminate object is such and such a thing. It is given a name which sets it apart from other objects that also bear names. It is in this context that every cognition, which is in effect a determinate perception, is said to be always shaped by words.[53] These two phases occur 'internally' or 'psychologically' and are designated the general, indeterminate (*nirvikalpaka*) perception and the specific, determinate (*savikalpaka*) perception. The distinction is implicit even in the swiftness with which cognition usually takes place—a swiftness which has to be attributed to the efficiency of the *manas*. The description which has just been given here is different from the case of doubt: here there is first a bare perception of something which is subsequently determined to be a specific thing; in the case of doubt, on the other hand, one is not able to decide—for reasons which do not necessarily relate to the perception of the object itself—whether what is perceived is this or that thing.

Another way of dealing with perception is to classify it as comprising three kinds and thereby accounting for the whole gamut of the function of man's faculty of perception. These are (a) the perception which is dependent on the sense organs (*indriya-sāpekṣa-pratyakṣam*), (b) the perception which is dependent on the internal organs (*antaḥ-karaṇa-sāpekṣa-pratyakṣam*), and (c) the perception which is not dependent on either of these two (*ubhaya-nirapekṣa-pratyakṣam*). Before dealing with these in detail, it is to be remembered that even in this classification, *cit śakti* alone is the only true means of cognition. The organs of the body merely provide a channel for the power of consciousness (*cit-śakti*) to manifest itself. The mere presence of an organ of perception and the object related to it (e.g., an ear and a sound) are not sufficient for the phenomenon of perception or cognition as such. The *Pauṣkara Āgama* (7:26) which Śivāgrayogin quotes states the case clearly:

> The association of an object and a sense alone is not regarded as perception since, without the association with *cit* [*śakti*] there is the production of nothing.[54]

3.2. (a) *Sense organ perception*

The perception that is dependent on the sense organs is the cognition of empirical objects. The things in the world are meant for man's experience of them. The objects are as real as they are validly cognized and their status can never be sublated. This is the case because the objects of experience in the world finally belong to the category of one of the three constituents of ultimate reality. When it is said that the objects are meant for the *ātman*'s experience of them, it means that they are got to be *known* by man, on account of the ignorance about the nature of things *as they are*. It is because of a veil or barrier—effected, as already seen, by *malam*—between the *ātman* and the objects of the world, that the instruments of the sense organs are required. They aid the *ātman* by providing a channel for the experience of the world of objects potentially removing, thereby, the barrier of ignorance about it. Contrasting this kind of perception with mental perception (described below) Śivāgrayogin quotes *Pauṣkara Āgama* (7:30) which furnishes a precise definition of it:

> [The perception which is] dependent on sense organs is different; it is the investigation of objects for the removal of the barrier through the channel [provided] by [*cit*] *śakti* which is dependent on the sense organs.[55]

Implicit in this kind of perception is the contact between a sense organ and an empirical object. *Cit śakti* uses the channel provided by the organ and is responsible for the 'illumination' of the object, which is identical with the cognition of it.[56] Śivāgrayogin makes a summary statement in the context of the discussion on perception which succinctly presents the Śaiva Siddhānta view on the matter. There is a *need*, he implicitly says in the following, for man's essentially independent power of consciousness (*cit śakti*) to be involved in the experiences of the world:

> ...on account of the obstruction of *malam*, it [*cit-śakti*], though self-dependent, is intent upon external objects for the sake of experience through the channels of the internal organs and the external senses, being manifested by *kalā* [*-tattva*], directed to objects by ignorance and coloured by *rāga* [*-tattva*].[57]

3.2 (b) *Internal organ perception*

The kind of perception which is dependent on the *antaḥ-karaṇas* (internal organs) of the *buddhi* (intellect), the *manas* (mind), and the *ahaṅkāra* (ego) is of a kind which rests on the entire psychological complex of man, moulded by the experiences of life in the world. That is to say, it is a kind of perception which depends on the *citta*, the function of which—as a single unit—is responsible for reason, intelligence, and thought. This type of perception is of two types: the perception of a *yogin* (*yogi-pratyakṣam*) and the common perception of joy, etc., (*prākṛita-sukha-ādi-pratyakṣam*). The second type is also called mental perception (*mānasa-pratyakṣam*).

The acknowledgement of the knowledge derived through yogic perception is based on the Śaiva Siddhānta acceptance—together with other schools, e.g., those of Vedānta—of the system of Yoga where, through a deliberate, austere training and practice, one can experience elevated states of consciousness. Śivāgrayogin's definition of yogic perception is that it is "a perception of the objects of the sense organs in the present, past and future by the mental faculty (*manas*), which is aided by the 'maturity of conduct'[58] acquired through the practice of Yoga."[59] In the perception which is dependent solely on the sense organs in their relation to an empirical object—as seen in the previous section—

the factor of time is restricted to the presence of the perceived object and to elements of this cognition in its relation to previous experiences (not necessarily recalled readily) concerning the object. In trained yogic perception, on the other hand, the time factor is claimed to be as evident as the presence of the object itself, i.e., a clear perception of the object is said to take place in terms, for example, of the nature of the object as it is now, what it was in the past, and what its nature will be in the future. The content of such a cognition is not dependent solely on the sense organs, but on a trained perception using the faculty of the *manas*. Further, such a perception, as with the one dependent on the sense organs, is also direct and immediate.[60]

What distinguishes the role of the mind (*manas*) here, from the one in mental perception (*mānasa-pratyakṣam*) described below—which also belongs to the kind called internal organ perception under discussion—is that in yogic perception the faculty of the mind (*manas*) is specially developed and trained by yogic exercises. This feature puts the mind (*manas*) at a level qualitatively different from its role when untrained, insofar as it functions without the trained awareness of its potential capabilities, which are said to be evident through special exercises. It may be said, as explained further in the description of mental perception that follows, that man's reflections on the nature of 'inner' perception points to the possibility of exercising the efficiency of the mind (*manas*) as developed through the training (*sādhana*) elaborated in the Yoga system (adapted to the Śaiva Siddhānta philosophical presuppositions).

Śivāgrayogin defines mental perception (*mānasa-pratyakṣam*) as 'the reflection on the experiences of joy and suffering.'[61] Such a perception is not vague or general (*nirvikalpaka*), but a direct, determinate (*savikalpaka*) one on the part of the mental faculty (*manas*) with the aid of the intellect (*buddhi*). Such a perception, it may be said in anticipating the contents of the next chapter, has significant soteriological implications. It is the outcome of man's involvement in life in the world of the existential experiences of joy and suffering. It is this involvement that makes evident the polarities, such as joy and suffering, of life's experiences. Insofar as such a perception is a 'reflection', it is a second order activity, but no less immediate as an 'internal' experience. The perception of a seemingly eternal, recurrent cycle of joy and suffering in human experience, is the outcome of a reflection on the nature of the *ātman*'s relation to the world of objects. An enquiry into the reason why the *ātman* is *made* to undergo such states of experience logically leads to an enquiry into the essential natures of both the world (*pāśa-svarūpa*) and of man in the world (*paśu-svarūpa*).

The outcome of mental perception (*mānasa-pratyakṣam*) may, therefore, be said to lead to the desire to be freed from the cycle of polarities, the experience of which vindicates itself. In other words, a break from *saṁsāra*, characterized essentially by suffering, is sought as a consequence of mental perception. Such a perception is not memory, which is merely the remembering of past experiences and which does not have the status of a valid cognition—as seen above where memory was discussed with doubt and error. Mental perception (*mānasa-pratyakṣam*) is, rather, a direct perception and a 'fresh' experience.

3.2 (c) *Independent perception*

The perception which is independent of both the internal organs and the sense organs 'has the form of the manifestation of consciousness.'[62] This perception occurs unmediatedly and is the direct outcome of *cit-śakti* as the *pramāṇa*. The soteriological function of this true means of cognition (*cit-śakti-pramāṇam*) is evident in this kind of perception. In other words, the transcendental role of *cit-śakti* becomes evident through an empirical and existential reflection on the view that *cit-śakti* operates behind all the organs of perception. When *cit-śakti* manifests itself independently of these organs, the resultant knowledge càn only be of the nature of its own manifestation, since *cit-śakti*—as already seen—is both the means of knowledge and the knowledge itself. Further, insofar as it constitutes man's essential nature, it is also intrinsically the subject that cognizes.

The knowledge which is a consequence of the perception which occurs through *cit-śakti* independent of the physical organs is said to be of two kinds: the knowledge of oneself (*sva-saṁvedana pratyakṣam*) and the knowledge of what is to be known by oneself (*sva-saṁvedya-pratyakṣam*). The distinction between these two kinds of perception has a direct bearing on both Śaiva Siddhānta metaphysics and theology. Implicit in the distinction is the ontological status of the *ātman* and *śivam*, on the one hand, and between the *ātman* and the world, on the other.

The involvement in the experiences of life in the world—as seen in the previous chapter with the analysis of verses three and four of the *Śivajñānabodham*—points to an *ātman* on account of 'the cognition of not-thisness, the excess of mineness, there being consciousness when the senses have ceased ...', i.e., it points to the existence of an *ātman* which is different from the internal organs, etc., although it is said to undergo the five states of consciousness in the way already discussed. In other words, the knowledge derived through a transcendental reflection on the essential nature of the world (*pāśa-svarūpa*) points to a knowledge of man as a bound being (*paśu-svarūpa*). A reflection, further, on the possibility of an unlimited expression of man's essential nature of consciousness (*ātma-svarūpa*) *leads* to a knowledge of the power of consciousness (*cit-śakti*) as the ground of all knowledge which, as already seen, is knowledge itself.[63] The *ātman*'s perception of itself by itself, i.e., through its own *cit-śakti* which is independent of the limiting factors wrought by the sense organs, is the *sva-saṁvedana-pratyakṣam* (the perception of the knowledge itself), referred to above.

The realm which this perception refers to is the ontological one, and in terms of the categories of ultimate reality *yet to be known* or experienced by the *ātman*, it is the essential nature of *śivam* that the *ātman* has to directly perceive or experience. It is this perception which the *ātman* has to have that is referred to as *sva-saṁvedya-pratyakṣam* (the perception of what is to be known by itself). Here too *cit-śakti* alone is the means by which this perception takes place directly and unmediatedly. Further details concerning the nature of this type of perception will be dealt with in the next chapter when the *ātman*'s unity-in-difference (*bheda-abheda*) relationship with *śivam* is considered.

The term *pratyakṣa* used in the context of the above discussion has a special connotation. Although it is generally rendered in English as 'perception', the words 'intuition' or 'experience' (i.e., synonymous with *anubhava*), are more appropriate for the specific context in which it is used here. The perception, or rather the apperception, here has the evident nature of consciousness (*cit* or *saṁvid*) and is qualitatively superior to the other kinds of perception, insofar as it is independent and unmediated representing, thereby, an unfettered expression of man's essential nature characterized by consciousness. In other words, it is a perception which takes place in the 'higher' states of consciousness and presupposes a transcendence of limitation and dependency. Such a perception which is independent of all organs is, as Śivāgrayogin says:

> ...the direct knowledge of oneself that is produced on account of the *ātman*'s eternal relation with *cit-śakti* that has its fetters removed.[64]

This position is maintained on the grounds of acknowledging the authority of the *Pauṣkara Āgama* (7:29) statement, about the different kinds of perception, that:

> Of these [the perception] independent of the [physical] organs is on account of the [*ātman*'s] indissoluble union with *cit-śakti* which has its bondages given up completely; the union [between the *ātman* and the *cit-śakti*] is considered to be natural.[65]

### 3.3 *Inference (anumāna)*

Apart from being the means of cognition using the internal and external sense organs as instruments, *cit-śakti* also manifests itself through the aid which constitutes the process of inference (*anumāna*). This is not *cit-śakti* as a *pramāṇa* which is independent of the sense organs, as discussed above. Inference is a process that is based on empirical observation and produces a cognition that is not directly and immediately evident. This is to say that whereas sense perception is immediate and produces a direct cognition of objects such as 'this is a pot', inference is mediate cognition as, for example, in the conclusion—arrived at indirectly—of the existence of fire, based on the direct and immediate perception of smoke which is previously known to be a sign (*liṅga*), invariably connected with fire.

Whereas the function of *cit-śakti* independent of the sense organs operates at the transcendental level, *cit-śakti* which operates through or in the process of inference had its function rooted in the empirical world of objects, the contact with which is made possible through the senses as instruments.[66]

Śivāgrayogin follows the Nyāya method of establishing the validity of inference on the grounds of clearly defining what constitutes invariable concomitance (*vyāpti*), which is inextricably connected with an inference. Insofar as his defence for the validity of inference rests on this important term, it is necessary to give his definition of it. He says: "The relation, which is not an adventitious condition, between the *probandum* and the *probans* is called invariable concomitance here."[67] It is on the basis of this definition that a clear notion of what inference is is given: 'The knowledge of invisible objects through well-established invariable concomitance is inference.'[68]

In defending inference as a valid means of cognition Śivāgrayogin discusses possible logical objections that may be raised by a prospective opponent (chiefly a Cārvāka). These objections, albeit somewhat lengthy, are best presented in his own words, since they furnish the context in which his defence of inference applies:

> Now, there is no means of valid cognition called inference because of the impossibility of perceiving the invariable concomitance [e.g., of smoke with fire] which is accepted as being responsible for that [inference]; there is an unremoved doubt of a [possible] violation [of invariable concomitance] in other places—even though there may be a correlation [between smoke and fire] in several places; and because, in removing this [doubt] by indirect argument (*tarka*), there arises infinite regress, since the indirect argument itself is rooted in [the acceptance of] invariable concomitance. For this reason [viz., that the argument depends on invariable concomitance], the view that there is an apprehension of invariable concomitance on account of the certainty that it is not an adventitious condition, is rejected. [This is rejected] because of the inadequacy of perception to grasp [the invariable concomitance] by penetrating the locus (*adhikaraṇa*) and cause (*sādhana*) when-

> ever there is [a case of] invariable concomitance; and also since there will be an infinite regress in regarding inference as being capable of grasping invariable concomitance.[69]

The main points of the opponent's objections which Śivāgrayogin has to deal with may be summarized as follows:

1. The knowledge of invariable concomitance—as, for example, between smoke and fire—which is based on perception, is an indispensable presupposition for the validity of an inference;
2. The invariable concomitance itself is not open to perception;
3. Even if the invariable concomitance were accepted in certain cases, there is always a logical possibility of it *not* being a universal rule;
4. This doubt cannot be removed through argumentation, which itself would be based on the knowledge of invariable concomitance, and so on;
5. It is humanly impossible to test every case of invariable concomitance;
6. Inference cannot be said to furnish the proof of all cases of invariable concomitance as it would lead to an infinite regress;
7. Therefore, inference as a valid means of cognition is rejected.

The opponent's argument is logically sound, but does not acknowledge—as Śivāgrayogin is quick to point out—that it contains elements of the very inferential process it attacks.[70] This refutation is based on what Śivāgrayogin says at the very outset, referring to the opponent's view that inference is not a valid means of cognition. He says:

> This is not so, since there would be the contingence of a cessation of [mental] activity as such in not accepting inference as a valid means of cognition—since [this] activity arises through the inference, etc., of effects of unknown objects which come within the range of [man's] activity. Thus, there need be no effort by one desirous [of verifying the existence] of the fire on the mountain, etc.[71]

With this point, Śivāgrayogin considers inference as a valid means of cognition on the grounds that it constitutes an essential factor of man's mental activity, based on the involvement in life in the world.

In other words, it is natural—be it through learned experience or through verbal testimony—to infer the existence, for example, of fire merely on the perception of smoke. Such a certainty is grounded on the realistic view of the invariable concomitance (*vyāpti*) of smoke with fire. The opponent's position does not acknowledge a cause (*kāraṇa*) for the existence of smoke on the grounds of the mere logical view that every instance of smoke alone need not necessarily attest the existence of fire—the fire itself would have to be seen in order to validate it as the possible cause of the smoke. This can be said to be a case of 'inverted' inference: whereas the Siddhāntin wants to prove the existence of the fire which is validly inferred through the perception of the smoke, the opponent, on the other hand, would be proving the validity of the smoke itself on the grounds of empirically verifying the existence of the fire. Therefore, Śivāgrayogin tells the opponent:

> It is not proper to say that there can be no inferential activity because of the absence of a cause, which is [in fact] grasped through invariable concomitance.[72]

This argument is based on the positive acknowledgement of man's situation in the world, and is characteristic of the Śaiva Siddhānta realism directed at the opponent:

> On account of the acceptance of the ability of the eyes or of the mind (*manas*), etc., in apprehending the universal concomitance with regard to objects which are unknown, etc., there is no contradiction of the perceptibility of that [invariable concomitance].[73]

In short, Śivāgrayogin feels that he has effectively defended the case of inference on the basis of the very method of argumentation employed by the opponent—who seems to reject it on a matter of principle. In this there is a failure to recognize a self-contradiction insofar as the rejection is justified in terms of a mechanism of argumentation which it wants to reject, viz., the process of inference as a valid means of cognition. In this sense, the opponent makes the case for inference even stronger.

After having established the validity of inference, Śivāgra-yogin continues with a division of it into two kinds: an inference for oneself (*svārtha-anumāna*) and that for others (*parārtha-anumāna*). Implicit in these two kinds of inference is the interesting distinction between a means of cognition valid to oneself and the same presented in a logical pattern to convey the validity of the cognition to others. The inference for oneself is defined as: '... the inference of fire, etc., after grasping the invariable concomitance between smoke and fire, on account of seeing the sign of the invariable concomitant [smoke] on the mountain.'[74] When this cognition is presented in the form of the five-membered syllogism, it constitutes an inference for another.[75] A noteworthy point implicit in this distinction is the possibility of the view that man first draws the conclusion, e.g., that there is a fire, although the smoke is in fact first seen—this would essentially be an inference for oneself. On the basis of this cognition the conclusion is then translated into a form intelligible to others. This would follow a logic built into man's use of language and it would be an inference for others, as referred to above.[76]

It was stated above (p. 119) that one of the conditions that needs to be fulfilled for a means of cognition to retain its unique character, is that it should furnish what is *new* and not attainable by any other means. There is no doubt that an inference involves the memory (*smṛiti*) of previous cases where, e.g., smoke was invariably concomitant with fire. However, it is emphatically stated that inference cannot be relegated to the function of memory which involves, exclusively or only, the revival of traces (*saṁskāras*) of previous experiences. Inference requires something more. That is, in addition to memory, it requires *parāmarśa*, a subsumptive reflection which, as already seen, is a cognition 'which arises from a combination of the knowledge of invariable concomitance (*vyāptijñāna*) and that of the presence of the reason (*hetu*) in the subject (*pakṣa*).'[77] In other words, in addition to memory, inference requires the knowledge of the relation between the middle and the minor terms of an argument which cooperate with the traces (*saṁskāras*) of previous experience, in relation to what is perceived. The role of memory alone, which is a mere recollection of past experience, therefore, cannot be equated with inferential thinking, which is also an intrinsic part of man's mental make-up.[78]

### 3.4 *Verbal testimony* (*śabda*)

It is the same opponent who, in providing the link into this section, calls for Śivāgrayogin's defence of verbal testimony (*śabda, śruti*) as a valid means of cognition (*pramāṇa*). It is very conveniently rejected on the grounds that it is said to follow logically from the previous objections: "Through the invalidity of inference [itself] there is also the invalidity of verbal testimony, which is dependent on the grasping of the relation [between words or statements] based on that [inference]."[79] Śivāgrayogin's answer in short—apart from the fact (which he does not state explicitly) that the opponent is again being self-contradictory by giving a testimony in verbal terms—follows from his defence as outlined above: "That [inference] being a valid means of cognition, there is the validity also of Nigama, Āgama, etc., which are established and grasped through the relationship [of statements] based on that [inference]."[80]

The Śaiva Siddhānta defence of verbal testimony as a means of valid cognition can be dealt with in the light of two related contexts in which it applies: (a) in the light of the Siddhāntin's earnest effort in defence of the Āgamas (in addition to the Vedas or Nigamas) as revealed, authoritative scriptures and (b) in the light of what constitutes meaningfulness in man's use of language. Before dealing with these separately the following points may be noted.

In both these contexts, *śabda* refers to words as a source of independent knowledge, not reducible to what can be obtained through inference and perception, as will be seen in more detail below. When words are derived from a source which the tradition regards as being infallible, they bear the stamp of authority or testimony. Implicit in the nature of this situation—which is a traditional acceptance and acknowledgement of a 'special' source of knowledge—is a defence of scripture as such. In other words, and in the context here, the Śaiva Siddhānta attempt to establish *śabda* as a *pramāṇa* (in the specific sense of the term, as already seen) constitutes a defence of scripture in general, and of the Āgamas in particular. In both the contexts of *śabda* referred to above, the knowledge furnished should not be contradicted (*abādhita*) by any other means, if it is at all to retain its validity. Further, the knowledge must be *new*, since this is a condition to be fulfilled by any separate means of cognition, as already seen.

It is claimed that *śabda* furnishes a knowledge of certain truths essential to man, which are not provided by perception and inference alone, e.g., the nature of man's essential definition, characterized as the *ātman*. In this context words function as a revelation insofar as they disclose or divulge a unique kind of knowledge. The fact that such a knowledge should not be contradicted by any other means, implies that the content of revelation must be internally coherent and that, though it may be *above reason*, it cannot go against it. Further, as already pointed out, the revealed truth has to be made intelligible in terms of human experience, for it to have any *use* at all. It is in this context that *śabda* plays a crucial soteriological function, which operates closely with *pratyakṣa* and *anumāna*, in divulging the condition of a possibility of unfettered existence, represented in the discussions on *mokṣa* (liberation) and the *jīvan-mukta* (liberated being). Also, it is here that the two senses (referred to above) in which *śabda* may be discussed, are closely related and even meet.

It is to be noted, further, that all the three instruments of knowledge accepted by the Śaiva Siddhāntin have a limited function:

> What is difficult to be indicated by these and other means of cognition, is *śivam*.[81]

This statement can be interpreted as representing a limitation inherent in words, and in the use of language as such, to adequately convey the nature of ultimate reality which—in the light of the discussions on *mokṣa*—can nonetheless be experienced. In this context, revelation functions as a reflection and, if metaphorical language may come to the rescue here, it may be said that: just as a reflection—the content of which is essentially unreal—serves the purpose or means of showing the facts concerning the object reflected, and just as the roaring of a lion in a dream may awaken one to the world, so too *śabda* as a *pramāṇa* *points* to the nature of the ultimate reality, which *śabda* itself is not. *Śabda*, in other words, is not the *content* of what it reveals, though it may be an indispensable instrument for it:

> Verbal testimony is the basis for the inference regarding the knowledge of *śivam*, only indirectly.[82]

3.4 (a) *The validity of the Āgamas*

The word Āgama is derived from the verbal root *gam* with the prefix *ā-* and literally means 'to come'. As a body of literature, Āgama means 'that which has come down' referring, thereby, to a body of knowledge that has been handed down from one generation to another in a traditional manner.[83] In this sense of the term, the word is a synonym for Veda. In order to distinguish the two—insofar as they constitute two separate bodies of valuable doctrinal literature (*śāstra*)—Veda is given the name Nigama as well. The issue which calls for an explicit defence of the validity of the Āgamas is over the concern whether this body of literature deserves the merit of being what is called revealed scripture (*śruti* or *śabda*)—a privilege accorded, without any doubt, to the Vedas. The discussion around this issue concerns the view that the two are currents of thought which are 'independent and antagonistic.'[84] On the other hand, there is also the view that the Āgamas are an essential—albeit independent—development of the Vedas themselves.[85] The debate on the validity of the Āgamas applies to the three branches of Hinduism that possess this vast body of literature.[86] It seems that at the time Śivāgrayogin wrote (sixteenth century) the question of the validity of the Āgamas was still a burning issue, which turned him into an apologist of the Śaiva Āgamas.[87] The numerous issues around this question, and the elaborate argumentation concerning them, are beyond the scope of this study.[88] What, however, calls for Śivāgrayogin's zealous philosophical defence of the Āgamas (as texts of revelation no less in stature than those which make up the Vedas) is chiefly because the revered and greatly honoured Śaṅkara (eighth century), the champion and propounder of Advaita Vedānta—which Śivāgrayogin accepts to a point permissible within the ontological and philosophical presuppositions of Śaiva Siddhānta—questions the authority of the Āgamas in his *Brahmasūtrabhāṣya.* Śivāgrayogin refers[89] to Bādarāyaṇa's *sūtras* 1:4.1, 2:2.1, and 2:2.37 which give Śaṅkara the platform to launch his attack on the validity of the Āgamas.[90] Suffice it to say, without entering into the intricacies of his arguments, that Śivāgrayogin sees the eternality of the Vedas and the Āgamas as being derived from a common authoritative source:

> Therefore, there is the validity of both the Vedas and the Āgamas, verily by being taught by Parameśvara [Śiva] who is: the supremely trustworthy person, the remover of man's bonds, the independent one, the perfect one, imperishable, perceiving things as they are, devoid of partiality, omniscient, flawless and eternal.[91]

What has been attempted above is a presentation of the Śaiva Siddhānta acceptance of the validity of the Āgamas, in addition to the generally accepted authority of the Vedas. In his commentary on the *Śivajñānabodham* Śivāgrayogin states this explicitly. However, it is a striking fact that his views are based almost entirely on the authority of the Āgamas alone and he liberally quotes them—particularly the *Pauṣkara* and *Mṛigendra Āgamas*—in justification of his ideas.

The Āgamas deal with a wide range of topics that encompass subjects such as architecture, consecration, rituals, rules for priests and devotees, and philosophy. These themes are conveniently divided into four sections, though this is not explicitly done in some particular Āgamas which may even omit certain sections, viz., the section dealing with philosophy or knowledge (*jñāna-pāda*); the section dealing with yogic practices (*yoga-pāda*); the section dealing with rituals (*kriyā-pāda*); and the section dealing with devotion (*caryā-pāda*). It is clear from this that Śivāgrayogin draws chiefly from the *jñāna-pāda* of the Āgamas he refers to. The divisions may be seen as a necessary convenience which adapts to man's decreasing capacities and limited vision on account of the untrained ability and faculty to see the manifold areas of the truth which the Āgamas reveal, as being intrinsically a single unit.[92] In other words, even if, for example, one were to uphold the supremacy of the philosophy and knowledge (*jñāna*) of the ultimate, ontological categories of *śivam*, *ātman*, and *malam*—usually dealt with in the *jñāna-pāda* of an Āgama—this should not be extricated from its essential applicability to the other areas. This is to say that no one section should be seen as being an exclusive, independent, and self-sufficient part of an Āgama. This seems to be the intention of the following *Mṛigendra Āgama* verse:

> Thus the three categories are dealt with together in the first [knowledge] section; with the devotional, yogic, and ritual sections their application will be explained.[93]

The implications of this unitary view of the content of the Āgamas are of special significance in the discussion concerning the enlightened being, liberated from a limited and fettered outlook. It means that such a person would see no essential distinction between *jñāna* and the other three branches of the Āgamas. Insofar as the other branches may be seen as what express the devotion (*bhakti*) of a devotee (*bhakta*), *jñāna* and *bhakti* may thus be said, finally, to be indistinguishable. For such a being—one for whom *immanent* transcendence becomes evident—all distinctions vanish and reality is seen *as it is*. This point will be dealt with further in the next chapter. What, however, is to be noted in the context of the discussion in this section, is that it is *śabda*, the word of revealed scripture (*śāstra*, *śruti*), that shows what the essence of man is, especially as a part of what ultimate reality is. It is both the Vedas and the Āgamas that fulfil this task.

### 3.4 (b) *The Śaiva Siddhānta theory of language*

The other context in which *śabda* may be discussed, as already pointed out, is in the light of what constitutes meaningfulness in man's use of language. Some of the issues involved in this context are, for example, what constitutes a sentence, what constitutes meaning, and what the relationship is between a word and the object to which it refers. Before attempting to present Śivāgrayogin's views on these issues, it will be useful to recall a few points already made.

It was stated that the ingredients of man's categories of experience constitute the scheme of the 36 *tattvas* discussed in the first chapter. These categories which encompass both the gross and subtle elements of experience and language, with sound and speech as its essential factors, also fall within this systematic scheme. It is to be remembered that all the categories are derived ultimately from *māyā*, which is a *malam* and, therefore, acts as a fetter (*pāśa*)—albeit with the express purpose of aiding (together with *karman*) the *ātman* to realize its intrinsic, essential nature of consciousness. It was in this context that the beneficent role of *māyā* (and *karman*) was discussed. The principles are instruments of experience at the disposal of the consciousness which is man's defining feature. They aid man and only *reflect* what, in fact, makes possible their role, i.e., the *ātman*. They are essentially insentient and, therefore, are not the content of experience as such. Experience is a privilege accorded to sentience which is *made* to become dependent on the instruments of experience and to be involved in life in the world, in which language plays a prominent part.

The instrument of language is perhaps the most basic tool of experience which permeates all the other categories of experience as the common principle. This would be the case insofar as language is said not only to 'reveal' itself but also to provide the means through which the categories of experience—including that of language itself—become intelligible to man. This is perhaps the Śaiva Siddhānta insight in postulating the category of *nāda* (sound), the essence of language and speech (*vāc*), as the first evolute of pure, unmixed (*śuddha*) *māyā*. It is from *nāda* that the *śuddha-aśuddha-māyā* evolves, which operates in close collusion with *karman*, to prepare the ground for man's involvement in the world. From this it follows that language not only functions as a tool of man's empirical life, but that it also has a role at the transcendental level of revealing man's essential nature. At this level, i.e., in the realm of the five *śiva-tattvas*, *nāda* is in 'closer' touch with the *śakti*—intrinsic to the nature of *śivam*—which is responsible, as already seen, for the evolution of *māyā*.

In view of the fact that man is 'condemned' to undergo worldly experience, and in view of the fact that perception (*pratyakṣa*) and inference (*anumāna*) cannot, by definition, reveal man's essential nature, verbal testimony (*śabda*)—which has its supreme expression in the Āgamas—serves as the indispensable tool which shows the possibility of a state of unfettered existence identical with the knowledge of ultimate reality. What this means is that the key to liberation is language, the word, or sound as such. Further, by definition *nāda*, even in its most subtle form, is not the content of the experience of ultimate reality, though it is necessary for the 'leap' from the realm of insentience to that of pure sentience.[94] It is only the power of consciousness (*cit-śakti*), the means of knowledge and knowledge itself (as already seen), which is really the content of any experience as such. The impact of this realization is a step through language beyond language.

It is useful to recall two further points which are related to the Śaiva Siddhānta theory of language. Firstly, that the evolution of the scheme of categories is instigated by *śakti* and that in the order of the discovery and knowledge of the categories, man proceeds from the gross manifestations of *māyā*, such as the objects of the world, to the subtle ones, such as pure sound.[95] Secondly, that the evolution of *māyā* has to be understood in the sense only of a change of state (*vṛitti*) of the one, self-identical material cause, and not as a transformation (*pariṇāma*) of it.[96] The implication here, to repeat, is that the essential nature of sound, even in its purest form as *nāda*, is basically insentient (*acit*) with a role no less significant in the scheme than that, for example, of the *buddhi*. It may be said, in other words, that the significance of the role of the *buddhi* in relation to the subsequent categories, is comparable to that of *nāda* in relation to the categories up to *kalā*. It is to be noted, nonetheless, that the role of *nāda* is most efficacious in the highest realm of the categories which constitute man's experience. Further, if man has to see the nature of things *as they are*, it follows that the nature of *pāśa* is 'complete' with the knowledge and experience of *nāda*. In this sense, the knowledge of *nāda* is a prerequisite for the realization of the essence of man, which is distinct from what constitutes the essence of the world.

Insofar as *nāda* stands for sound, it represents the basic element of speech (*vāc*) which has its grossest manifestation in man's everyday use of it. It is in this sense that *nāda* and *vāk* may be seen as synonymous terms. In keeping with the degrees or levels of manifestation, characteristic of the evolution of the Śaiva Siddhānta categories, speech or sound is also spoken of in terms of subtle or gross forms. Śivāgrayogin speaks[97] of four such levels which mark the evolution of speech: *paśyantī-vāk* is *nāda* itself, which is the first modification of *śuddha-māyā* in the scheme of the categories, and it is the differentiated speech principle in which the capacity for revelation is inherent but not explicit; *madhyamā-vāk* is the modification of speech that is an intermediary level, where the dynamism or the manifestation of speech is in the mode of thought; *vaikharī-vāk* is the uttered, articulated speech of man. A fourth level is also postulated. It is called *parā-vāk*, the unmanifested ground of all levels of speech and represents the essence of speech itself. It is the seminal mode of speech, which is a speech beyond speech—if such metaphysical language may be employed—which inheres in the basic stuff of *māyā*. In this sense *parā-vāk* is synonymous with *śuddha-māyā* which, as already seen, is also called *bindu* and *kuṇḍalinī*.

Śivāgrayogin furnishes a clear description of the significance of speech for man by giving the following account of its origin:

> *Śiva-tattva* is the first modification of *kuṇḍalinī* which: is also called *nāda*; is of the nature of meaning; is the locus of the lord's *śakti* which manifests in degrees of great, greater, and greatest [what is] in the brightness of the *cit* in one who is desirous of liberation; is also the locus of *kalās* such as *indhika*, etc., which are limiting adjuncts; is also alone [responsible] for removing *malam*, having been controlled by it [the lord's *śakti*]; and is a modification of speech which is known as subtle.[98]

From this syntactically pregnant construction several noteworthy points emerge. Language, which is based on sound (*nāda*) as such, is a double-edged sword insofar as it serves as a substrate not only for adjuncts of limitation, but is also the ground through which this limitation—which is due to *malam*—is lacerated. In this process, *nāda* may be said to open itself to the power which makes its own operation possible. It reveals its own essence by pointing to what gives it itself the means and power of expression, namely, *cit-śakti*. *Nāda* thus serves as the platform for the leap into transcendence or, by tearing itself up, permits a withdrawal of *cit-śakti's* association with it. It is the medium through which the *śakti* intrinsic to *śivam*, manifests itself in degrees depending on the intensity of the desire for liberation.[99] Following from this point is the implication that while *cit-śakti*'s ability to effect its own dissociation from *malam* is potentially present—and eternally so, insofar as *cit-śakti* (as already seen) is essentially indestructible—the responsibility for the keen desire to be liberated from a limited and dependent existence, rests on man. In other words, a reflection on the nature of man's predicament at the empirical level points to freedom and liberation from bondage as such—a state which is essentially characteristic of the power of consciousness evident in perception, inference, and preeminently in *śabda* or Āgama (which alone gives an awareness of this possibility). It is man's own responsibility to see the wisdom of the word which, as the locus of *śakti*, can inflame to the greatest degree the consciousness of the one desirous of liberation.

The word as a category of revelation[100] retains its special feature particularly in man's use of language, where its efficacy may be said to be consciously put to use. As is explicitly stated in the above quotation, the word in this context has the nature of meaning, i.e., there is an inextricable relation between a word and the meaning inherent in it.[101] The significance of this point, which evidently applies at the empirical level, is an extension of this essential role at the transcendental level as well. In both these realms, the following may be said to be the case: the meaning of a word is dependent on the word itself; whilst the word is of the nature of meaning, i.e., it points to what furnishes meaning, the word itself is incapable of effecting anything apart from the means through which meaning is revealed, i.e., *cit-śakti* as the *pramāṇa*; this is to say that the word is not the 'thing' it means, yet the word itself is indispensable for the knowledge of what ultimate reality is. In short, *śabda* is man's instrument for what constitutes and yields meaning in life.

*Śabda* or verbal testimony is made up of words and Śivāgrayogin provides a definition of a word and its meaning in the context of the present discussion:

> A collection of letters is called a word. Since letters perish instantaneously and since, [therefore], there cannot be an apprehension of meaning, there is to be recognized—for the sake of apprehending meaning—such a thing called *sphoṭa* within letters, which is eternal and which is the meaning of a word.[102]

Śivāgrayogin does not elaborate the theory of meaning known as *sphoṭa-vāda* and a few brief remarks concerning it from the Śaiva Siddhānta perspective will not be out of place here.[103] The theory is an intricate and elaborate one, and only a brief clarification will be attempted here for the purpose of the present discussion.

The word *sphoṭa* is derived from the verbal root *sphuṭ* which, among several things, means: to burst or split open, to expand or blossom, and to appear suddenly. Applied in the context of language, *sphoṭa* stands for the 'bursting forth' of the meaning of a word or sentence—a meaning which presents itself instantaneously and as a single unit. Śivāgrayogin says above that this instantaneous capacity of meaning to burst forth through the word is eternal. In the light of what has already been said about the Śaiva Siddhānta essential nature of sound (*nāda*), the basis of verbal testimony, the letters themselves (which make up a word) are devoid of any power of their own. Whatever efficacy they may be said to have, has to be credited ultimately to *śakti*, the power inherent in consciousness (*cit*). This is to say that, as an evolute of *māyā*, *nāda* is 'perishable', although the stuff out of which it evolves remains as an insentient, eternal category. In other words, the eternality of *sphoṭa*—which is always responsible for the meaning of a word—is to be seen as synonymous with *śakti* as the means of cognition and knowledge as such, i.e., the bursting forth of meaning is the thrust of *cit-śakti* revealing itself by illuminating the meaning inherent in the word. It is only this *śakti* that can rend the veil of ignorance about things as they are and, further, it is the means to obtain the knowledge which it in fact is, as already seen. In other words, inasmuch as the word is its meaning, *cit* is the *śakti* which makes possible what may be called a two-in-one kind of knowledge: on the one hand, a knowledge of the word which points to a meaning and a knowledge of the word which *is* its meaning—the meaning inherent to it; and, on the other hand, the knowledge of both these as a single unit. This is equivalent to *śakti* pointing to *cit* and *śakti being* the *cit* to which it is intrinsic and essential, on the one hand, and, on the other hand, the unitary knowledge that this awareness is identical with the knowledge which distinguishes *cit-śakti* from insentience.

The question now is: in what precise sense is verbal testimony a means of knowledge in Śaiva Siddhānta? In the clear words of Śivāgrayogin the answer, which also defines man's use of language, is:

> Valid verbal testimony is the knowledge which is the outcome of the words of a trustworthy person. A person who is one who sees things as they are and teaches them as they are, is called a trustworthy person.[104]

In elaborating this basic definition, Śivāgrayogin says: "The statement of such a one is a group of words which possess mutual expectancy, compatibility, and proximity."[105] Mutual expectancy (*ākāṅkṣā*) is defined as: 'the employment of the proper case suffixes, etc., in the syntax of this or that [statements.'[106] What this presupposes is a knowledge of grammar, and although Śivāgrayogin does not emphasize it the way in which the grammarians do[107], its significance for meaningfulness in man's use of language is evident. Another definition he gives of mutual expectancy is interesting to note: it is 'the desire for gaining knowledge.'[108] At least two points seem to be presupposed here: firstly, a desire on the part of a listener to know about the nature of a particular subject and, secondly, it presupposes that the one who teaches it, obtained the knowledge through an identical attitude. The second point, by extension, may be said to imply a desire on the part of the one who knows, to teach the knowledge that is gained. Implicit in all these points seems to be a theory of communication inherent in the Śaiva Siddhānta theory of language.

Compatibility (*yogyatā*) is defined negatively as: 'the absence of the certainty that there is a lack of connection.'[109] Put in positive terms, this definition means that there should be an absence of any contradiction in what is said. The example that Śivāgrayogin gives in this context is the absurd and meaningless statement: 'he sprinkles with fire' (*agninā siñcati*), instead of: 'he sprinkles with water' (*jalena siñcati*). This definition of compatibility as what is intrinsic to meaningfulness in man's use of language, evinces the point that verbal testimony (*śabda*) should be made intelligible in terms of human experience and this applies particularly, as already indicated, to the transcendental truths of the Āgamas and Nigamas, if they are to have any *use* at all.

Proximity (*sannidhi* or *āsatti*) is defined as: 'the presence of two words uninterruptedly.'[110] By referring to two words, Śivāgrayogin implies a complete sentence as, for example, the simple one: 'Bring the cow' (*gām ānaya*). That these words be uttered without a lapse of time and that they follow the rules of grammar—with the word for cow being in the accusative case in this instance—are essential factors of what constitutes meaningfulness in the use of language. In other words, a statement should be uttered in one grammatically correct sequential unit and it is this single, complete unit of speech (or language) that makes the meaning burst forth (*sphoṭa*) and, thus, makes the truth of the statement evident. Whereas compatibility dealt with the grouping of compatible words, in order to avoid absurdity, proximity now defines the use of compatible words which should be uttered in an appropriate time sequence, for the meaning to become evident.

The above elements of meaningfulness are implicit in the use of language by a trustworthy person. Whereas in the ordinary use of language man's limitations are unavoidable, in the case of scriptural statements, however, this problem is said not to arise because the author is the supremely trustworthy lord of all beings (*paśu-pati*) who is incapable of erring. What is presupposed here is the traditional acknowledgement of scriptural authority as being infallible. Apparent 'errors' would have to be attributed to man's limitation in being able to grasp the truth of the statements concerning reality itself. This does not preclude man's attempt to interpret and reinterpret these texts in a manner intelligible in terms of human experience—albeit in keeping with the *intention*[111] of the author or speaker. In other words, a trustworthy person, in the nature of the case, has to be said, in tautological terms, to be trustworthy and, hence, credibility and meaningfulness have to be a priori assumed.

A point that is not explicitly stated by Śivāgrayogin in the context of the present discussion, but one which may be said to attest the eternality of scripture as such, is the 'readiness and maturity' of man to grasp the meaning of the truths expressed by a trustworthy person.[112] It is life's experience in the world and a reflection on it—i.e., the awareness that without a desire for liberation, the recurrent cycle of worldly experience perpetuates itself—that prepares man to perceive the eternal wisdom which previously was meaningless. The desire for liberation, in Śaiva Siddhānta's terms, is a conscious attempt and effort on man's part to follow the behaviour and attitude of the Āgamic view of reality which promises the fruit of the labour, viz., the realization or experience of the nature of ultimate reality itself.

As a limited being involved in experiences which vindicate dependency, man is prone to error. An awareness of this fact—namely, man's fallibility—is a step towards a realization of what trustworthiness means insofar as it not only leads to an understanding of the validity of verbal testimony (*śabda*) which has an infallible source, but it also serves as a means towards gaining a knowledge of things as they are. The only means through which man can know is through *cit-śakti*. Its association with the instruments of perception, inference, and verbal testimony is what limits it. Nonetheless, they are indispensable to man for life in the world and it is through these limiting adjuncts that error can creep into man's cognition of things. Śaiva Siddhānta has its own theory of error and insofar as it forms a part of the philosophical anthropology of the school, it will be useful to make a few brief remarks concerning it, in order to put into proper perspective this entire chapter which deals with the Śaiva Siddhānta theory of cognition.

### 3.5 *Śaiva Siddhānta Theory of Error*

Implicit in the concern with epistemology in Indian thought are theories of error, i.e., taking into account the generally accepted possibility of human fallibility, Indian thinkers sought to explain this phenomenon of man's life in the world. Indeed, the soundness or success of a theory of truth is commensurate with the success with which the fact of error is explained.[113] Indian thinkers have propounded several theories of error and this study attempts to deal with selected aspects from the Śaiva Siddhānta view of it.[114] A few preliminary remarks will be useful to continue the attempt toward understanding man as a knowing and cognizing being in Śaiva Siddhānta.

In the light of the discussion on perception, inference and verbal testimony, the unique character of *cit-śakti* can hardly be over-emphasized: 'since in every case, it has been established that *cit-śakti* alone has the nature of being the valid means of knowledge.'[115] Bearing in mind its special feature as the conscious principle in man, the responsibility for the occurrence of error in man's cognition cannot be put on *cit-śakti*—it only 'illuminates' the data obtained through the organs of cognition. If perception is accepted as man's most basic instrument of cognition, a description of this process would be the following. *Cit-śakti* provides the organs of the body with the ability to 'reach out' for the objects that come within their range. In other words, the internal organs (*antaḥ-karaṇas*) 'go out' to an object via the sense organs (*indriyas*) which the internal organs in fact guide, through the power of consciousness (*cit-śakti*). On reaching the object, the internal organs assume the form of the object. In effect, and in summary, this situation is a mode or modification of the intellect (*buddhi-vṛitti*), subsequent to the indeterminate (*nirvikalpaka*) cognition that takes place, as already seen, in the mind (*manas*). This mode of the intellect which takes on the form of the object, however, is not by itself sufficient to be called a case of cognition. It needs to be illumined by the *ātman*, which is the epitome of *cit-śakti*. In the context of Śaiva Siddhānta, there are a few points implicit in this summary description of cognition through perception.

The organs of the body are capable of functioning only in the presence of, or through the contact with, an object (*viṣaya*).[116] What is presupposed here is the three-fold structure of cognition (*tripuṭi-jñāna*), viz., the *ātman* which cognizes, the object cognized, and the means through which the cognition takes place. In terms of Śaiva Siddhānta realism, the status of the object as 'real' needs to be acknowledged. Further, the self-validity (*svataḥ-prā-*

*māṇya*) of the process of knowledge is a significant, fundamental thesis of Śaiva Siddhānta epistemology, as already seen. In other words, to ask how we know what we know, is to beg the question and to lead to an infinite regress in attempting to answer it. Whatever factor is responsible for the validity of cognition, is itself accepted at the very outset, i.e., it is the power of consciousness (*cit-śakti*) which, by definition, reveals itself, its object, and the consciousness (*cit*) in which the experience takes place. The question now is: where does the occurrence of error fit into the structure of man's process of cognition? The answer to this question is especially significant if the intended seriousness of the metaphysical foundations of Śaiva Siddhānta epistemology, and of the system as a whole, is to have any philosophical justification and credibility.

The answer, in fact, has already been provided in the discussion concerning *cit-śakti* and the modification (*vṛitti*) of the intellect (*buddhi*), in the first section of this chapter. Two quotations may be repeated here for the link and continuity they provide in the present context:

> *Cit-śakti* which is free of doubt, etc., is acknowledged as the valid means of cognition.
> By the fact that it is impossible for *cit-śakti* to be identified with a *buddhi-vṛitti* which is ridden with doubt, etc., and since this would give rise to a contradiction in the phrase "[*cit-śakti*] free of that [doubt, etc.]", the meaning is: "only after the conditioned *buddhi-vṛitti* is free of that [doubt, etc.]", because this is the necessary conclusion.[117]

It may be noted that the word 'etc.,' in both the above quotations refers to misapprehension and memory, i.e., it is *cit-śakti* which is devoid of doubt, misapprehension, and memory that is verily the means of cognition, in the proper sense of the term as Śaiva Siddhānta sees it. These three factors (already defined above, p. 104) are the limiting agents of man's intrinsic power of consciousness (*ātma-cit-śakti*) and their efficacy is attributed to the *ātman*'s association with *malam*. What this means is that the Śaiva Siddhānta theory of error involves a further consideration of these factors in the context of the present discussion.

In the mechanics of cognition, as described above with reference to perception, the intellect (*buddhi*) is the decisive factor which determines the cognition of such and such an object presented to it via the senses, and illumined through the means of consciousness' power. The occurrence of cognition, therefore, is identical with the judgement passed by the intellect as regards what the object is said to be—it is to be noted that *cit-śakti* impartially *permits* the intellect to operate in this decisive role as regards the cognition of an object. It follows from this that the occurrence of error—whenever such a case is in point—is still an instance of a judgement passed by the intellect with regard to the object concerned. Now, the intellect (*buddhi*) is manifested through its modification (*vṛitti*) that moulds a judgement or decision. In the human context, this applies in every act of cognition and implies that cognition, by definition, is what is conditioned, coloured, and determined by the mode or modification of the intellect (*buddhi-vṛitti*). Further, this situation represents man's condition as a bound being (*paśu*) who is involved in life in the world within the periphery of what the intellect (*buddhi*) can determine, as regards the objects of experience which come within its range.

The *need* for man to undergo experience, as already seen, is to provide the *ātman* an opportunity for the experience of the nature of things as they are. Experiencing the world means knowing the world, seeing it *as it is* (the identity between experience and knowledge is intended here and will be taken up again in the next chapter). The cognitive experiences are a representation of the state of man's limited knowledge (*kiñcijjñatva*) and these experiences themselves provide the possibility for man to get to know the nature of things as they really are. The symptom of man's limitedness is the restricted scope of the *buddhi*'s role—which has its clear sign in the occurrence of error—and the cause for this condition is the effect of *malam*. The knowledge of this state of affairs is not given by perception and inference alone but as they apply, and optimally so, in the case of verbal testimony—credibility to which is accorded on the presupposition of such testimony having a trustworthy source. Ironically, it is the 'trained' *buddhi* itself—the *buddhi* involved in life in the world—that is *made* to arrive at this decisive conclusion (*siddhānta*) through the very power that is itself the means of man's cognitive experiences, viz., *cit-śakti*.

As indicated already, the intellect (*buddhi*) is man's indispensable instrument for life in the world, i.e., for the manifestation of the consciousness (*cit*) which constitutes man's essential nature. It is the experience of objects that broadens, as it were, the scope of the *buddhi*'s function. Whilst this is in every case a limited experience, experience itself furnishes the insight into the nature of things. It is an awareness of this condition, i.e., a reflection on man's limited state, that is the first step for the possibility of a conscious effort to eradicate a limited outlook through the very instruments which effect limitation. For man in the world, the journey through the different states of consciousness (*ātma-avasthās*) is plotted, so to speak, on the *buddhi* in the form of traces (*saṅskāras*) which the experiences leave behind. In this sense, the experiences either limit further or expand the efficacy of the *buddhi*, i.e., these experiences are directly responsible for the decisive role of the *buddhi* in subsequent experiences. This state represents a seemingly endless, recurrent cycle—a cycle which, as already seen, has a beginningless (*anādi*) origin—of experiences determining experiences.

The impact of the significance of this predicament needs to be seen together with the role of the category of *karman*, which operates in close collusion with man's categories of experience. The judgement concerning the nature of objects is based on experience, and the condition which determines the present situation under which man experiences the world is *prārabdha-karman* that operates inexorably, as already seen. *Karman* is the unseen (*adṛiṣṭa*) factor that accumulates through experience, and itself determines experience. It is built into the structure and framework of man's experience. Further, it is reflected in the judgement which the *buddhi* passes as regards the nature of things. The occurrence of error, therefore, entails the role of *karman* as well.

Doubt, misapprehension, and memory are responsible for error in cognition, as already seen, and these are modes or modifications of the intellect. Their effect is that they limit the already limited function of the *buddhi* to the point of causing error. Error is the cognition of the object as 'otherwise' (*anyathā-khyāti*), i.e., as what it is not. The occurrence of error is no reflection on the status of the object nor on the nature of consciousness which is *made* to cognize it erroneously. It may be noted in this context, that the existence, as such, of an object is not in question—it is only whether the cognition of it is valid or not, that is the issue here. When error occurs, it represents the condition or state of the *buddhi* alone. In other words, the object is *as it is* (*yathā*)—and always so—and consciousness is the eternal principle that makes the occurrence of cognition at all possible. The only variable factor in the judgement of an object is the *buddhi*. It is assumed that whenever the *buddhi* passes a judgement concerning an object, that this judgement is valid. This does not preclude the possibility of a subsequent judgement which invalidates the previous one.[118] This theory—without compromising the Śaiva Siddhānta contribution to the analysis of error—is based on the intrinsic validity of knowledge (*svataḥ-prāmāṇya*), as already seen. This point may be seen more closely in the light of the following remarks on the three limiting agents of the *buddhi*.[119]

### 3.5 (a) *Doubt* (*saṁśaya*)

As already seen, doubt is the inability on the part of the *buddhi* to come to a conclusive judgement regarding an object. In terms of the description, given earlier, of determinate (*savikalpaka*) and indeterminate perception (*nirvikalpaka-pratyakṣa*), doubt would be a factor in the *buddhi* which mediates between the two. There are a few points involved in this situation. Insofar as a judgement cannot be reached concerning the object, one would have to admit that this itself is a judgement. Further, this judgement would have to be described as an indeterminate (*nirvikalpaka*) one. In the light of the description of the perception process, this state would represent a vague perception that usually takes place at the level of the mind (*manas*), as already seen. In this context, doubt would be a mental (*mānasa*) perception which, in the nature of the case—taking into account the specific role of the mind (*manas*)—is an undecided or indeterminate one. In other words, the mind presents to the intellect different sets of data, all of which appear valid. It is the *buddhi*'s role to pass judgement on the data and the decision it comes to is a doubtful one. The cause for this would have to be attributed to the 'source' of the data, namely, the sense organs.

What these points mean is that the modification of the intellect (*buddhi-vṛitti*) is one of indecision or even error, since the object is not seen as it is. *Cit-śakti* only illuminates this condition of the *buddhi*. This is to say that doubt is a kind of cognition where the object is seen as otherwise (*anyathā*), and this point may be said to be what constitutes the factor of 'error'. It is the *buddhi* that is responsible for this and not the *cit-śakti* itself.

The solution to the doubt situation would be a subsequent cognition which resolves the ambiguity. Of course, this may itself be a repetition of the doubt situation and one may have to take recourse to inference or verbal testimony for an appropriate conclusion. What the situation of doubt emphasizes is the limitation of the human situation. It calls for a reflection on the nature of things as they are (*yathā*) and a discipline which promises, through training, a knowledge of the nature of ultimate reality. This point, which also applies to error due to misapprehension and memory, anticipates the discussion of the next chapter.

3.5 (b) *Misapprehension* (*viparyaya*)

Whereas doubt (*saṁśaya*) was seen to be a case of oscillation between two alternatives—both of which may be erroneous—misapprehension (*viparyaya*), on the other hand, is a clear case of cognition where the object is taken to be something else (*anyathā*) as, e.g., mistaking a rope for a snake or perceiving silver in the mother-of-pearl. The knowledge of this error, of course, can only come from a subsequent perception of the same object, which contradicts the previous experience of it. What this case of error signifies is that as long as the original cognition is not vitiated by a subsequent one, the 'validity' of the original judgement concerning the object remains unquestioned.

This case of error, which only subsequently attests the incorrect view of an object, is not identical with the case of the error regarding the objects of dream experience. Whilst the dream objects appear real *in* the dream and are only subsequently realized as having been unreal, in the case of error through misapprehension, on the other hand, the sense organs are involved in both the original misapprehension and also in the subsequent apprehension. Their similarity lies only in that both are invalidated by subsequent experiences and that both retain their 'validity' as long as they are not contradicted.

As in the case of doubt, here, too, in the case of misapprehension, the *cit-śakti* is not responsible for the fact that the senses perceive aspects unrelated to the nature of the object concerned.

3.5 (c) *Memory* (*smṛiti*)

In saying that memory is a case of error, the Siddhāntin implies that it is not a means or instrument of valid cognition. This point is a consequence of the conditions which have to be fulfilled, as already pointed out, for a means of cognition to be valid. The condition which rules out the case of memory as such a means, is that memory does not furnish a cognition that is *new*. As is clear from the definition already given (p. 104 above), memory is merely the revival of impressions of past experience. On this theory, the 'correctness' of the memory, i.e., the recollection of the past experience, is itself not in question. The point is that the object of cognition to which the memory refers, is not immediately open to verification, i.e., it is not presented *as such*, as an object, to sense perception—the most basic instrument of cognition and the ground for the validity of cognition as such.

Further, memory implies an original perception which, at the time it occurred, may have been valid. The impressions of this experience are retained in man's psychological complex, viz., the *citta*, and are subsequently recalled. But the memory of the recalled experience is not itself a perception and, hence, the status of memory is in question here.

The specific context of these criticisms notwithstanding,[120] i.e., that memory constitutes a case of erroneous or non-valid cognition in the sense explained above, the positive significance of memory may be noted—which does not apply to the other two cases of error already discussed. As seen earlier, memory collaborates with perception in cases of valid inference as, for example, it is the memory of the universal concomitance (*vyāpti*) between smoke and fire, that leads to the conclusion of the presence of fire, on the basis of the perception of smoke (it may be repeated that memory alone is insufficient for this conclusion, as pointed out in the discussion on subsumptive reflection, *parāmarśa*, p. 108 above). Its role here is obviously a positive one insofar as inference is regarded as a valid means of cognition. However, memory per se is for all intents and purposes, a case of error for the Siddhāntin.

## 3.6 *Summary*

In all three cases of error, the question still remains as to why they occur in the forms they do. In some cases, it could evidently be due to some extraneous cause, such as defective eyesight. The basic question, however, applies here as well: why is man in a condition such that objects are not seen as they are? That man is a being who possesses limited knowledge (*kiñcijjña*) is not itself the answer, insofar as it points to the question about the cause for this limitation itself. For the Siddhāntin, the root cause is *malam*, as already seen, and the cases of error are only the signs that point to it. The instruments of cognition—which presupposes that the roles of *māyā* and *karman* are in operation—afford the *ātman*, i.e., man's essential nature characterized as consciousness, a scope to manifest itself. In so doing, it copes with the otherwise overwhelming role of *malam*. Every instance of experience, which is invariably a case of knowledge about the nature of things implies, as already seen, a removal of the veil of ignorance caused by *malam*—in this context, *malam* and ignorance (*avidyā*, *ajñāna*) are used synonymously. Although the removal of this veil is partial, insofar as man's knowledge is limited by the role of the instruments of cognition, nonetheless, a glimpse is provided into the nature of things. The only means, in the proper sense of the term, through which this takes place is *cit-śakti*.

The limitation of man's knowledge determined by the role of the intellect's modifications (*buddhi-vṛittis*), points to the significance of the *buddhi*'s function. It was seen in the first chapter that the basic quality of the *buddhi* is what is called *sattva-guṇa*, the quality responsible for calmness, tranquility and clarity of experience as such. These features are positive ones and imply that when this basic quality essential to the *buddhi* predominates, then the factors of error are practically non-existent. In other words, it is the mode of the *buddhi* dominated by the quality responsible for clarity, which is the ideal medium for the manifestation and expression of man's powers of consciousness (*ātma-cit-śakti*) and results, thereby, in the knowledge of things as they really are.

The realization of this feature of the *cit-śakti* is crucial for the Śaiva Siddhānta understanding of man. It is the outcome of a transcendental reflection on man's role as a cognitive being undergoing the states of consciousness which constitute life in the world. Such a transcendental reflection implies a discipline and training, identical with a conscious effort on the part of man to exploit the categories and instruments of experience at man's disposal, to their full capacity. In this process, man's consciousness (*ātma-cit-śakti*) may be said to be unleashed furnishing, thereby, a knowledge of man's essential nature as opposed to the nature of insentience, on the one hand and, on the other hand, revealing man's essential nature in relation to the ultimate reality of *śivam* as the underlying principle of existence as such. Here Śaiva Siddhānta philosophical anthropology and Śaiva Siddhānta theology meet. The next chapter attempts to deal with the discipline which leads to this wisdom of the Āgamas.

## NOTES

1. The special emphasis on *prāmāṇyavāda* (epistemology) marks a significant phase in the very early development of the systems of Indian thought, with its strong rationalistic tendency. Closely related to this is the emergence of *sūtra* literature, and particularly the commentaries on them. Jaimini's *Mīmāṁsāsūtra* is traditionally believed to have been the earliest, it is by far the longest, and is assigned the date of about A.D. 200.
2. In this context one can speak of the soteriological function of epistemology in Indian thought. Cf., also M. Hiriyanna, *Outlines*, pp. 182-183, when he says, speaking about the results or aims of the means of cognition: "...what the Indians aspired after in philosophy was not a mediate knowledge of the ultimate truth but a direct vision of it..." and the "insistence that one should not rest content with a mere intellectual conviction but should aim at transforming such conviction into direct experience." See also his book *Values*, p. 27, where he is concerned "with the nature of knowledge as a fact of mental life or with its validity as pointing to an object beyond itself."
3. There is a great deal of difference among the schools of Indian thought

over the number (and nature) of the means of valid cognition. See note 48 below.

4. Speaking about *jñāna* and *pramā*, D.M. Datta, *The Six Ways of Knowing* (Calcutta: University of Calcutta, 1960, p. 19), says: "Consequently knowledge, strictly speaking, should always stand for a cognition that is true, uncontradicted or unfalsified. The ordinary division of knowledge into true knowledge and false knowledge should therefore, be considered as an instance of loose thinking; the word true as applied to knowledge would then be a tautology, and the word false positively contradictory—false knowledge being only a name for falsified knowledge, which is another name for no knowledge."
5. Cf. K. Sivaraman, *Śaivism*, p. 297: "When self too knows itself and knows other selves and their knowledge, its knowledge is not of the epistemologically cognisable category of *pramāṇa*." Also, *ibid.*, "...there is no *pramāṇa* by which to know God except as he is revealed to self by *Śivaśakti;* the 'means' and the 'end' of knowledge coincide there."
6. In the light of what has already been pointed out, the word *mithyā-jñāna* should be construed as "erroneous cognition" rather than 'erroneous knowledge'.
7. The question for the Nyāya school, whose favourite topic is one of *pramāṇas*, is not how knowledge comes to be true or false but how we become aware of its truth or falsity, for which we require fruitful activity (*saṁvādi pravṛitti*) as an additional condition, i.e., its appeal to facts. Thus, for Nyāya all knowledge is either true or false, there being no 'neutral' knowledge—doubt is a kind of knowledge that one has, the truth or falsity of which is not yet seen.
8. M. Monier-Williams, *op.cit.*, s.v., *pramā.*
9. *Ibid.*
10. Na kasya-api padārthasya yad-vinā bhavati pramā / Tad-eva mānam-eṣṭavyaṁ cakṣur-ādi na tādṛiśam iti // *Pauṣkara Āgama* 7: 13-14, quoted in *Śaivaparibhāṣā* (Mysore: University of Mysore, 1950), p. 4.
11. Yan-meyaṁ na hi tan-mānaṁ yato mānena mīyate. *Pauṣkara Āgama*, 7:12, quoted *ibid.* Also in *SB*, p. 19, and p. 97. This quotation is repeated in the context of the discussion, p. 112 below.
12. Cakṣṇr-ādi-indriyāṇāṁ sva-sva-viṣaya-vyatirikta-viṣaya-grāhakatva-ayogāt sarva-grāhakaṁ kiñcit-pramāṇam-eṣṭavyam. *Śaivaparibhāṣā*, *op.cit.*, p. 4.
13. Na cakṣuḥ śabda-saṁvittau na śrotram rūpa-vedane / Sarvatra grāhikā saṁvit-saiva mānam-ato matam // *Pauṣkara Āgama*, 7:15, quoted *ibid.*, p. 5.
14. Tac-ca cic-chaktir-eva. *Ibid.*, p. 4.
15. Tatra pramāṇa-sāmānya-lakṣaṇaṁ tu saṁśaya-viparyaya-smṛiti-vyatiriktā pramā-paraparyāyā ātma-cic-chaktir-iti. *Ibid.*, p. 2. This point is on the authority of the *Pauṣkara Āgama* (7:4) statement which Śivāgrayogin quotes, *ibid.*: "*Cit-śakti* which is devoid of doubt, etc., is said to be the means of valid cognition" (Saṁśaya-ādi-vinirmuktā cic-chaktir-mānam-

ucyate). See section 3.5 below for details as to why memory, doubt and misapprehension have to be excluded.

16. Tatra saṁśayo nāma sādhāraṇa-dharma-darśanātkoṭi-dvaya--avalambinī buddhiḥ yathā sthāṇur-vā puruṣo vety-ādi. *Ibid.*, p. 2.
17. Viparyayas-tu atasmiṁs-tad-buddhiḥ yathā śuktikāyāṁ rajatam-ity-ādi. *Ibid.*
18. Pūrva-anubhava-janita-saṁskāra-janyā buddhiḥ smṛitiḥ yathā kāmukasya kāminī-sākṣātkāra-ādi. *Ibid.*
19. Etat-tritaya-vyatirikta cic-chaktir-eva pramāṇam. *Ibid.*
20. The discussion beginning here follows Śivāgrayogin's argument closely, with practically a word by word translation and exegesis. In the original, the discussion goes on into several pages, *SB* pp. 95-98, and for the sake of convenience his entire argument is given in Appendix 3—the specific sentences are referred to in the notes that follow. The section dealt with here is entitled "Defining *cit-śakti*'s validity as the means of cognition." The discussion ends on p. 117 below. See also the end of note 47 below.
21. See Appendix 3, the sentence beginning: "Tvan-mate cic-chakter-eva..."
22. *Ibid.*, "Cakṣur-ādy-asannikarṣe'pi..."
23. *Ibid.*, "Saṁśaya-viparyaya-āsāder-api..."
24. See also K. Sivaraman, *Saivism*, p. 299: "This means that the advocate of *cit-śakti* is not very far from including the senses also under *pramāṇa*."
25. See Appendix 3, "Na-ādyaḥ sukha-ādiṣu..."
26. *Ibid.*, "Na dvitīyaḥ..."
27. The term *parāmarśa* is a logical one and the Nyāya school provides a clear definition of it:

    "*Parāmarśa* (subsumptive reflection) is a cognition which cognizes the presence of the invariably concomitant factor denoted by the middle term (*probans*) in the thing denoted by the minor term. For instance, the cognition, 'This mountain has smoke which is invariably concomitant with fire' is a subsumptive reflection; and the cognition resulting from it and taking the form 'mountain has fire' is inferential cognition." S. Kuppuswami Sastri, *Indian Logic*, *op.cit.*, p. 188. The significance of the term is evident in the following two clarifications: "*Parāmarśa* is a complex cognition which arises from a combination of the knowledge of invariable concomitance (*vyāptijñāna*) and that of the presence of the reason (*hetu*) in the subject (*pakṣa*)—technically known as *pakṣadharmatājñāna*. In the stock example of inference—'The hill has fire; because it has smoke', the *parāmarśa* takes the form—'The hill has smoke, which is invariably concomitant with fire' (*vahnivyāpyadhūmavān parvataḥ*); and it is contended by the Naiyāyikas that, in the absence of such a *parāmarśa*, *anumiti* does not arise." *Ibid.*, p. 194. See also *Ibid.*, p. 196: "...the Naiyāyikas insist that subsumption is the essential feature of inference and insist therefore that every *anumiti* should be taken to be preceded by *parāmarśa* which is but a subsumptive reflection subsuming the smoke in the hill under the pre-established *vyāpti*."
28. See Appendix 3, the sentence beginning: "Tasya atīta-anāgata..."

29. *Ibid.*, "Ata eva na tṛitīyaḥ..."
30. *Ibid.*, "Na ca kāraṇa-antara..."
31. *Ibid.*, "Evaṁ sati sarvasya-api..."
32. *Ibid.*, "Karma-ādāv-ativyāpteś-ca. Karma-ādikam-api anena rūpeṇa kara-ṇam-eva..." This argument may be said to refute both the Nyāya and the Grammarian standpoints, where the results of acts performed are loosely taken as instruments of acts. There are five kinds of *karman* in Nyāya (see S. Kuppuswami Sastri, *Indian Logic*, p. 34 and p. 263): *utkṣepaṇa* (the act of throwing upwards); *avakṣepaṇa* (throwing downwards); *ākuñcana* (the act of bending); *prasāraṇa* (stretching); and *gamana* (moving). Pāṇini (i, 4,49) talks of four kinds of *karman: nivartya* (when anything new is produced, e.g., he makes a mat); *vikārya* (implying change as, e.g., redu-cing fuel to ashes or, e.g., fashioning gold into a ring); *prāpya* (when any desired object is attained, e.g., going to the village); and *anīpsita* (when an undesired object is abandoned, e.g., he leaves the wicked).
33. See Appendix 3, the two sentences beginning from: "Tathā sati rūpa-ādy..."
34. See note 27 above.
35. K. Sivaraman, *Śaivism*, p. 302.
36. See Appendix 3, the sentence beginning: "Cakṣur-ādy-avyāpteḥ..."
37. See also K. Sivaraman, *Śaivism*, p. 303. Śivāgrayogin's argument here is based on what the *Pauṣkara Āgama* (7: 19-21) says. The translation of the verses which appear in Appendix 3 is: "Now, who would not acknowledge a collection [of causes] since a pot is ascertained only when there is [the collection] beginning with the cognizer and ending with the pot? There should be a suspension of the common usage of the cognizer, the cognized, etc., [here] since it is established that the cognizer, the means of cognition and the thing cognized are included in that [collection]—apart from these, there is no collection to be seen."
38. See Appendix 3, the paragraph beginning: "Atrocyate..."
39. *Ibid.*, the two sentences beginning from: "Cākṣur-ādi-karaṇaka-buddhi..."
40. K. Sivaraman, *Śaivism*, p. 306.
41. See p. 104 above for their definitions.
42. See Appendix 3. This line is a slight variation of the same quoted in Śivāgrayogin's *Śaivaparibhāṣā*, *op.cit.*, p. 6. There the word *vibhinnā* is used instead of *vinirmuktā* here, without any semantic difference.
43. On a point of grammar and semantics, the editor of the text suggests that the word *saṁśaya* should be read as *saṁśayatva*, because it is logical to say that one should speak of a *buddhi-vṛitti* which is *doubting* the nature of an object, rather than it being "identified with doubt." In other words, even when a *buddhi-vṛitti* is under the influence of doubt, there is still a manifestation of an object, the nature of which is in doubt. This mani-festation itself is on account of *cit-śakti* and it is inadmissible to identify *cit-śakti* with the *doubting buddhi-vṛitti*. See next note for the exact sentence in question.

44. See Appendix 3, the sentence beginning: "Cic-chakteḥ saṁśaya-ādi buddhi-vṛitti.."
45. *Ibid.*, the sentence beginning: "Na caivaṁ buddhi-vṛitti..."
46. *Ibid.*, the sentence beginning: "Buddhi-jaḍatvena..."
47. *Ibid.*, the sentence beginning: "Atra buddhi-padena..." Śivāgrayogin quotes *Mṛigendra Āgama* 11:8 to justify this statement. The translation of this verse which appears in Appendix 3 is: "This light of *buddhi*, which has the nature of determination and dispositions, is known as intelligence, because it is the source of the manifestation of the *paśu*'s intelligence." In a footnote to the text, the editor of the text points out that the "light of *buddhi*" is to be understood as the *vṛitti* of *buddhi*, which is the cause for the production of cognition in man. It is only in this sense that the *buddhi* appears as the "light" which in fact is derived from *cit-śakti*.

    This concludes the section that closely follows Śivāgrayogin's commentary, supplied in Appendix 3. See also note 20 above.
48. There is no general consensus in the schools of Indian thought about the number (and nature) of the means of cognition. Thus, the Cārvāka accepts the priority only of sense perception (*pratyakṣa*); the Buddhists and Vaiśeṣikas accept only two, adding inference (*anumāna*) to perception; Sāṅkhyans, Śaiva Siddhāntins, and Viśiṣṭa Advaitins accept only three, including scriptural authority or verbal testimony (*śabda, śruti*) in the list; the Nyāya school accepts only four, including comparison (*upamāna*); the Prābhākara Mīmāṁsakas accept only five, including presumption or the supposition of a fact (*arthāpatti*); the Advaitins accept the six of the Bhāṭṭa Mīmāṁsakas which include non-cognition or non-apprehension (*anupalabdhi* or *abhāva*) in the list; some schools accept nine by adding equivalence (*sambhava*), tradition or fallible testimony (*aitihya*), and gesture (*ceṣṭā*). The Paurāṇikas accept only eight, excluding the last one mentioned in the list.
49. It is to be noted that for the Siddhāntin, only *cit-śakti* deserves the label of being a means of valid cognition, in the Śaiva Siddhānta sense of the term as already seen. Whilst the term "means" is also used here for the three means of valid cognition accepted by the Siddhāntin, its derivative sense is to be noted, i.e., perception, inference and verbal testimony serve as means of cognition only through the *cit-śakti* which makes their operation possible.
50. Tatra sākṣātkāri-pramā pratyakṣam. *SB*, p. 108.
51. Sākṣātkāritvam-akhaṇḍo dharma-viśeṣaḥ. *SB*, p. 109.
52. Vastu-svarūpa-mātrasya grahaṇaṁ nirvikalpakam / Nāma-jāty-ādi-saṁbandha-sahitaṁ savikalpakam // *Pauṣkara Āgama* 7: 28, quoted in *Śaivaparibhāṣā*, p. 6.
53. ...sarvam savikalpaka-jñānaṁ śabdollekhi. *SB*, p. 110.
54. Na cendriya-artha-mātrasya saṁyogo'dhyakṣam-iṣyate / Cit-saṁyoga-vihīnānām-akiñcitkaratā yataḥ // *Pauṣkara Agama,* 7: 26, quoted in *Śaivaparibhāṣā*, p. 8.
55. Anyac-cendriya-sāpekṣaṁ sva-ācchādana-nivṛittaye / Indriya-apekṣayā

śaktyā tad-dvāreṇa-artha-vīkṣaṇam // *Pauṣkara Āgama*, 7:830, quoted *ibid.*, p. 7.

56. Śivāgrayogin, *ibid.*, pp. 8-9, speaks of six kinds of association (*saṁbandha*) between a sense organ and an object. These constitute varying levels of cognition which may be enumerated below:

(a) The relation which is a mere conjunction (*saṁyoga*) between the sense organ and the object, e.g., when there is a simple cognition of an object such as a pot.

(b) The relation of inherence in the conjoined (*saṁyukta-samavāya*), e.g., the cognition of the generality and its quality (such as being the colour blue);

(c) The relation of inherence in what is inherent in the conjoined (*saṁyukta-samaveta-samavāya*), e.g., the cognition of the quality-ness of the object, such as the blueness of the pot;

(d) The relation of inherence (*samvāya*), e.g., hearing inherently implies the cognition of sound;

(e) The relation of inherence in what is inherent (*samaveta-samavāya*) e.g., the cognition of soundness from the cognition of sound;

(f) The relation of qualification and the qualified (*viśeṣaṇa-viśeṣya-bhāva*), e.g., the cognition of non-existence as inherent in the object which serves as the qualification of the object or as its substrate.

Cf. V.A. Devasenapathi, *Śaiva Siddhānta*, p. 30, says that the Siddhāntin "does not accept this classification as it is based on the view that perception is generated solely by the contact of the sense with object." See also note 54 above.

57. ...mala-āvaraṇa-vaśāt-sva-niṣṭhā-api sā kalayā vyañjitā avidyayā viṣaya-abhimukhī-kṛitā rāgeṇa rañjitā ca satī antaḥ-karaṇa-bāhyendriya-dvārā ātma-bhogāya bāhya-arthe pravartate. *Śaivaparibhāṣā*, pp. 7-8.

58. This point will be dealt with in the next chapter.

59. Yogi-pratyakṣaṁ yoga-abhyāsa-samāsādita-dharma-paripāka-sahakṛitena manasā atīta-anāgata-ati-indriya-artha-parijñānam. *SB*, p. 111.

60. Yogi-jñānaṁ nāma atīta-anāgata-vartamāna-sākṣātkāraḥ. *SB*, pp. 19-20.

61. Prākṛita-sukha-ādi-jñānaṁ nāma sukha-duḥkha-anubhava-anusandhā-nam. *Ibid.*, p. 20.

62. Tatra nirapekṣaṁ cit-prakāśa-rūpam. *SB*, p. 111.

63. At the transcendental level referred to here, the distinctions of *pāśa-jñāna*, *paśu-jñāna*, and *ātma-jñāna* are a matter of experience (*anubhava, bhoga*) which, in the nature of the case, is in fact inadequately expressible in terms of the categories of man's fettered existence. The distinctions serve only a descriptive attempt, in the light of the philosophical presuppositions of Śaiva Siddhānta, to make the transcendental realm intelligible within man's limited scope.

64. (Tatrendriya-antaḥ-karaṇa-nirapekṣaṁ) nirasta-bandhayā cic-chaktyā āt-mano, nitya-saṁbandhāj-jāyamānaṁ sva-ātma-aparokṣa-jñānam. *Śaiva-paribhāṣā* p. 7.

65. Tatrendriya-anapekṣaṁ ca sarvathā tyakta-bandhayā / Cic-chakty-ānan-

tya-yogāc-ca yogaḥ svābhāviko mataḥ // *Pauṣkara Āgama*, 7:29, quoted *ibid.*

66. It may be noted here that *cit-śakti* as a *pramāṇa* at the transcendental level presupposes a knowledge of its own nature as constituting the knowledge which it itself perceives or experiences. The knowledge about the possibility of such a perception is derived from scripture or from teachers. The knowledge derived through inference, on the other hand, is grounded in experience and life in the world which determine its validity as, e.g., it is perception which verifies the inference of fire from smoke. Whilst the same word *pratyakṣa*, is used for both these two kinds of perception, the essential difference between them, as already seen in the previous section, is to be noted.

67. Tatra vyāptir-nāma sādhya-sādhanayor-anaupādhikaḥ sambandhaḥ. *Śaivaparibhāṣā*, p. 9. Śivāgrayogin's definition of what constitutes an adventitious condition is :

   "And an adventitious condition is the being pervasive of the *probandum* while not being pervasive of the *probans*, e.g., the association, etc., with wet fuel [the adventitious condition] when the smoke is to be proved by fire. It [the adventitious condition] is pervasive of the smoke, the *probandum*, on account of existing wherever there is smoke. It is not pervasive of the fire, the *probans*, on account of not existing in an iron ball, etc., which possess fire. And this is the ascertained adventitious condition." (Upādhiś-ca sādhana-avyāpakatve sati sādhya-vyāpakatvam. Yathā vahninā dhūme sādhye ārdrendhana-saṁyoga-ādiḥ. Sa hi sādhyasya dhūmasya vyāpakaḥ, dhūmavati sarvatra vṛitteḥ. Sādhanasya vahner-avyāpakaḥ, vahnimaty-ayo-golaka-ādāv-avṛitteḥ. Ayaṁ ca niścitopādhiḥ.)

   *Śaivaparibhāṣā*, p. 10.

68. Anumānaṁ dṛiḍha-vyāptyā parokṣa-artha-avabodhakam. *Pauṣkara Āgama*, 7: 37, quoted *ibid.*, p. 9.

69. Nanv-anumānaṁ nāma pramāṇam-eva na-asti. Tad-dhetutva-abhimatasya vyāpti-grahasya-asambhavāt. Katipaya-sthale sāmānādhikaraṇya-grahe'pi sthala-antare vyabhicāra-śaṅkāyā anivṛitteḥ. Tarkāt-tan-nivṛittau tarkasya-api vyāpti-mūlakatvena-anavasthā-āpatteḥ. Ata eva-anaupādhikatva- niścayāt-vyāpti-graha iti nirastam. Vyāpter-yāvat-sādhana-adhikaraṇa-garbhatvena tad-grahe pratyakṣasya-asāmarthyāc-ca. Vyāpti-grahasya ca-anumānikatve'navasthā-āpatteḥ. *SB*, pp. 13-14.

70. In Śivāgrayogin's own words: "Thus you are self-contradictory because your words are used in the form of an inference [itself]." (Asyaiva tvadīya-vacanasya-anumāna-prayoga-rūpatvena sva-vyāhateḥ) *Ibid.*, p. 14.

71. Maivam, anumāna-prāmāṇya-anaṅgīkāre pravṛitti-mātroccheda-prasaṅgāt. Pravṛitteḥ pravṛitti-gocara-anāgata-viṣayaka-kāryatā-anumity-ādi-janyatvāt. Evaṁ parvata-ādau vahny-arthinaḥ pravṛittiś-ca na syāt. *Ibid.*, p. 14.

72. Na ca vyāpti-grahasya kāraṇasya-abhāvena-anumāna-pravṛittir-eva na sambhavati iti yuktam. *Ibid.*

73. Anāgata-ādi-viṣayake vyāpti-grahe manasaś-cakṣur-āḍer-vā sāmarthyasya klṛiptatvān-na tasya pratyakṣatva-anupapattiḥ. *Ibid.*
74. ...vahni-dhūmayoḥ vyāpti-grahaṇa-anantaraṁ parvata-ādau vyāpya-liṅga-darśanād-vahny-ādy-anumānam. *Śaivaparibhāṣā*, p. 10. On this point the Siddhāntin seems to follow the Nyāya view that inference takes place as involuntarily as the sudden perception of a thing. For the Advaitin, on the other hand, inference takes place either when there is a doubt or, at least, when there is a want of knowledge regarding what is to be inferred. See D.M. Datta, *op.cit.*, p. 230 and p. 231.
75. Here Śaiva Siddhānta follows the Nyāya school in accepting five members necessary for a valid inference. Śivāgrayogin quotes *Pauṣkara Āgama* 7: 37-40 as his authority. The five components as he mentions them in *Śaivaparibhāṣā*, pp. 10-11 are: (1) the proposition or assertion to be proved (*pratijñā*), e.g., there is a fire on the hill; (2) the reason (*hetu*) for the assertion, e.g., because the hill has smoke on it; (3) the example or instance (*udāharaṇa* or *dṛiṣṭānta*) that serves as the reason, e.g., wherever there is smoke, there is fire, as in the fire-place; (4) the application (*upanaya*) of the invariable concomitance between the smoke and the fire, as in the case of seeing smoke on the mountain; and (5) the conclusion or restatement of assertion (*nigamana*) in the light of the application of the invariable concomitance as, e.g., therefore, there is a fire on the hill.
76. Cf. also Datta, *op. cit.*, p. 218: "In inference, it is not always the case that the premises are *given* and the conclusion is to be *found*. It is very often the case that the conclusion is presented first to the mind, and we are required to find the premises that justify it. This latter process is mostly in evidence when we adduce arguments in justification of our instinctive beliefs. The order of reasoning, therefore, may take either form; the premises first and the conclusion last, or the conclusion first and the premises last. In the latter case it is, of course, a misnomer to call the proposition proved a conclusion. It should rather be called a *probandum*, for until the premises are adduced it is not a conclusion but only a proposition to be proved. Hence the Indian logicians call it a pratijñā (*probandum*)."
77. See note 27 above.
78. The aim of the discussion on inference in this section is only to show its validity as a means of cognition (in the special Śaiva Siddhānta sense of the term *pramāṇa*) as defended by Śivāgrayogin. For this purpose, it has not been necessary to deal with the intricate details of inference which presupposes a thorough acquaintance with the development of Indian logic. Thus, further details, e.g., of *hetvābhāsa*, which entail an elaborate clarification of the *sādhya*, *sādhana*, and *hetu*, together with the term *pakṣatā*, are beyond the scope of this study.
79. Anumāna-aprāmāṇyena ca tan-mūlaka-saṅgati-graha-sāpekṣasya śabdasya-apy-aprāmāṇyam-iti. *SB*, p. 14.
80. Tat-prāmāṇye ca tan-mūlakasya saṅgati-grahasyopapatter-nigama-āgama-ādir-api pramāṇam. *Ibid.*
81. Evam-ādi-pramāṇais-tu durlakṣyaṁ tac-chivaṁ smṛitam. *Suprabheda*

*Āgama* 1: 18a, quoted in B. Dagens (ed.), *Śaivāgamaparibhāṣā-mañjarī* (Pondichèrry: Institut Francais D'Indologie, 1979), p. 255.

82. Śabdas-tu pāramparyeṇa śivajñāna-anumāpakaḥ. *Pauṣkara Āgama* 7: 74, quoted in *Śaivaparibhāṣā*, p. 23.

83. Cf. also: "...the word '*āgama*' can be taken to imply the handing down of knowledge from teacher to pupil, and thus to denote traditional (*sampradāya*) knowledge. Then the word '*āgama*' can be taken to mean what the *Āgamas* stand for." V. Varadachari, *Āgamas*, p. 10. The following is also noteworthy: "A Science which comes from teacher to disciple from time immemorial is called Āgama. That which gives needed knowledge and describes the means for the welfare here in this world as well as in the other is called Tantra. Any methodically arranged collection of Texts or verses is called Saṃhitā. So Āgama or Tantra or Saṃhitā speak about the same variety of Texts." N.R. Bhatt's Introduction to *Kāmikāgama* (Madras: C. Swaminatha Gurukal, 1975), p. i.

84. "From a very early stage in the history of Indian Philosophic speculation, there would seem to have been two currents of thought, the Vedic and the Āgamic, apparently independent and antagonistic. It is not possible to fix definitely the period when the Āgamas came into being. Some of them that exist now go in for a criticism of Jainism and Buddhism, the Sāṁkhya and the Mīmāṁsā and the Advaita Vedānta, and could have been evolved only after these systems; but some at least of these, the Pāśupata and the Pāñcarātra Āgamas, should have been current before the compilation of the *Vedānta Sūtras*, as those two systems are refuted by Bādarāyaṇa in the second pāda of the second chapter of the *Sūtras*." S.S. Suryanarayana Sastri, *The Śivādvaita of Śrīkaṇṭha*, (Madras: University of Madras, 1972) p. 1.

85. "It has been suggested that the Āgamaic systems were developed out of the Brāhmaṇas in the same way as the Upaniṣads, though at a much later stage, and that some of the later Upaniṣads like the Śvetāśvatara, which address the Supreme Being by a sectarian title and not *param Brahman* as of yore, probably grew up under the shadow of the Āgamas." *Ibid.*, pp. 1-2. See also *ibid.*, p. 3 where the writer quotes and translates the following Āgamic passages which claim Vedic authority for their doctrine:

> "*Siddhānto vedasāratvāt*, "as the siddhānta consists of the Veda": (*Suprabhedāgama*).
>
> *Vedasāram idaṁ tantram*, "this tantra is of the essence of the Veda": (*Makuṭāgama*).
>
> *Vedāntārtham idaṁ jñānaṁ siddhāntaṁ paramaṁ śubhaṁ*, "This siddhānta knowledge which is the significance of Vedānta is supremely felicitous": (*Makuṭāgama*)."

Cf. also V. Varadachari, op.cit., p. 12: "The *Āgamas* have an independent development of theory and practice and should be taken as a system of philosophy and religion based on the *Vedas*. The theoretical side represents a continuation of the results of philosophical enquiries which the *Vedas* deal with. The controversies and discussions which mark these enquiries are left out in the *Āgamas*. Greater attention is paid here to the cultural discipline which is sought to be inculcated through practical religion." As regards the date of Āgamas, the writer just quoted says, *ibid.*, p. 42: "Anyway, the *Mahābhārata* which must have taken a specific shape by 3000 B.C. should justify this date as the lowermost limit for the prevalence of the Āgamic doctrines."

86. The three branches are: Śaivism with its Śaiva Āgamas which consider Śiva as the supreme deity; Vaiṣṇavism with its Vaiṣṇava Āgamas which consider Viṣṇu as the supreme deity; and Śāktaism with its Śākta Āgamas which consider Śakti or the Goddess as the supreme deity. Whilst there are several features which are common to all Āgamic literature—including the debate on its validity—the discussion here pertains to the 28 Āgamas, and the numerous subsidiary Āgamas (*upāgamas*) basic to the Śaiva Siddhānta school. The research by the French Institute of Indology in Pondicherry, India, has thrown a great deal of light to allay the allegation that the names and contents of these Āgamas are largely legendary. See the complete list provided in N.R. Bhatt (ed.) *Rauravāgama*, table 1, facing p. xix, and the numerous publications of Āgamas, either in part or in full (apart from those which are still in MS form) which bear evidence to the fact that these Āgamas did indeed exist.

87. It is clear that the problem turned into a philosophical issue at least as early as the tenth century. Yāmunācārya (918-1038), predecessor and grand teacher of Rāmānuja, wrote a special treatise justifying the validity of the Āgamas in his *Āgamaprāmāṇya*. Although his is a defence of the Vaiṣṇava Pāñcarātra Āgamas, the question of validity applies to Āgamas in general. It has been said about Yāmunācārya's work that: "Though short, this is perhaps the only early work solely devoted to this question." M. Narasimhachary (ed.), *Āgamaprāmāṇya of Yāmunācārya* (Baroda: University of Baroda, 1976), p. xiii. An earlier edition with a translation preceded this critical edition: J.A.B. van Buitenen, *Yāmuna's Āgama Prāmāṇyam*, (Madras: Ramanuja Research Society, 1971).

88. Some of the issues are: that the Āgamas go against the Vedas by strongly recommending the exclusive worship of one specific deity; that contrary to Vedic practice, the Āgamas permit women and people of all castes to perform worship; and that in addition to the sacred thread initiation (*upanayana*) the Āgamas, without Vedic injunction, make mandatory a second qualification for worship, called *dīkṣā* (initiation).

89. *SB*, p. 18.

90. This is the reason why Yāmunācārya also defends the Pāñcarātra Āgamas in his *Āgamaprāmāṇya*. See M. Narasimhachary, *op.cit.*, Preface p. xiii.

91. Tasmān-nitya-nirmala-sarvajña-pakṣapāta-rahita-yathā-artha-grāhaka-avyaya-paripūrṇa-svatantra-paśu-pāśa-hantṛi-parama-āpta-parameśvara-praṇītatvenaiva vedānām-āgamānāṁ ca prāmāṇyam. *Śaivaparibhāṣa*, p. 21. This quotation also makes evident the difference in the elaborate debate between, for example, the Mīmāṁsaka view that the Veda is eternal and cannot be said to be composed by any being (*apauruṣeya*), and the Śaiva

view here that both the Veda (Nigama) and the Āgama are the work of the supreme lord (Parameśvara, i.e., Śiva) "the supremely trustworthy person."

92. Bearing in mind that the Āgamas were taught by Śiva, the point here may be said to be a legitimate extension of the following: "The first *Ṛṣis* realised *dharma*, that is, they acquired it. It is implied that they acquired the *Mantras* also, without being taught by anybody. Their successors were of inferior calibre and could not realise the *dharma* nor acquire the *Mantras* by themselves...When they [the *Ṛṣis*] saw the gradually decreasing capacity of the later generations, they diversified the *Veda* for the sake of facility in learning. They also handed down the auxiliary sciences of the *Vedas* (the *Vedāṅgas*)." K.A. Subramania Iyer, *Bhartṛhari* (Poona: Deccan College, 1969), p. 95.

93. Iti vastu-trayasya-asya prāk-pāda-kṛita-saṁsthiteḥ / Caryā-yoga-kriyā-pādair-viniyogo 'bhidhāsyate// *Mṛigendra Āgama*, 2:8, p. 68. I am indebted to Pandit N.R. Bhatt of the French Institute of Indology, Pondicherry, for this reference and the point made here.

94. This point represents an obvious rejection of the *śabda-brahmavādin's* standpoint, viz., that the essence of speech or sound is the ultimate reality. For the Śaiva Siddhānta rejection of this theory, see also. K. Sivaraman, *Śaivism*, p. 229.

95. See chapter one, p. 21 above.

96. *Ibid.*, p. 21 above.

97. *SB*, p. 149.

98. Tatra sūkṣma-abhidhānāyāḥ vāg-vṛitteḥ mumukṣu-gate cit-prakāśe mahattva-mahattaratva-mahattamatva-abhivyañjikāyā īśvara-śakter-niyojya mala-nivartikāyāś-ca tasya evopādhi-bhūtānām-indhika-ādi-kalānāñca-āśrayī-bhūtā nāda-pada-vyapadeśyā artha-ātmikā kuṇḍalinyāḥ prāthamikī vṛittiḥ śiva-tattvam. *SB*, p. 149.

99. This point has a direct bearing on the soteriology of Śaiva Siddhānta theology, which will be dealt with in the next chapter.

100. This phrase is the title of an article by K. Sivaraman which deals with the Śaiva Siddhānta theory of *nāda* especially in the light of *Nāda Kārikā* by Rāmakaṇṭha (12th century). The text and its translation are given in the article. See H. Coward and K. Sivaraman (eds.), *Revelation in Indian Thought* (California: Dharma Publishing, 1977), pp. 45-64.

101. Cf. also: "With the emergence of the word emerges the meaning and not *vice versa*. It is the word which has to be used even when the meaning has to be explained." K. Sivaraman, *Śaivism*, p. 229.

102. Padaṁ nāma varṇa-samūhaḥ. Varṇānāṁ kṣaṇa-bhaṅguratvāt artha-pratyāyakatva-abhāvāt artha-pratyayanārthaṁ varṇeṣu sphoṭo nāma kaścit-padārtho nityo'ṅgīkaraṇīyaḥ. *Śaivaparibhāṣā*, p. 24.

103. The speculations on language in the *āstika* schools of India may be said to be the following three important theories of meaning that, as a consequence, have been propounded: *anvitābhidhānavāda*, advocated by Prabhā-

kara; *abhihitānvayavāda*, advocated by the Nyāya school generally, by Kumārila, and by the Advaitins (including Śaṅkara, though he nowhere mentions it specifically); and *sphoṭavāda*, generally held by the grammarians, especially Bhartṛihari (Maṇḍana Miśra is also a staunch upholder of the doctrine and in his *Sphoṭasiddhi* he defends it from attacks by Kumārila and Śaṅkara). According to the first theory, the words of a sentence simultaneously retain their individual meanings in conjunction with one another, while at the same time produce a single constructed meaning of the whole sentence, i.e., the collection of *words* gives a unitary sense of the sentence. According to the second theory, the words hold their individual meanings in isolation but subsequently combine (*saṅghāta*) to express a single sentence-meaning, i.e., the recollection of the meanings of individual words gives a unitary sense. According to the third theory a sentence is an indivisible unit (*akhaṇḍa*), presenting or thrusting forth itself as such (*sphoṭa*) and the meaning of a sentence as a whole, as a single unit, is achieved through a flash of insight or intuition (*pratibhā*)—thus, a *sphoṭavādin* is a *vākyavādin*, with the emphasis on the sentence as a whole. For further details, see especially: G. Sastri, *The Philosophy of Word and Meaning*, Calcutta: Sanskrit College, 1959; K. Kunjunni Raja, *Indian Theories of Meaning*, Madras: Adyar Library, 1963; G. Kaviraj, *Aspects of Indian Thought*, Burdwan: University of Burdwan, 1966; and K.A. Subrahmania Iyer, *Bhartṛhari*, Poona: Deccan College, 1969.

104. Āpta-vākya-janyaṁ jñānaṁ śabda-pramāṇam. Āpto nāma yathā-artha-darśī yathā-arthopadeṣṭā puruṣaḥ. *Śaivaparibhāṣā*, p. 20.

105. Tad-vākyaṁ tu ākāṅkṣā-yogyatā-sannidhi-matāṁ padānāṁ samūhaḥ. *Ibid.*

106. Ākāṅkṣā ca tat-tad-anvaya-anukūla-vibhakty-ādi-samabhi-vyāhāraḥ. *SB*, p. 20.

107. Cf. the following quotations from K. Raghavan Pillai (ed. and tr.) *The Vākyapadīya* (Delhi: Motilal Banarsidass, 1971), p. 3: "*Arthapravṛittitatt-vānāṁ śabdā eva nibandhanam / Tattvāvabodhaḥ śabdānāṁ nāsti vyākaraṇādṛite.* Words are the sole guide to the truths about the behaviour of objects; and there is no understanding of the truths about words without grammar. *Taddvāramapavargasya vāṅ malānāṁ cikitsitam / Pavitraṁ sarvavidyānāmadhividyaṁ prakāśate.* A gateway to liberation, a cure to the blemishes of speech, purifier of all (other) disciplines, it shines as being applied to them. *Yathārthajātayaḥ sarvāḥ śabdākṛitinibandhanāḥ / Tathaiva loke vidyānāṁ eṣā vidyā parāyaṇam.* Just as all thing-classes depend upon word-classes similarly, in this world, this (grammar) is the basis of all disciplines."

108. Ākāṅkṣā nāma pratipattur-jijñāsā. *Śaivaparibhāṣā*, p. 20.

109. Ananvaya-niścaya-abhāvo yogyatā. *Ibid.* The same definition is put in other words: Yogyatā tv-ananvaya-niścaya-virahaḥ. *SB*, p. 20.

110. Āsattiḥ padayor-avyavadhānenopasthitiḥ. *Ibid.*

111. For more details on this from the Śaiva Siddhānta perspective, see K. Sivaraman's article "The Word as a Category of Revelation", *op.cit.*, p. 52.

112. This point is associated with the 'ripening' of *malam* and will be considered in the next chapter.

113. Cf. also, M. Hiriyanna, *Values*, p. 48.

114. The theories of error may be divided broadly into 'realistic' and 'idealistic' ones. The realistic theories are the following:

(a) *Akhyāti-vāda*, the theory that error is a lack of knowledge, i.e., that error is partial or incomplete knowledge. In other words, there is really no error as such and one should speak, rather, of a failure to distinguish the positive features of an object from the negative ones. The criterion that decides the issue, finally, is the applicability of the knowledge to practical life (*vyavahāra*). This theory is mainly associated with the Prābhākara school of Mīmāṁsā and, with significant variations, also with the Sāṅkhya school and Viśiṣṭādvaita, propounded chiefly by Rāmānuja (his version of the theory is also called *yathārtha-khyāti* or *sat-khyāti*).

(b) *Anyathā-khyāti-vāda*, the theory that error is the cognition of the object as "otherwise", i.e., as other than what it is in fact. The theory is also called *viparīta-khyāti* or cognition that is "reversed", i.e., reverse apprehension. This theory is advocated by the Bhāṭṭa school of Mīmāṁsā, the Nyāya-Vaiśeṣika school, the Yoga school, and the Śaiva Siddhānta school. It is this theory that will be discussed from the Śaiva Siddhānta point of view.

The idealistic theories may be divided into three groups:

(a) *Ātma-khyāti-vāda*, the theory that all experience in its objectivized mode is as such illusory and, by extension, the 'error' that occurs in everyday life is a 'double-error'. This theory is advocated chiefly by the Yogācāra or Vijñānavāda school of Buddhism.

(b) *Asat-khyāti-vāda*, the theory that error is the cognition of the non-existent. This theory is advocated wth significant differences in its interpretation by the Mādhyamika school of Buddhism and the Madhva school of Vedānta.

(c) *Anirvacanīya-khyāti-vāda*, the theory which points to an object which cannot be said to be this or that thing, i.e., the object is indeterminable.

It is beyond the scope of this study to deal with these theories in their manifold ramifications. As already stated, only the Śaiva Siddhānta view of *anyathā-khyāti* will be considered. For the Śaiva Siddhānta defence of this theory based on a critical rejection of the rival views on error, see K. Sivaraman, *Śaivism*, pp. 323-335.

115. Sarvatra cic-chakter-eva prāmāṇya-samarthanāt. *Śaivaparibhāṣā*, p. 23.

116. This theory, which Śaiva Siddhānta shares with Vedānta, is also called *prāpyakāri*.

117. See p. 116 above.

118. Cf., K. Sivaraman, *Śaivism*, p. 342: "Till such time as a judgment is contradicted by another judgment it is necessarily known as a valid judgment."

119. See also the definitions given on p. 104 above.

120. Cf. also the following: "Memory indeed admits of classification into valid memory (*yathārtha smṛti*) and erroneous memory (*ayathārtha smṛti*) on parity with valid and erroneous knowledge, and its exclusion from 'valid knowledge', as such seems on purely technical grounds." K. Sivaraman, *Śaivism*, p. 320.

CHAPTER 4

# *Man and the Discipline (Sādhana)*

## 4.1 *Gnosis as the only means for man's freedom*

The discussion that has been so far undertaken may be said to rest on one basic thesis: that there is the condition of the possibility of man's unfettered existence. In other words, the impact of the definition of man as a bound being (*paśu*) in the world, is to find its significance in what constitutes the meaning and definition of liberation (*mokṣa, mukti*). Seen from this perspective, it may be said that the endeavour to arrive at the nature of man's defining characteristic, as being one essentially of consciousness—described as the *ātman*—culminates in the realization, the knowledge, or the experience of this fundamental fact, as Śaiva Siddhānta sees it. The definition of man was arrived at through a transcendental reflection on the human condition, viz., of man possessing limited knowledge and of being involved in life in the world, both of which vindicate and perpetuate the apparently unending cycle of experiences (*saṁsāra*). To live in the world without perceiving things *as they are* is to live in ignorance, to be a victim of one's own deeds, and to live a life that is thereby couched in suffering.

A knowledge of this predicament of man is provided chiefly through a reflection on the categories of experience diversified, for example, in man's role as a cognitive being within the framework of the different states of consciousness (*ātma-avasthās*), together with man's use of language as the preeminent instrument or vehicle for the expression of consciousness. In attempting to follow Śivāgrayogin's systematic exposition of Śaiva Siddhānta through his commentary on the *Śivajñānabodham*, and particularly in attempting here to extract from it some aspects which lead to an understanding of man in Śaiva Siddhānta, the metaphorical language of man undergoing a journey proved useful. In several places, as will be seen, this metaphor is even explicitly stated. The metaphor of man undergoing a spiritual journey is very commonly used in Indian philosophy. Crossing the ocean of life is also usually mentioned. Metaphors, analogies and parables are fascinating linguistic techniques to make intelligible certain concepts which, in the nature of their cases, cannot be adequately explained by a purely theoretical use of language. It will be noticed that several such techniques are employed in this chapter. Many of the metaphors, etc., belong to a 'pool of images' that many schools draw from to express their philosophical insights. What this means is that at some point—if the metaphor is to be taken as realistically as it seems to be intended—the journey has to come to an end. Having said this, it is to be borne in mind that the journey is paradoxically a return to one's original and natural state, to the point from which one in fact unawares started. The metaphor is, however, a useful tool for this chapter which deals with the end of man's so-called journey.

The journey analogy, encompassing the end of the journey as well, is obvious in verse eight of the *Śivajñānabodham*, which may be a good starting point for the contents of this chapter. The verse reads:

> Being taught by a guru thus : "Having lived with the hunters, the senses, you do not know yourself," the blessed one, not different [from *śivam*] attains that state [of śivahood], having abandoned these [senses].[1]

Śivāgrayogin goes into an exegetical detail on the word 'taught' (*bodhitaḥ*) with which to begin his commentary on this verse. In his preamble to the verse he clearly states his position that the end of man's journey is reached only through gnosis (*jñāna*).[2] This standpoint is implicit in his exegesis on the word 'taught' and elaborated in the rest of his commentary on this verse. In analysing the word grammatically, he points out that it is a passive participle, which means two things simultaneously: that the person who is taught is also the one who is understood to be the agent who knows. In other words, such a one is the knower who has grasped the meaning of the teaching.[3] This conclusion is necessary to complete the meaning of the word grammatically and, semantically, it applies specifically to man's ability, having been taught, to know. There are certain conditions under which not only is this teaching given but, also, under which it serves the medium through which its meaning—which is identical with reaching the end of the journey—has the intended soteriological function. The conditions pertain to the exegesis on 'the blessed, or fortunate, one' (*dhanyaḥ*), to be dealt with presently.

The syntax associated with the word 'taught' is complete by construing it along with 'attains that state' (*prāpnotitat-padam*), which refers to the state of śivahood. This is to say that the one who is taught, attains the realization of being non-different from the nature of *śivam*. The question that this point raises is crucial to Śaiva Siddhānta ontology. It is persistently emphasized, as has already been indicated, that man essentially shares the nature of ultimate reality—the *ātman* and *śivam* are identical insofar as both are characterized as being of the nature of consciousness. In the light of this basic standpoint, how can it be said, as 'Śivāgrayogin points out anticipating the query, that man 'attains' or reaches that state of identity which, at the outset, is already presupposed as being 'eternally attained' (*nitya-prāptam*)? Śivāgrayogin's answer is that, for man in the world, it is '*as if* not attained' (*aprāpta-kalpam*).[4] Therefore, having been taught 'it is *as if* attained, like one obtains [again] the forgotten ornament seen around the neck; thus it is said that one attains this [state].[5]

In elaborating this point Śivāgrayogin arrives at a perceptive semantic conclusion in interpreting this part of the verse:

> Therefore, in saying that the one who *knows* attains that state, it follows that there is a cause for the reaching of that [state] of knowledge; and on account of the teaching, the subject is the same of both the reaching and the knowing through the idiom of mentioning together 'the one who has effected what has to be done'—[that is] on account of the teaching being the cause for the reaching of that [state], which is distinguished by knowledge through the application, generally, of the maxim concerning 'the distinguished and the distinction.'[6]

The above is a summary statement of what is the means for the realization of man's essential nature. There are several points implicit in it which are noteworthy.

From what has already been said, it is clear that the subject who is taught is the same as the one who 'attains' the state of śivahood which, as stated, is rather a recovery of an apparently 'forgotten' essential nature. This is to say that what is attained is not a 'new' state but, nonetheless, has the 'freshness' of an experience of what is in fact always known but, as it were, always forgotten to have existed, as with the forgotten ornament around the neck. What is particularly noteworthy here from the Śaiva Siddhānta perspective, is that one has to be taught, to be made aware of the presence of what is already there. The maxim of 'the distinguished and the distinction' referred to above, applies to one who is distinguished by a particular distinction. One is distinguished by having acquired the knowledge which has been taught. The distinction pertains to what qualifies one for the teaching, a certain preparation—as will be seen below—which calls simply, but no less profoundly, for an indication of what is already known. From what Śivāgrayogin says here, three significant points emerge: (a) that only the one who has the special quality of knowledge can attain the state of śivahood; (b) that it is this knowledge which leads to it; and (c) that, in fact, it is this knowledge *alone* which is responsible for it.

The manner in which the teaching is conducted is an important point for Śivāgrayogin, which he says is expressed in the verse by the word 'thus' (*iti*). The word indicates direct speech and carries with it the impact of the active voice which, grammatically, and semantically, seems to balance the deliberate use of the passive form 'being taught.' The contextual significance of this lies in being told 'you do not know yourself'. The cause for this state of ignorance is what forms part of this teaching, viz., 'having lived with the hunters, the senses.' Although the verse uses the verbal noun, gerund, construction to state the cause of the ignorance, it is clear from the context that it has to be construed as what is generally evident in an ablative construction. The cause for man's ignorance, therefore, is said to be the living with the senses, which are analogously regarded as being hunters.

If an illustration is sought which simply conveys the profound insight of man's predicament and the teaching, through it, which leads to a knowledge of man's essential nature, then this will be found in the hunter analogy which Śivāgrayogin gives in exegeting the words 'senses' and 'hunters.'[7] The analogy may be paraphrased here since it helps in following his application of it toward an understanding of man. It is a story concerning a prince who lived with hunters since his childhood. It is said that for some reason or the other (*kutaś-cit-kāraṇāt*), soon after his birth, a certain prince had to be brought up by a family of hunters who were friends of the king. The charm of the story lies obviously in the fact that the prince was reared as a hunter's child and, quite unaware of his royal birth, grew up as a hunter himself. At a dramatic moment, if the story were enacted, the king appears. He says to the prince: "you do not belong to the group of hunters, but are my son, verily [now] the king."[8] Thus, the prince is no longer under the control of the hunters whom, in fact, he now commands and, having left them, goes to his kingdom.

Śivāgrayogin applies this parable to the human situation in the following way: by living with the senses ever since creation (*saṁsāra-ārabhya*), man is ignorant of being essentially non-different from the nature of *śivam*. Later, 'when there is a maturity of *karman* and *malam*', Śiva appears in the form of a guru, with grace (*anugraha*), and says: "you are verily I" (*aham-eva tvam*).[9] Before discussing the maturity of *karman* and *malam*, it may be interesting to see how Śivāgrayogin elaborates this analogy. Just as hunters use baits to lure animals they wish to capture, so too the senses present to the *ātman* objects of enjoyment which fetter it. Ignorant of its essential nature, the *ātman* is made to identify itself with what is alien to it and, in this process, becomes entrapped. Therefore, man needs to be taught and what is significant about receiving the teaching is that the teacher (guru) is the epitome of Śiva and, thus, represents the status of one who is the supremely trustworthy person.[10]

Further, being told that one does not know oneself is by itself insufficient, insofar as the impact of the knowledge that the *ātman* is non-different from *śivam* needs to be established by a teacher through the use of reasons, etc., thereby making direct teaching indispensable: "The meaning is that the knowledge is established, devoid of [any] impossibility of understanding, through a teacher alone."[11] At this point, Śivāgrayogin points out that the injunctions of Vedic and Āgamic scripture concerning sacred study (*adhyāyana*) are implicit in the verse, viz., that a teaching must first be heard (*śravana*), then it must be reflected upon (*manana*) and, finally, that there should be a deep contemplation or meditation (*nididhyāsana*) on it, which leads to an intuitive experience of its meaning.

One of the crucial points concerning man's qualifications to become a candidate for and recipient of the teaching of ultimate reality, pertains to what has been called above the 'maturity of *karman* and *malam*.' Implicit in this statement is the overcoming not only of the primordial, overwhelming and malevolent fetter of *āṇava-malam* but, also, of the fetters of *karma-malam* and *māyā-malam* which, as already seen in the first chapter, serve a 'beneficent' role. Since the latter are needed on account of the first, what is called for in effect is basically a removal of or dissociation from *āṇava-malam*'s malevolence. As will be seen in more detail below, this has to be done in stages through the means of knowledge leading, via the inefficacy of *karman* and *māyā*, to the state of non-contact with *āṇava-malam*, i.e., to the pure state (*śuddha-avasthā*). The position is stated without equivocation:

> ...by taking into consideration the Nigamas and the Āgamas, the manifestation of *śivam* is only by first rending *malam*. As already stated this [manifestation] is not possible without gnosis.[12]

In view of the fact that man is inescapably involved in life in the world and in view of the fact, also, that the human situation is the outcome of an act of grace on the part of the lord of all beings (*paśu-pati*), it may be said that man's experiences in the world are themselves a discipline, or rather, will be transformed into it through a knowledge of this fact, as Śaiva Siddhānta sees it. Without a conscious reflection on the nature of things as they are, man suffers the polarities and extremes of involvement in the world. It is a suffering which seems to go on in endless, recurrent cycles. In this context, one can speak of the dialectics of freedom and determination in the human situation. Through the inexorable operation of the law of *karman*, man is self-condemned to a life of suffering. On the other hand, this situation itself represents an exercise of man's freedom to do one thing or the other. The key to the expression of man's essential freedom would be an exploitation of the freedom to get to know the nature of ultimate reality. The attempt to do this signifies an involvement in the world which is qualitatively different from an ignorant involvement in the inescapable discipline of life.

The aim of life in the world according to Śaiva Siddhānta is progressively and consciously to lead to an unfettered and unlimited expression of man's essential nature. This is identical with a withdrawal of the *ātman*'s association from the factor of limitation, viz., *malam*. The discipline involved in this task is a gradual dissociation, in stages, from the influences of *karman,* of *māyā* and, finally, of *āṇava-malam*. It has already been seen that it is beyond the *ātman*'s ability to overcome the overwhelming power of *āṇava-malam* which is 'born with' (*sahaja*) the *ātman.* However, insofar as *karman* and *māyā* serve the *ātman* by providing a modicum of scope for an expression of its powers of consciousness (*ātma-cit-śakti*), the *ātman* is potentially able to consciously direct them (on the analogy of the prince commanding the hunters). In other words, man is capable of taking advantage of the benevolent role of *karman* and *māyā* for the very purpose—with their own aid and with a knowledge of their nature, role and function—of nullifying their influence. The influence of *malam* itself, i.e., of *āṇava-malam,* is removed, as already stated and as will be seen again below, through *śivam*'s power of grace (*anugraha-śakti*). It will be convenient to discuss the stages of the discipline separately, i.e., with reference to the stages involved in the dissociation from fetters.

## 4.2 *The dissociation from karman*

The ingenuity of the theory of *karman* is that its own 'destruction' is built into its inexorable operation. According to the theory, *karman* thrives on the attachment to experiences in the world. In other words, the involvement in experiences leaves behind traces which, like seeds, bear fruit at the appropriate time, as already seen in the first chapter. It follows that without the attachment to experiences, the operation of *karman* is theoretically rendered useless. This point is an intricate and delicate issue. It is useful, in the present context, to recall some aspects of the theory already discussed.

The mechanics of *karman* involve the operation of three kinds of *karman*, viz., the accumulated (*sañcita*) *karman*, the presently operating (*prārabdha*) *karman*, and the *karman* which is yet to come (*āgāmi*). It is *prārabdha-karman* that is responsible for the present conditions of man's existence. Further, the operation of this type of *karman*, by definition, can only be nullified by experience (*bhoga*) in the world itself, i.e., only life in the world, for which it is itself responsible, can consume it. The impact of the reflection and knowledge of this fate of man's existence is crucial to the discipline (*sādhana*) which reconciles man with the so-called self-imposed condition of life in the world. The implications of this point for a liberated being in the world (*jīvan-mukta*) will be considered presently. What is to be noted here is the significance of *prārabdha-karman* for man, viz., that it has to follow its own course to self-annihilation, that with a knowledge of its inescapability man can cope with the human predicament, and that, consequently, *prārabdha-karman* is not necessarily an obstacle to the realization and expression of man's essentially unfettered nature of consciousness.

It is on the basis of the theory that *prārabdha-karman* is the cause for man's present situation, in the sense already seen, that the other types of *karman* are postulated. In the present context, the elimination of *sañcita-karman* is important to consider—with the treatment of *prārabdha-karman*, it is assumed that future (*āgāmi*) *karman* is of no significance, i.e., with a detached attitude towards the inescapable involvement in life in the world, *karman* is not generated, it has no 'soil' in which to implant its seed-like traces and, hence, future *karman* is effectively treated on the grounds that there can be no question of its efficacy. In view of the fact that *karman* has to be completely annihilated, the question arises as to how the accumulated (*sañcita*) *karman* can be got rid of. It is at this point that one would have to concede an 'exterior' factor, viz., a special initiation or ritual, called *dīkṣā*, in bringing to nought all the accumulated *karman*.[13] It is not necessary to enter into the elaborate details concerning *dīkṣās*. Suffice it to say in short that for Śivāgrayogin *dīkṣā* itself is not sufficient for liberation. Its function in the present context is limited only to the annihilation of *sañcita-karman*. It serves here as a purificatory aid to gnosis, which alone yields liberation.[14]

The *sañcita-karman*, as already seen (Chapter 1, p. 33), is the stock of meritorious and unmeritorious deeds in seminal form, which have to mature before the *ātman* can be said to step out of the cycle of *karman*. The inefficacy or annihilation of *sañcita-karman* is spoken of as a balance of the twin-fold *karman* (*karma-sāmya*). What exactly this means is a matter of considerable debate.[15] However, as a prerequisite for the dawn of knowledge concerning ultimate reality, the following is a noteworthy assessment of the concept:

> *Karma-sāmya* as a preliminary to the slackening of the grip of *mala* should be understood to imply a condition when accumulated merits and demerits and their fruits come to entail no difference to the affective reactions of man.[16]

In terms of the schematic framework of the categories of experience (*tattvas*) the 'journey' of the *paśu*, in progressively freeing itself from fetters (*pāśas*), 'reaches' the level of *śuddha-aśuddha-māyā*. This means that it is beyond the scope of the influence of the factor of time (*kāla*) and, more importantly, that of *rāga* which is responsible for the attachment to experiences that perpetuates *karman*.

### 4.3 *Dissociation from māyā and āṇava-malam*

Together with the balance or equanimity (*sāmya*) of the twin-fold *karman*, goes what is referred to as a maturation or ripening (*pāka, paripāka*) of (*āṇava*) *malam*. In a sense this ripening is a logical, concurrent occurrence of the systematic process which leads to the balance of *karman*. It is a disciplined, yogic attitude on the part of man—an attitude characterized by a constant reflection on the nature of things and on what constitutes man's essential nature—that serves as the prerequisite qualification for grasping the knowledge of ultimate reality. The concept of *mala-paripāka* interestingly implies a dialectical involvement in the world: on the one hand, man has to be involved in the world so as to feel the suffering (*duḥkha*) of the seemingly unending cycle of the polar experiences tacit in worldly life and, on the other hand, to be involved in the world, paradoxically without being identified with what, by definition, affords a limited expression of consciousness, viz., the instruments of the senses which make life in the world at all possible. The journey of the *ātman* is a process of maturation, of growing up, so to speak, which leads to a 'detached' involvement in the world. It is a spiritual journey in which man attempts to overcome and, thereby, to leave behind the obstacles in the journey. It is an attempt which in the Yoga system is a disciplined, psychological attitude striving to overcome man's greatest obstacle, viz., that of 'I am-ness' (*asmitā*).

As in the Yoga system, Śaiva Siddhānta regards the attitude of self-assertion as the most subtle hindrance to liberation. In the nature of the case, man's self-assertion is generally a limited expression. The root cause for limitation as such is *āṇava-malam* which imperceptibly manifests itself as an independent and exclusive 'I', not as the 'I' which, as will be seen, is essentially dependent on *śivam*. The form in which the limitation of *āṇava* is evident to man, i.e., through a transcendental reflection, is that of the intellect (*buddhi*) which operates in close collusion with the 'I'-maker (*ahaṅkāra*). In a sense, for man in the world, the progress of the journey to liberation may be said to be taken up with man's attempt to grasp the nature, function, and role of the intellect (*buddhi*) and that the 'purification' of the *ātman* begins with a purification of the *buddhi*.

In the analysis of man's role as a cognitive being, it was seen that the intellect is responsible for error in the form of doubt, misapprehension and memory. It is only the intellect which, by definition, is said to function ideally when its inherent quality of clarity (*sattva-guṇa*) dominates. In this way, devoid of error, it serves as the 'most appropriate' medium for the *ātman*'s manifestation in the world. With the balance of *karman* (*karma-sāmya*) the intellect's function is 'unhindered' by the polarities of aversion and attachment, which the category of *rāga* imposes on it. The yogic discipline involves a clear perception of things as they are with a sharp, cautious psychological analysis of not becoming a victim of what, in fact, should facilitate the 'loosening' of fetters, i.e., man has to contend with the possibility of believing to be non-assertive, what may well be a subtle, but no less powerful, self-assertion.[17] The coming to terms with such a predicament may be said to promote or advance the ripening or maturity of *malam*. In short, what the Siddhāntin calls for, is a mature attitude.

The mature attitude of the *paśu* elevates its status in the hierarchy of *paśus*[18] and corresponds to the degree of *malam*'s maturation. The maturity of *malam* is defined as the special state in which 'the dissociation [from fetters] is anticipated.'[19] Śivāgrayogin emphasizes the point that the maturity of *malam* (with the balance of *karman*) is a necessary precondition to receiving the teaching in the manner described in the verse quoted above. It is man's own efforts to take the first steps, as it were, which lead to the eligibility for being taught—on a review of the efforts from the enlightened position, however, it is acknowledged that the *śakti* intrinsic to *śivam*, is what serves as the force behind man's endeavours. In elevating its status the *paśu* 'reaches' the realm of *śiva-tattvas* which, as already seen, belong to *śuddha-māyā*. This is the threshold to liberation and is the realm in which *śivam* operates directly through the inherent *śakti*. In this context one can speak of a 'descent of *śakti*' (*śakti-pāta* or *śakti-nipāta*). It may be said that the discipline which makes the *paśu* 'ascend' to the pure realm (*śuddha-māyā*) converges with the descent of *śakti*. The signs of this status which marks the *paśu*'s eligibility to receive the knowledge of ultimate reality are clearly defined:

> Aversion to the cycle of worldly experience, the desire for liberation, the devotion to *śivam*, etc., are the characteristics of *śakti*'s descent.[20]

The outcome of such a state is that it brings fortune.[21] Hence, as the verse says, man is a fortunate or blessed being to be eligible for the teaching which leads to the state of oneness with *śivam*. In Śivāgrayogin's own words:

> The meaning here is "being fortunate and thereafter being taught"; and not "being taught and thereafter being fortunate, one attains that state."[22]

At least two points are noteworthy in the *ātman's* journey to shake off its fetters. Firstly, the teaching that is received is verbal testimony which by itself does not effect liberation (*mokṣa*). Apart from the fact that the teaching needs to be meditated upon; as seen above, it was also seen in the discussion on the Śaiva Siddhānta theory of language, that verbal testimony only *reflects* a reality which it itself is not. Moreover, it operates within the realm of *māyā* and, therefore, has a limited function. Secondly, as is implicit in the verse, the attainment of the state presupposes an abandoning of the senses which, in effect, means surpassing the limitations of the categories of experience (*tattvas*). The direct vision of *śivam* is an intuitive experience (*anubhava*) which, to use tautological language, can only be experienced. Such an experience, by definition, has to be free of the limitations which characterize life in the world. In other words, it is an experience which occurs not only with a dissociation from *māyā* but, also, from (*āṇava*) *malam*. (For more details on the latter, see 4.6 below.)

With the last quotation cited above, what Śivāgrayogin is making out a case for, is the emphasis on deep contemplation or meditation (*nididhyāsana*) which effects the direct experience. In his commentary on verse nine of the *Śivajñānabodham* (see Appendix 2) he makes the point clearly:

> From statements [in scripture] such as "the one who is Śiva is the same as I;" "one should always think about the non-difference;" and "one gets liberated through concentration and gnosis," the means of liberation is [clearly] a deep contemplation in the form of the apperception of non-difference.[23]

In elaborating his point here, and in explaining further the teaching which leads to the direct experience of *śivam* as a consequence of passing beyond *māyā* and *āṇava-malam*, Śivāgrayogin merely mentions[24] the moral of the analogy about the 'tenth person'. The story (which may be briefly stated here) goes that after crossing a violent river a person counts only nine people instead of the ten who were on the boat together. It is only when the person is made to realize that he omitted himself, that the knowledge of his error dawns in him. Śivāgrayogin's point in referring to this didactic parable is to show that one needs to be taught and that one has to experience the truth of the teaching. It may be said to apply to the context of the present discussion insofar as one does not realize the unity of oneself with *śivam* and that this ignorance is due to the association of the *ātman* with *karman, māyā* and *āṇava-malam.*

### 4.4 *The concept of non-difference (ananyatva)*

The verse under discussion says that the fortunate or blessed one is non-different. Śivāgrayogin says that the statement means the *ātman* is non-different from *śivam.* This conclusion is arrived at by taking into account the context of the statement and the hint given by the word guru or teacher used in the verse. The teacher here, according to the tradition, stands for *śivam.* The identity between the teacher and *śivam* is representative of the ultimate identity to be realized by the one being taught, the one who has yet to realize it. Śivāgrayogin raises a crucial question here, one which directly bears upon Śaiva Siddhānta ontology, viz., how is the non-difference between *śivam* and the *ātman* to be understood?[25]

In answering this question he begins by saying explicitly in which sense it is *not* to be understood. That is, the non-difference between *śivam* and the *ātman* is *not* the kind of non-difference between, for example, an object and its reflection through such means as a mirror or water, as in the case of a face and its reflection, or the sun and its reflection; nor is it the non-difference that is determined by the presence or absence of a limiting agent, such as the form of a pot which separates the inner and outer space; nor, again, is the non-difference to be understood as an absolute identity.[26] The interpretation of non-difference as, for example, between gold and a gold ornament or a snake and its coil, is not acceptable either since these examples signify basically an absolute identity, which is clearly rejected. The coexistence between space and time, which may be regarded as one unit, on the other hand, signifies an absolute difference insofar as the two parts of the unit are intrinsically different. The example of unity as between a word and its meaning is a subtle extension of two things that are basically different and is also unacceptable. The case of the unity of being that is the outcome of the realization of superimposing (*āropita*) a false reality as, for example, the form of a snake on a rope, is rejected on the grounds that the one cannot exist without the other[27] and also, it may be added, that what is superimposed does not constitute the essential nature of the substrate of the superimposition.

In arriving at the Śaiva Siddhānta interpretation of the non-difference between *śivam* and the *ātman*, Śivāgrayogin points out that Bādarāyaṇa in his *Brahmasūtras* (on which Śaṅkara bases his philosophy of absolute monism, Advaita Vedānta) mentions three ways in which non-difference is interpreted. Śivāgrayogin quotes *Brahmasūtras* 3:2, 27-29 which, in summarizing the interpretations of non-difference, give the following three examples: that of a snake and its coil, that of light and the locus of light, and that of an object and its reflection.[28] By applying the 'maxim of what is stated in the middle' (*madhyama-nyāya*) as being most important and by acknowledging that this is acceptable 'even from a superficial view' (*sthūla-dṛiṣṭeḥ*)—and, it may be added, since it seems to avoid extreme interpretations—Śivāgrayogin says that the non-difference between *śivam* and the *ātman* is to be interpreted and understood on the analogy of light and the locus of light.

The understanding of non-difference (*ananyatva*) is central to Śaiva Siddhānta and marks the special contribution of the school to the views on liberation (*mokṣa*).[29] The impact of its interpretation on the analogy of light and its locus is that it provides a scope for the unique Siddhānta view of difference (*bheda*) and non-difference (*abheda*) together as one, single representation of ultimate reality as such. In this sense, Śivāgrayogin interprets *ananyatva* (non-difference), as *advaita* or *tādātmya* (identity), on the basis of what is said in verses two, ten and eleven of the *Śivajñānabodham* (see Appendix 2). His interpretation, therefore, stands for the postulation of a unity of being as constituting both difference and non-difference combined, to the point where it is inadmissible to emphasize exclusively one or the other aspect which make up the single unit of being. In Śivāgrayogin's own words:

> Therefore, that state [of unity between *śivam* and the *ātman*] is verily one of non-difference albeit having 'a little' difference.[30]

What Śivāgrayogin is striving towards here is an interpretation of non-difference which can, theoretically at least, tolerate some kind of difference such as that between a quality (*guṇa*) and what possesses the quality (*guṇin*) on the example of light and the locus of light.

It is difficult to explain precisely the philosophical justification of the Śaiva Siddhānta insistence of non-difference which accommodates a *slight* difference (*īṣad-bheda*). The contribution and significance of this position may be said to lie in the emphasis on Śaiva Siddhānta theology over against Śaiva Siddhānta philosophical anthropology. The analysis of the school's philosophical anthropology evinces man's limitedness in respect of both the knowledge and the expression of consciousness, evident in the *ātman*'s succumbing to the influence of *malam*. The motivating force behind man's limited expression, nonetheless, has to be attributed to a power which itself provided a scope for manifestation through a 'superior' power. This force is the *śakti* intrinsic to *śivam* which, in qualitative terms, is referred to as the power of grace (*anugraha-śakti*) of Śiva or God, the lord of all beings (*paśu-pati*). The recognition and acknowledgement of man's limitedness, which leads to the postulation of a being essentially unlimited, may be said to be an act of humility occurring indeed, according to the Siddhāntin, through the grace of God. In this act the Siddhāntin upholds the sovereign and supreme status of God, albeit within man's limitations. Without the grace of the divine, man would remain in the forlorn, desperate and abandoned condition, represented in the Śaiva Siddhānta understanding of the *kevala-avasthā*. The divine, through its divine power, permeates the very essence of man and in this sense man is eternally in relation (*sambandha*) with the divine—a relation that represents a unity of being that humbly acknowledges a little difference between the divinity in man, the *ātman*, and the divinity that is termed God or *śivam*. Śaiva Siddhānta theology and Śaiva Siddhānta philosophical anthropology thus coalesce to represent a single unity of being—a unity that is paradoxically described as a unity-in-difference (*bheda-abheda*).

Man's essential non-difference from the nature of *Śivam* is obscured by superimposing the nature of the insentient senses on the *ātman*. The error derives from the involvement in worldly experiences. Man falls prey to the senses which, like hunters, entrap the sentient principle in man—the principle which, in fact, furnishes the senses with the very power to act according to their nature. Man needs to be taught, as the verse quoted earlier says, that: 'having lived with the senses, the hunters, you do not know yourself.' There is no question of interpreting this predicament of man as being unnatural (*adharma*) in itself; rather, it should be acknowledged that the senses act according to their nature as fetters and that to be liberated from the limitations they impose, implies knowing their essential nature (*pāśa-dharma*). In other words, man has to realize that the senses themselves have to be subjugated, instead of succumbing to their shackling efforts. In this way, the senses would be utilised for what is accepted to be man's highest aim (*puruṣārtha*), viz., liberation (*mokṣa*).

The expression of man's essential nature is under subjection 'on account of being overpowered by insentient things, etc., beginning with the senses, whose actions—through proximity—are limiting adjuncts superimposed [on the *ātman*], even as the clarity of a crystal [is superimposed upon] by the redness of a rose.'[31] What is important to note here, is the use of the term 'limiting adjunct' (*upādhi*). The word is derived in Sanskrit from the prefix *upā* with the verbal root *dhā* meaning 'to place upon', 'to seize' and 'to lay hold of.' As a noun the word means several things which apply in the present context: that which is put in the place of another thing; a substitute or substitution; anything which may be taken for or has the mere name or appearance of another thing.[32] The significance of Śivāgrayogin's use of the term lies in the view that 'by living with the senses.' man is controlled by them to the point where they superimpose their insentient nature on the essential clarity of consciousness (*cit*). The analogy of the crystal taking on the colour of the rose near it effectively conveys the idea of man's tarnished vision of things as they are.[33]

What Śivāgrayogin is making out a case for here is not a denial of the senses—which are indispensable to man in the world—but, rather, for the view that the essential nature of the senses not be identified with man's essential nature. Not to 'live with the senses' thus implies 'not to be identified with them.' It may be said that the closeness of the senses to the *ātman* is only symbolic of the *ātman*'s essential closeness to *śivam*. This is to say that the *ātman* should realize its relation to *śivam*—a relation which intrinsically, as already seen, is one of difference-in-non-difference. The word *upādhi* signifies the view that whilst the senses do indeed afford a defining characteristic of man, they are, nonetheless, not essential to the definition of man's intrinsic nature. In other words, man's essence can, and should, be defined without reference to the senses. Such a definition leads to the view of the *ātman* as pure consciousness which is identical with *śivam*, whilst at the same time accommodating a little difference, as already pointed out.

### 4.5 *The discipline seen as 'ten actions' (daśa-kāryāṇi)*

The discipline which leads to the knowledge of ultimate reality may also be described in terms of what is called the ten actions or 'things to be done' (*daśa-kāryāṇi*).[34] The theory may be said to be a summary of Śaiva Siddhānta insofar as it deals with the knowledge—in various stages or levels—of all the categories which make up the structure of the Śaiva Siddhānta system of thought. It was seen that liberation is effected ultimately only through gnosis (*jñāna*). What this means for a study that deals with the philosophical anthropology of the system is that in order to have a knowledge of ultimate reality, man must have a knowledge of all the categories which constitute it, as postulated by the system. The possession of such a knowledge is identical with living a life of unfettered existence. In this sense, as will be seen, the *ātman* is the orienting principle for an understanding of the ten actions of knowledge.

It has already been pointed out that ultimate reality, according to Śaiva Siddhānta, is constituted of the three ontological categories of *malam*, *ātman* and *śivam*. What is presupposed in this basic position is that without knowing one, the other categories cannot be known; or, that knowing any one of them entails a knowledge of the other two. Although schematically one may divide knowledge into stages or degrees of clarity, or of 'levels' of knowledge, in itself the knowledge or experience needs to be seen as a unitary one, as will be shown below.

For man in the world, knowledge is the order of the discovery concerning the nature and role of the categories of experience, i.e., the *tattvas* which are derived ultimately, as already seen, from *malam*. In the scheme of the 'ten actions' of knowledge, the number 'ten' is derived thus: each of the three categories of ultimate reality is 'known' in three different ways, thereby making up nine kinds of knowledge, together with a tenth called the culminating experience of ultimate reality (*śiva-bhoga*). It was seen in the discussion of man as a cognitive being that knowledge involves the perception of things *as they are* (*yathārtha*), meaning by that that such knowledge is devoid of misapprehension (*viparyaya*) and doubt (*saṁśaya*). The order and stages of the discovery concerning the nature of ultimate reality is said to correspond to this epistemological distinction (the other form of 'error', viz., memory, is not relevant to the scheme being discussed here). This is to say that in the knowledge of the *tattvas*, for example, there is what may be described as a progression from a misapprehension of their essential nature, to a doubt about them, and, finally, to a clear perception of them *as they are*. The corresponding terminology for this 'journey' towards the knowledge of *tattvas* is *tattva-rūpam*, *tattva-darśanam* and *tattva-śuddhi*. The same terminology is used for the knowledge of the *ātman* as well, viz., *ātma-rūpam*, *ātma-darśanam* and *ātma-śuddhi*. In the case of the knowledge of *śivam*, however, the following terminology is used: *śiva-rūpam*, *śiva-darśanam* and *śiva yoga*. The final experience which constitutes ultimate knowledge, as already mentioned, is *śiva-bhoga*. Before attempting to describe these ten stages of knowledge in more detail, the following points are to be noted.

The categories of *śivam*, *ātman* and *malam* correspond to a classification of ultimate reality in terms of what is *sat* (pure being itself), *sadasat* (both being and non-being) and *asat* (non-being). These are characterized respectively by *cit* (pure consciousness), *cidacit* (both consciousness and non-consciousness), and *acit* (non-consciousness). In terms of what has already been said about the terminological framework of Śaiva Siddhānta, the descriptions of *śivam* as *sat* and *cit*, and of *malam* as *asat* and *acit*, do not require further discussion. The description, however, of the *ātman* as *sadasat* and *cidacit* is of special significance not only for the Śaiva Siddhānta understanding of man but, also, for the ten actions of knowledge, insofar as they apply specifically to man who needs the knowledge of ultimate reality. This unique description of man's nature may be said to be extracted from what is stated in verse seven of the *Śivajñānabodham*: 'That which knows *śivam* and the world is the *ātman*, which is different from these two.'[35] That the *ātman* is different from both *śivam* and *malam* (the use of the word 'world' here is synonymous with *malam*) means that it is not exclusively one or the other—in the sense to be shown presently—and that it has the special status of knowing both. Its central position in the ontological framework signifies that it is capable of 'directing' its power of consciousness to both. Further, its unique status represents what has been referred to several times, viz., that the essential nature of the *ātman* is its eternal relation (*nitya-sambandha*) to *śivam* which becomes veiled through the factor of *malam*. On account of this, the *ātman* has an 'unnatural' relation to the things of the world. In either case, one of the essential defining features of the *ātman* is that it does not exist in isolation, but is always in some kind of relation. What the journey through the ten actions of knowledge leads to is the *ātman*'s awareness of this feature of its relation and, more significantly, to the awareness which is described rather as the 'recovery' of the knowledge of its unity of relation with *śivam*.

It is the *ātman*'s nature to be in relation to some factor that furnishes a clue to the understanding of the Siddhāntin's definition of it as *cidacit* and *sadasat*. Śaiva Siddhānta is unequivocal in defining the essence of man, the *ātman*, as consciousness (*cit*), as already seen. However, in the light of the *ātman*'s predicament such that it *becomes* bound and fettered by *malam*, its definition merely as consciousness needs to be qualified. The *ātman*, by definition, is not and cannot be *śivam* nor *malam*, yet it occupies a curious status in between both these two categories of ultimate reality. Viewed from the perspective of its liberated state, it is *cit* (*ātman*) in relation with an eternally unfettered *cit* (*śivam*). Viewed from the perspective of its bound state, it is a *paśu* (intrinsically still retaining its *cit* nature) in relation with *malam* (which is intrinsically insentient, i.e., *acit*). Therefore, an adequate description of its *cit* nature has to accommodate both these aspects. In other words, and in taking these points into account, Śaiva Siddhānta attempts to provide an adequate definition of man's essence, viz., the *ātman*, in a way which accounts for the *ātman*'s nature such that it could be a *paśu*—a fettered being in the world—and such that it could recover its essential unity with *śivam* through what constitutes a liberation from *pāśa*—for which, in fact, the ten actions of knowledge are intended.

The terms *cidacit* and *sadasat*, which qualify the unique nature of man's essence, are the special contribution of Śaiva Siddhānta to Indian thought. In the epistemological context, a knowledge of *acit* and *asat* must be said to take place through an agent that 'possesses' these very natures—without such a 'becoming' of the nature of what it experiences[36] knowledge cannot be said to take place. It is because the *ātman* 'becomes' a *paśu* on account of *pāśa* that it is in relation to *pāśa*, which is described as being *acit* and *asat*. That the *ātman* is in a fettered state does not preclude its expression and manifestation through its inherent power of consciousness, limited though the power may be. In this way *cit* 'becomes' *cidacit* in order to know what is *acit* (and, also, finally to know *cit*, i.e. *śivam*). The knowledge of what is *acit* contrasts it with what is of the nature of *cit*. In other words, the *cit* of *cidacit* is isolated from what is of the nature of *acit*. At this stage, through the power (*śakti*) inherent to consciousness (*cit*), it is possible, on the one hand, to have a knowledge of *acit* and, on the other, to experience the relation between *ātma-cit* and *śiva-cit* which, as seen, is one of unity in difference.[37]

The above points are summarized in the terminology of the ten 'things to be done' or actions of knowledge in the following way. *Tattva-rūpam* is a general comprehension of the categories of experience, without any self-critical understanding. Such a knowledge 'is useful practically and is the function of reason or intellect which enumerates and categorises in the interest of comprehension and control.'[38] *Tattva-darśanam* is a 'metaphysical reason' which is knowledge that is an awareness of knowledge being in 'subordination to something higher or deeper which is the condition for the very possibility of its functioning as knowledge.' Such a knowledge is indeed an insight which is 'self-critical and contemplative yet it does [not] amount to integral knowledge.' It is "prone to 'misplaced concreteness', as the knowing self detaches itself and views things abstractly." This kind of knowledge may be said to be a knowledge of the categories that still retains a vestige of the influence of the *tattvas*. In other words, such a knowledge is not yet 'purified'. This happens in the stage of *tattva-śuddhi* where knowledge is undistorted by hindrances of impurity.' In terms of the scheme of the categories of experience such a knowledge goes beyond the *tattvas* and cannot be termed knowledge as used in the empirical sense. It implies an intuitive vision which is cleansed of all impurity (*malam*) and is in this sense beyond or 'above knowledge.'

In *tattva-rūpam* and *tattva-darśanam*, the first two acts of knowledge, the knowledge in the form of *ātma-rūpam* is implicit. With *tattva-śuddhi* there is *ātma-darśanam*, with *śiva-rūpam* implicit in these kinds of knowledge. When *ātma-śuddhi* takes place, *śiva-darśana* goes with it. These phases of knowledge constitute the means (*sādhana*) for liberation (*mokṣa*) that is identical with *śiva-yoga* and *śiva-bhoga*. The above description may be schematically represented as follows:

| | | |
|---|---|---|
| 1 tattva-rūpam<br>2 tattva-darśanam } | 4 ātma-rūpam | |
| 3 tattva-śuddhi | 5 ātma-darśanam | 7 śiva-rūpam |
| | 6 ātma-śuddhi | 8 śiva-darśanam |
| | | 9 śiva-yoga<br>10 śiva-bhoga } mokṣa |

It has already been pointed out that the only means of knowledge, in both the transcendental and empirical realms, is *cit-śakti*. It 'belongs' intrinsically to *śivam* and is common to *ātman* as well. The linking thread in all the ten actions of knowledge called *daśa-kāryāni*, is *cit-śakti*. It is the means through which the union with *śivam* is effected. This stage corresponds to the *ātman* reaching the state of purity (*śuddha-avasthā*) and in terms of the *ātman*'s states of consciousness, *śiva-yoga* is the fourth (*turīya*) state of this pure realm. The culminating experience called *śiva-bhoga*, is the final state beyond the fourth (*turīyātīta*). It is the element of bliss (*ānanda*) that distinguishes these latter two states:

'A distinction is thus evident between manifestation of Grace and the ensuing manifestation of Bliss.'[39] Further:

> The constitutive element of Bliss is the *advaita*-experience. The inner significance of *advaita* consists in its being not merely a relation or union but a resulting experience of the relation. We may accordingly distinguish between the stage of 'advaitic' relation with *śakti*, and an ensuing *advaita* experience of *Śivatva*.[40]

The unity between *śivam* and the *ātman* is also analogously compared to the unity in man between the organs of the body, which serve to express sentience, and the principle of sentience. This is unambiguously stated in verse eleven of the *Śivajñāna-bodham*: 'Śiva is the guide of this [*ātman*], like the *ātman* is the guide of sight.'[41] In other words, life is permeated through and through by the underlying power of supreme divinity. This fact is obscured to ordinary man who requires to be taught it. The teaching calls for a discipline which prepares man for the culminating experience which is the knowledge of man's śivaness (*śivatva*), represented by the doctrine of the ten actions of knowledge.

One more point, finally, is relevant to the discussion in this section, viz., the noteworthy distinction between *śivam* and *śakti*. How the two are distinguished in Śaiva Siddhānta is crucial for the understanding of man's culminating experience of *śiva-bhoga* through the means of *śakti*, which operates in the ten occurrences of knowledge. Bearing in mind the Śaiva Siddhānta distinction between a quality (*guṇa, dharma*), and the possessor of the quality (*guṇin, dharmin*), the following is how *śakti* and *śivam* are distinguished. The difference between them:

> ...is the (1) polarity of causal agency (kartṛtva) and the causal means (karaṇatva), (2) of being the supporting ground (aśrayatva) and the supported or grounded (āśritatva), (3) of being the unproved or the unknowable (sarva-viṣayanirūpyatva) and the provable or the knowable (sarva-viṣaya-nirūpyatva). The last point is significant: the argument from the world (nirūpaka) to the world cause (nirūpya) is of the dharmāt dharmi

anumāna type [i.e., an inference of the possessor of a quality from the quality]. God combines within Him the inaccessible depth (Śivam) as well as the element of cognitive accessibility (Śakti) or the aspect of self-giving but for which it would not be possible to approach God through reason or revelation. The latter is the gift of śakti.[42]

The essence of man is the *ātman* which is essentially defined as *cit-śakti.* In other words, man is basically defined in terms of *śakti,* which ultimately 'belongs' to *śivam.* The culminating experience, *śiva-bhoga,* may thus be described as *śivam* 'drawing' within itself the *śakti* which served as the manifesting means of the divinity permeating existence as such. To see the *ātman* as synonymous with *śakti* is to realize the unity or identity between *śivam* and *śakti.* The words 'unity' and 'identity' are used cautiously so as to maintain the Śaiva Siddhānta insistence on the little difference between *śivam* and the *ātman.* This is necessary in order not to slide into the position of the Śivādvaitins, where the identity between the two is regarded as an absolute one. Such an absolute unity between *śivam* and the *ātman* is categorically opposed to Śaiva Siddhānta ontology.

### 4.6 *On the non-contact with malam*

The key factor in the realization of the *ātman*'s unity with *śivam* is the removal of the obscuring veil of *malam* which has the effect of 'disuniting' the two. There are several implications concerning the status of *malam,* particularly with regard to the liberated being (*jīvan-mukta*), and it is necessary to discuss a few relevant aspects of Śivāgrayogin's 'thoughts on the non-contact with malam' (*mala-asaṁsparśa-vicāraḥ*).[43] What prompts these thoughts is the use of the word 'untouched', or the being without contact, used in verse ten of the *Śivajñānabodham:*

> Untouched by *malam, māyā,* etc., the perfected one—become one with *śivam*—is one who has self-knowledge, and has [his] own activity dependent on that [*śivam*].[44]

In commenting on this verse, he says it is clear that "on account of the removal of *malam* through an intuitive perception (*sākṣātkāra*) [of *śivam*] there is non-contact [with *malam*]."[45] By the dissociation or non-contact with *malam* is *not* to be understood that there is a 'destruction of *malam*'s power' (*mala-śakti-vināśa*).[46] To regard *malam* as being destroyed is to contradict the ontological status it is given in Śaiva Siddhānta, i.e., as one of the three constituents of ultimate reality. Further, in order to accommodate the possibility of liberation from *malam*, granting its ontological status, liberation is not to be seen as becoming actual on account of 'the non-pervasive existence of *malam*'s power' (*mala-śakter-avyāpya-vṛittitva*).[47] If this were the case then there need not be any discussion of the *ātman*'s bound condition. That is, if *malam* were non-pervasive—and if this non-pervasiveness were to account for the possibility of liberation—then it would also be non-pervasive in the so-called bound state. In this case, the *ātman* would have to be regarded as being, in fact, liberated. This view is rejected because life in world is a bound state of existence, as already seen in the foregoing chapters, and man's goal is to be liberated from fettered, worldly existence. To see *malam* as non-pervasive is to lead to the contradiction of the bound state being the liberated state.

To regard *malam* as being all-pervasive and possessing manifold *śaktis* or powers, on the other hand, has other implications. In the first place, this would point to the impossibility of liberation, on the theory of the all-pervasiveness of *malam*. If it is suggested that one of its powers vanishes to make liberation possible, then it would have to be acknowledged that the other powers are still operative (besides, it could be argued that at some point *malam* would vanish with the vanishing of its powers). On this theory, granting *malam*'s ability to obscure the *ātman*'s nature, not a single *ātman* can ever be liberated because *malam*, at the outset, is said to be all-pervasive.

The crucial question now is: if liberation means that there is no efficacy of *malam*'s power of obscuration over a particular *ātman*, how is such liberation possible and how is it to be explained? It is to be remembered that all the three categories of ultimate reality, including *malam*, are all-pervasive, eternal and indestructible. The basic problem under discussion amounts to the need to explain how two all-pervasive categories, the *ātman* and *malam*, are no longer in any relation or union—the explanation would also in fact account for the ontological status of all the three categories of ultimate reality, as will be shown. There is no doubt, according to Śaiva Siddhānta, that liberation involves a separation, dissolution or disjunction between the two. In this sense only can one speak of a 'destruction' of *malam*. In Śivāgrayogin's own words: "Therefore, the separation is the destruction of the contact" (*taṣmāt-saṁyoga-nāśo viśleṣaḥ*).[48] The words used here are carefully selected and are consistent with the ontological status of both *malam* and the *ātman*. Śivāgrayogin's explanation entails a destruction of the *union* between the two and not the destruction of *malam* itself—if *malam* were destroyed the question arises as to how it came to exist in the first place and, further, if it were destroyed now, in liberation, then there can be no logical guarantee that it could not exist again. By saying that the *union* is destroyed, the Siddhāntin obviates the problem of accounting for the origin of *malam* which, in any case, is said to be eternal and all-pervasive.

However, the objection above may be levelled against the view of the very disjunction itself of *malam* from the *ātman*, i.e. what 'guarantee' is there that the two would not be conjoined again? If this were to be acknowledged, the entire justification of the possibility of liberation is in jeopardy, insofar as man's bound condition would return. In other words, liberation would be encompassed within the framework of *saṁsāra*, the recurrent cycle of existence couched in pain—liberation then would be a temporary state of bliss equivalent to a period of joy in the world.

Śivāgrayogin's answer to these problems is:

> It cannot be said that there is the contingency of an obscuration through a recurrence of the union, because of the absence of [any] other *karman*, etc., which are the cause for the union.[49]

Underlying this answer is the entire analysis of Śaiva Siddhānta philosophical anthropology and the discipline which leads to the equanimity of the two-fold *karman*, leading to the maturity of *malam*, and culminating in the divine grace (*anugraha*) which, once and for all, blissfully unites the *ātman* with *śivam*. *Malam* exists eternally and its disunion from the *ātman* marks the unveiling of the eternal union between *śivam* and the *ātman*, which was obscured by the power of *malam*. This is to say that the positive role of *malam* indicates a life of fettered existence, its negative role implies a life of freedom or liberation.

The state of liberation, which occurs when there is the absence of any contact between *malam* and the *ātman*, can be explained in the metaphorical terms of light and darkness. Darkness may be said to be 'conspicuous' by its very absence in the presence of light. It cannot be said to be destroyed once and for all because it reappears when the light is withdrawn. In applying this analogy to liberation, *śivam* would be the light that keeps darkness at bay, so to speak. The light of *śivam* is all-pervasive, all-powerful, eternal and untouched by any other factor. In the state of liberation the *ātman* shines in unison with *śivam* and, together, both remain untouched by *malam*—*śivam* eternally so and the *ātman* through the grace of *śivam*. *Malam* cannot be said to lurk around the periphery of the range or potency of the light and thereby, in fact, 'encompass' the light—in this case, the light-darkness analogy is inadequate. *Śivam*'s light is beyond human comprehension and one can only repeat the superlative descriptions of the power of *śivam* contained in scripture. *Śivam* is the light beyond all lights, the power beyond all powers, the light of all lights, the power of all powers. Light and power are potent only through *śivam*'s light and power. And it is because *śivam* is the *ātman*'s guide that there is the advice: "therefore, supreme devotion should be had to this one who is the *ātman*'s aid."[50]

### 4.7 *The liberated being* (*jīvan-mukta*)

The description of one who, through the success of the discipline with the aid of grace, is liberated in the world, is given in verse ten of the *Śivajñānabodham* quoted at the beginning of the previous section.[51] The question that arises over such a being concerns the evident association with the world, the body and the apparent involvement in experiences like other beings. One who has the knowledge of ultimate reality, i.e., the wise, perfected one, is not expected to be involved in 'the mirage of worldly existence.'[52] Such an existence seems to contradict the basis of the discussion on liberation, with the tacit implication of being rid of the very instruments which signify a fettered life.

Śivāgrayogin's explanation accounting for the life in the world of a liberated being is implicit in the words, quoted above, about there being no 'other *karman*.' What this means is that apart from *prārabdha-karman*, there is no other *karman*, i.e., such a being has neither *malam* nor *sañcita* and *āgāmi-karman*. This is to say that *prārabdha-karman* alone is responsible for the wise one's continued existence in the world, while in fact being liberated. The understanding of the liberated being's state rests on grasping the full impact of the *karman* theory. In all the schools that accept the theory, particularly insofar as it pertains to the discussions on liberation (*mokṣa*), there is the acknowledgement of one basic thesis, which Śivāgrayogin quotes, viz., that "*prārabdha* is destroyed by experience, the rest [*sañcita* and *āgāmi*] is burnt by knowledge."[53] This thesis is based on the law of *karman* which requires the fruit of past actions, i.e., those which are already in the process of maturation, to find their end only by reaping their effects in the world. This accounts for the wise one's continued existence in the world. Despite the law, the fruit of the discipline, viz., the acquisition of the knowledge of ultimate reality, is not denied.

In other words, gnosis serves two functions in the context under discussion. It effects the achievement of man's final goal, viz., liberation (*mokṣa*), which constitutes the highest value to be sought by man (*puruṣārtha*). Gnosis also makes possible the reaping of *karman* without perpetuating it, as would otherwise be the case, i.e., in the state of ignorance, prior to the dawn of knowledge. There is a qualitative difference in the *attitude* with which man is involved in the two states, which appear to be the same at first sight. Firstly, as verse ten of the *Śivajñānabodham* says, the activity of the perfected one is 'dependent on that [*śivam*].' In other words, it is not dependent on the attachment and aversion characteristic of worldly life, which vindicates and perpetuates life in the world. Here, in the world, the process of reaping *karman* involves the accumulation of further *karman* in the process. However, with *śivam known* to be the guide of the *ātman*, as the *ātman* is the guide of the senses (as already seen), the status of such a being is in fact not of this world.

Such a being undergoes the experiences of joy and suffering in the world as a formality, so to speak, as required by the law of *karman*. Life no longer oscillates between the extremities of experience but is a constant, steady flow of the experience of *śivam*'s bliss (*śiva-ānanda*), ever fresh and ever new.[54] It is a life of eternal wakefulness to the reality of *śivam*. The world is seen in the light of the light of all lights. Man's entire journey which, willy nilly, is already in progress, is perceived as being possible only through an act of divine grace for man's own benefit. The end of the journey is the recovery of man's essential unity with *śivam*. In this sense, experience in the world (*prapañca-bhoga*) is transformed into the bliss of the experience of *śivam* (*śiva-bhoga*).

The enlightened being is beyond all limitations, beyond the influences of worldly existence, and beyond the discipline which vouchsafed the prize. The continued life in the world is the outcome only of *prārabdha-karman*. It was already seen that *karman* is described as a *malam*, albeit, a beneficent one. The *prārabdha-karman* of the liberated being has to be understood in a special way, i.e., as a kind of *karman* that entails only the removal of the traces or vestiges (*vāsanā*) of *malam* and not, as with ordinary beings, as effecting or causing any further accumulation of *karman*. Therefore, *prārabdha-vāsanā*, literally the impressions left behind by *prārabdha-karman*, is to be understood as *mala-vāsanā*, the lingering traces of impurity although the root cause, viz., *malam*, has been removed.

Two analogies are generally given to explain the phenomenon of *vāsanā* as it applies to the liberated being. One is in terms of a spice container—and the spice called asafoetida is generally mentioned because of its intense smell—which retains vestiges of the spice's aroma, even when the container is empty. In the same way, *prārabdha-karman* is, for all practical purposes, defunct in that it cannot take root and thereby germinate at any appropriate time—it is in fact as useless as the aroma of an empty spice container. It is only its traces, the lingering vestiges, that are a harmless cause of worldly desire 'through sheer force of habit.'[55] The other analogy that is used to explain the liberated being's continued life in the world is that of the potter's wheel. When the potter is finished with his creation, the wheel continues to rotate for a time, by the sheer force of the momentum that was originally built up by the potter himself. When its own force is spent or dissipated, the wheel comes to rest of its own accord, well after its rotating power is withdrawn. In the same way, the liberated being continues to live in the world until the lingering force of the involvement in the world is spent. The driving force of life in the world, viz., the attachment (*rāga*) to transitory experiences, is withdrawn but life continues—as if normally—until the dying force comes to a standstill. In both analogies there is a tacit recognition of the power of knowledge (*jñāna*) which makes possible the life in the world which is not of the nature of the world.

Verse nine of the *Śivajñānabodham* recommends a contemplation of the five sacred syllables[56] and this needs to be explained. The liberated being is by definition free from all obligations and free to act in accordance with the 'free will' that goes with any definition of liberation. The recommendation is to be seen in the spirit in which it is made, viz., as a recommendation. The verb 'should contemplate' (*dhyāyet*) is to be taken literally, i.e., as an optative form which is deliberately used over against the imperative form that carries the force of an injunction. The contemplation is recommended for 'warding off the lingerings of Impurity (*vāsanā-mala*).'[57]

The sacred formula comprises two words which make up five syllables, viz., *śivāya namaḥ* (obeisance to Śiva). Although grammatically speaking the meaning is the same in whichever order the words are put, esoterically, however, it is auspicious in the sequence given—it is interesting to note that the word *śiva* also means 'auspicious' and in its personified form means 'the auspicious one', viz., Śiva. In this form it is also called the five sacred syllables which lead to liberation (*mukti-pañcākṣara*). This formula contains the entire philosophy of Śaiva Siddhānta: *śi* stands for *śivam*, *vā* for *śakti*, *ya* for the *ātman*, *na* for the obscuration power (*tirodhāna-śakti*), and *ma* for *malam*. It is significant to note that while the *ātman*, represented by the syllable *ya*, here too—as in the ontological framework of the three categories of ultimate reality—occupies a central position (in this case, between the two syllables on either side of it), it *belongs* to the word *śivāya*. In other words, the essential unity of the *ātman* with *śivam*, and not with *malam*, is what is represented in the sacred formula and is what is to be meditated upon. The liberated being perceives this state of unity and its recommended contemplation serves the purpose of showing obeisance for the grace of liberation, i.e., the removal of the *ātman*'s *malam* through the power integral to *śivam*.[58] Further:

> The recital of *pañcākṣara*...carries with it a total disvaluation or depreciation of self, disvaluation in respect of its very being as an independent thing, and a complementary appreciation of Śiva as the Supreme Being and value.[59]

The liberated being in the world (*jīvan-mukta*) is one who is purified of all taints (*malam*) and, by virtue of the knowledge of ultimate reality, reaches the state of purity (*śuddha-avasthā*). It marks the end of man's journey. Scorched by the travails of the journey through life in the world, the perfected being now experiences the bliss of 'the shade of the state of *śivam*.'[60] When the *prārabdha-karman* is dissipated the *jīvan-mukta*'s body perishes and there is what is called *videha-mukti* (bodiless liberation). Once the threshold of the pure state is reached, the point of no return has been achieved. The divine grace that was obscured is now experienced in its unfettered glory. It is this grace that eternally makes evident to the *ātman* its eternal, blissful unity with *śivam*.

## NOTES

1. See Appendix 2.
2. ...jñānam-eva sākṣāt-tat-prāpti-sādhanam...*SB*, p. 351. It may be noted here that Śivāgrayogin's emphasis on gnosis is a reinterpretation, and not a rejection, of the Āgama theory of *mokṣa* through *dīkṣā* alone. For Śivāgrayogin, *dīkṣā* is a ritualistic purification which is an aid to *jñāna*, the only means for *mokṣa*, according to him. Referring especially to the *Sarvajñānottarāgama*—a text which he often refers to and one which is held in the highest esteem by the specific tradition to which Śivāgrayogin belongs, viz., Skanda-paramparā—he says (*SB*, p. 353), about the means for liberation, that "there, gnosis is the cause for obtaining it" (*Tatra jñānasya tat-prāpti-hetutve*...). He immediately quotes the following from

this text: "The one who in fact knows the *ātman*, being superior, is one who—being in whatever state—is set free without effort" (*Ātmānaṁ paramo bhūtvā yo vijānāti tattvataḥ. Sa mucyate tv-ayatnena sarva-avasthāṁ gato'pi sann-iti...*). For the importance of *dīkṣās* in the Āgamas, see especially the two articles by H. Brunner: "Importance de la littérature âgamique," *Indologica Taurinensia*, vols., III-IV, 1975-76, *Proceedings of the Second World Sanskrit Conference*, 9-15 June, 1975 (Torino: Instituto di Indologia), pp. 107-124; and "Le mysticisme dans les āgama śivaites," *Studia Missionalia*, vol. 26 (1977): 287-314.

3. Tataś-ca boddhā ity-apy-artho labdhaḥ. *Ibid.*, pp. 351-352.
4. *Ibid.*, p. 352.
5. ...prāptam-iva bhavati vismṛita dṛiṣṭam kaṇṭhasya-graiveyakam-iveti prāpnoti-ity-ucyate. *Ibid.*
6. Tataś-ca boddhā tat-padaṁ prāpnoti-ity-utsargataḥ prāpta-viśiṣṭa-vaiśiṣṭya-nyāyena bodha-viśiṣṭasya-tat-prāpti-hetutva-bodhanāt-siddha-sādhya-samabhivyāhāra-nyāyād-bodha-prāptyoḥ samāna-kartṛikatva-bodhanāc-ca bodhasya tat-prāpti-hetutvaṁ pratīyate. *Ibid.*
7. *SB*, pp. 356-357. The hunter analogy also appears in *Bṛihadāraṇyaka Upaniṣad*, 2: 1-20, which Śaṅkara refers to in his *Brahmasūtrabhāṣya*, 1:1,4.
8. ...na tvaṁ vyādha-jātīyaḥ kintv-asmad-apatyaṁ mahārāja eva...*SB*, 356.
9. ...paścāt-karma-mala-paripāke saty-anugraha-pūrvakaṁ guru-rūpeṇa śivenokta-prakāreṇa-aham-eva tvam-iti.., *SB*, p. 356.
10. Cf., *Śaivaparibhāṣā*, p. 135, where it is said that, apart from possessing virtues and being without faults (*doṣa-hīna*): "A guru is also one [who is] not a bound being, but one who has acquired the nature of Śiva through direct intuition, arising from the fruition of listening to, reflecting on, and deeply contemplating the Vedas, Āgamas, etc." (Guruś-ca na paśutva-yogī. Kiṁ tu nigama-āgama-ādi-śravaṇa-manana-nididhyāsana-paripāka-adhīna-sākṣātkāreṇa sampanna-śiva-bhāvaḥ.)
11. Asambhāvanā-rahita-dṛiḍha-avabodho guruṇaiva saṁbhavati-iti-bhāvaḥ. *SB*, p. 355.
12. ...nigama-āgama-paryālocanayā mala-vidāraṇa-pūrvikā śiva-abhivyaktir-evā. Sā ca jñānaṁ vinā na sambhavati-ity-uktam. *SB*, p. 353.
13. Sivāgrayogin defines *dīkṣā* as what gives one the eligibility for Śaiva practice. Three such initiations are compulsory rituals in Śaiva Siddhānta: *samaya-dīkṣā* and *viśeṣa-dīkṣā*, both of which make one eligible for rendering services in the Śaiva temples and the observance of obligatory duties; the third, *nirvāṇadīkṣā*, is what makes one eligible for the study of the Āgamas. See also next note.
14. For details on *dīkṣā* according to Śivāgrayogin, see especially the relevant sections of his commentary on verse eight of the *Śivajñānabodham*, *SB*, pp. 374-420; and chapter five of his *Śaivaparibhāṣā*, pp. 132-136. See also K. Sivaraman, *Śaivism*, pp. 380-388; V.A. Devasenapathi, *Śaiva Siddhānta*, pp. 236-245; J. Gonda, *Change and continuity in Indian Religion* (The Hague: Mouton and Co., 1965), pp. 429-435 (these pages deal with *dīkṣā* in Śaivism and form part of Chapter X, which is concerned with *dīkṣā*

as a whole, analysing its origins and performance in various religious groups).

15. Cf. also: "The meaning of the term *karma-sāmya* has been a matter of great controversy in the writings of Śaiva Siddhānta." K. Sivaraman, *Śaivism*, p. 394.
16. *Ibid.*, p. 395.
17. Whilst Śaiva Siddhānta freely adopts the yogic discipline expounded by Patañjali, the basic ontological difference between the two is to be especially noted. The Yoga system would not concede the Śaiva Siddhānta view of the *ātman* being non-different from, and even dependent on, *śivam*. Further, as already pointed out, there are three categories of ultimate reality according to the Siddhāntin, as opposed to the two of the Yoga system.
18. Śaiva Siddhānta speaks of three kinds of *paśus:* the *sakala-paśu*, which has been referred to as man, associated with all the three kinds of *malam*, viz., *āṇava*, *māyā* and *karman;* the *pralayākala-paśu*, associated with *āṇava* and *māyā;* and the *vijñānākala-paśu*, associated only with *āṇava-malam*. See especially *Śaivaparibhāṣā*, pp. 65-67 for further details.
19. Malasya paripāko hi viśleṣaunmukhya-avasthā-viśeṣaḥ. *Ibid.*, p. 134.
20. Asya ca śakti-pātasya saṁsāra-vidveṣa-mumukṣā-śiva-bhakty-ādīni cihnāni. *Ibid.*
21. In the technical language of Śaiva Siddhānta, this means that *karma-sāmya* and *mala-paripāka* lead to a removal of *tirodhāna-śakti* (the obscuration power). This is identical with *śakti* acting as *anugraha-śakti* (the power of grace). When this takes place, it is called *śakti-nipāta* (the 'descent' of *śakti*, i.e., of grace). See also, K. Sivaraman, *Śaivism*, pp. 394-396.
22. Atra dhanyas-san paścād-bodhita-iti sambandhaḥ. Na tu bodhitas-san paścād-dhanyas-tat-padaṁ prāpnoti-iti. *SB*, p. 360.
23. Tatra yaś-śivas-so'ham-eveti advaitaṁ bhāvayet-sadeti dhyānāj-jñānāt-pramucyata-iti ca vacanād-advaita-bhāvanā-rūpa-nididhyāsanaṁ mokṣa-sādhanam. *SB*, p. 445.
24. *SB*, p. 446.
25. This question is central to Śaiva Siddhānta and what is presented here are some aspects of the discussion on it by Śivāgrayogin, taken from his commentary on verse eight of the *Śivajñānabodham*. For a general, critical analysis of the *advaita* doctrine from the Śaiva Siddhānta perspective, see K. Sivaraman, *Śaivism*, pp. 141-152, pp. 412-415, and see also the fifteen kinds of identity given on pp. 616-617.
26. *SB*, p. 354.
27. ...āropito vā-ananyatvaṁ tad-vad-atraikaṁ vinā'nyasya-avasthāna-abhāvāt...*Ibid.*, pp. 354-355.
28. *Ibid.*, p. 355. The three *sūtras* are: "But because of the twofold reference (in the Scriptures) (the relation of the Highest Self with the Jīva-Self) is like (the relation of) a snake to its coils"; "Or else it is like the light and its source, inasmuch as both are Teja (luminous)"; and "Or rather (the relationship between the Jīva-Self and the Highest Self, is) as has been stated

earlier (in Sūtra 25)", translated by V.M. Apte, *Brahma-Sūtra Shāṅkara-Bhāṣya*, pp. 604-605.

29. What follows is basically the Śaiva Siddhānta view of *mokṣa*, as represented by Śivāgrayogin in *SB*. For his refutation of the views of other schools of thought, see especially, *SB*, pp. 470-481, and *Śaivaparibhāṣā*, pp. 153-160.
30. Tasmād-īṣad-bhede saty-abheda eva tattvam. *SB*, p. 354.
31. Āropitair-indriya-ādy-upādhi-sannidhāna-kṛitair-jāḍya-ādibhir-abhibhavāt japā-lauhityeneva sphaṭikagatā svacchatā. *SB*, p. 355.
32. M. Monier-Williams, s.v., *upādhi.*
33. The language of superimposition is used with caution, especially since the Śaiva Siddhānta use of it here differs radically from that of the Advaitins. For the Advaitin, *brahman* is the only reality. On account of ignorance, man superimposes on it qualities alien to its intrinsic nature. The stock example of such a case is the superimposition of snake's features onto a rope. Ultimately, however, both the snake and the rope are unreal for the Advaitin—the analogy serves the function only of pointing to the substrate of all existence, viz., *brahman*, which alone is the single, ultimate reality. For the Śaiva Siddhāntin, on the other hand, the world (the word is used as a synonym for *malam*), the *ātman*, and *śivam* are the three categories which constitute ultimate reality. The language of superimposition is used in the present context only to distinguish the sentient nature of the *ātman* from insentient things, such as the senses. What it demonstrates is the view that man's perception is coloured by the senses as a crystal's appearance is tinged by the colour of the flower near it—the analogy is no reflection on the ontological status of the categories of ultimate reality postulated by Śaiva Siddhānta.
34. The analysis here is based on K. Sivaraman, *Śaivism*, pp. 372-418. The significance of the "ten actions" for Śaiva Siddhānta is that: "This doctrine sums up in a single formula the philosophy of spiritual life—Means (*sādhana*) as well as the Fruit (*phala*)." *Ibid.*, p. 373. Although Śivāgrayogin does not elaborate the scheme quite in the way elaborated here, it may be referred to because it clearly captures the stages of the discipline, taking into account the whole of Śaiva Siddhānta thought.
35. See Appendix 2.
36. K. Sivaraman, *Śaivism*, p. 379.
37. *Ibid.*, p. 375: "It is knowledge of *ātman* that holds the key for comprehending the sphere of tattvas on the one side and the sphere of spirit on the other."
38. *Ibid.*, p. 373. Until otherwise indicated, the subsequent quotations are taken from the same place.
39. *Ibid.*, p. 412.
40. *Ibid.*
41. See Appendix 2.
42. K. Sivaraman, *Śaivism*, p. 519. Expressed, *ibid.*, in technical language, the difference is: "Śiva signifies the dharmas of (i) kartṛtva, (ii) āśrayatva, (iii) sarva-viṣayānirūpyatva, (iv) parameśvaratva, (v) mahattva, (vi) vyāpakatva.

Śakti, in contrast is: (i) karaṇatva, (ii) āśritatva, (iii) sarvaviṣaya-nirūpyatva, (iv) paramaiśvaryatva, (v) mahimārūpatva, (vi) vyāptitva. The two sets are not synonyms of each other, and hence *different*."

43. *SB*, p. 461.
44. See Appendix 2.
45. Tatra-malasya tāvat sākṣātkāreṇa-apasāritatvād-asaṁsparśaḥ. *SB*, p. 461.
46. *Ibid.*
47. *Ibid.*
48. *Ibid.*, p. 462.
49. Na ca punas-saṁyogotpattyā-āvaraṇa-prasaṅga iti vācyam. Saṁyoga-kāraṇasya-anyatara-karma-āder-abhāvāt. *Ibid.* See the next section for the explanation of "other karman."
50. Verse eleven of the *Śivajñānabodham*, see Appendix 2.
51. See also *ibid.*
52. Verse nine, *ibid.*
53. Prārabdhaṁ bhogato naśyec-cheṣaṁ jñānena dahyate. *SB*, p. 495.
54. Cf., "...there is an eternal novelty, a perpetual freshness about the experience." K. Sivaraman, *Śaivism*, p. 415.
55. *Ibid.*, p. 411.
56. See Appendix 2.
57. K. Sivaraman, *Śaivism*, p. 403.
58. Tathā-ca śivaṁ sva-śaktyā ātmano mala-nivartakatvena dhyāyed-ity-arthaḥ. *SB*, p. 451.
59. K. Sivaraman, *Śaivism*, p. 403.
60. Verse nine of the *Śivajñānabodham*, see Appendix 2.

# *Conclusion*

On the basis of the foregoing investigation into Śivāgrayogin's *Śivāgrabhāṣya*, the Śaiva Siddhānta analysis of man may be said to rest on the distinction between sentience and insentience. The proof that there is an *ātman*, the principle of sentience, in the body, therefore, is of crucial significance not only for the essential definition of man but, also, for what is expressed or manifested in man's everyday experiences. Without the principle of sentience, viz., consciousness, so-called man would be reduced to a corpse. For man, life in the world involves a close relationship between the organs of the body and the conscious, sentient principle which makes their functions possible. The unity of being between sentience and insentience is indispensable for a meaningful life in the world. Crucial to such a life is a 'harmonious' relationship between the two which derives from a knowledge of their essential natures.

It has been said, in a somewhat dramatic way, that the senses are like hunters, making a concerted effort to trap sentience. The attraction of their ploys leads to a subjection to their influences. The Śaiva Siddhānta analysis of this predicament implies that the way in which the senses 'act'—the power of action being derived, in fact, from the sentient principle—is in accordance with their essential nature. As hunters, the senses can do nothing but hunt and, to extend the analogy, their prey can only be sentience, with which they have a close relationship. The sign of their influence is the passion (*rāga*) for certain kinds of experiences, i.e., an attachment to what is pleasing, with a tacit aversion or repugnance (*dveṣa*) to what is unpleasing. Without a knowledge of what constitutes the essential nature, role and function of the insentient categories of man's experience—including, most immediately, the senses—man is in the throes of life, oscillating between the extremes of experiences and, thereby, feels life in the world to be one of suffering or pain (*duḥkha*).

The principle of sentience, or consciousness as such, is a

victim of the limiting effects of the senses, in the manner already elaborated according to the Śaiva Siddhānta standpoint. The close relationship between them, making up what constitutes the unity of being referred to as man in the world, is no reflection on the essential nature of the two, i.e., the all-pervasive, eternal essence of consciousness is not at stake or at risk on account of the limiting adjunct of insentience. The senses are not only indispensable for life in the world but are, also, the instruments through which consciousness is given a scope for expression and manifestation. A reflection on the positive role of the senses is the first step toward coming to grips with man's predicament. Such a reflection presupposes an inquiry into why man is subject to passion (*rāga*), with its inbuilt structure of attachment and aversion to certain kinds of experiences—a structure which splits the nature of what in fact belongs to one category. This is to say that passion (*rāga*) is a category that is of the nature of insentience, with a single function. To desire what is 'pleasant' and, thereby, to avoid what is 'unpleasant' is an inadmissible separation—based on ignorance—of a category function which, in fact, should be regarded as being essentially one, insofar as both are effects of a single factor.

No sooner is the nature of life in the world seen to be what involves both kinds of so-called desirable and undesirable experiences than one strikes at the heart of the mechanism which is responsible for the perpetuation and vindication of polar or extreme experiences, viz., of the law of *karman*. In other words, the craving for certain things and the aversion to others, leads to an unending accumulation of desires. The striving toward what is desirable only, is an attitude to life which ignores an integral part of the nature of what influences worldly life, i.e., of what also causes so-called undesirable experiences. The law of *karman* inexorably presupposes a reaping of the results of all kinds of actions and deeds. The problem for man, who possesses limited knowledge, is the inability to know precisely which actions are meritorious, which previous actions are responsible for the present conditions of existence, and what effects are yet to take place. In any case, to exploit such knowledge serves the purpose mainly of indicating what probably is meritorious leading, thereby, to the harvest of so-called pleasant effects. However, this is not the solution to the problem of man's fettered existence. To desire what is pleasing is still to be a victim of the law responsible for continued fettered life. What is called for is a balanced, mature attitude where life's joys are to be taken *in the same spirit* as life's sufferings. The basis of this theory is that one is responsible for one's own situation. To realize the impact of this point is the first step to achieving a balanced attitude, where the effects of one's deeds are borne with equanimity.

The senses exploit man's weakness and limited knowledge—which they themselves contribute to causing—to the point where man becomes subjugated. The sign of their influence is most striking in their role in cognition, i.e., in man's subjection to error in the perception of things. There is no gainsaying that without the role of the senses life in the world is impossible. There is no doubt either that, as instruments of perception, the senses have a limited capacity, that they themselves cannot perceive things *as they are*. The senses share the essential nature of the insentient things which they apparently perceive. The indispensability of the senses for life in the world does not put them in a state of authority—the senses perform as they do only through the power of the consciousness, which makes their function at all possible. To consciously direct them, and not to be directed by them, constitutes the attempt not to fall into the pattern, and thus become a victim, of their hunter-like behaviour. In other words, one attempts not to fall prey to the senses' caprice in indicating what is pleasing, making it appear as a value to be sought. In this way, the mechanism of the *karman* law is interfered with, insofar as an attempt is made to withdraw the fuel for *karman*, viz., *rāga* or passion, which is responsible for the attachment to what is pleasant, with the implicit *dveṣa* or aversion to what is unpleasant. This is to say that the senses are made to turn direction. Instead of their usual outgoing attitude, they are consciously directed 'inwards' so as to 'reveal' their nature. This attempt involves a discipline which exploits the full—albeit intrinsically limited—capacity of the senses, i.e., consciousness takes command.

From what has been said above, the unity of being for man entails a constant juxtaposition of the sentient and the insentient. To be involved in the world, swayed by the whims of the senses is to fasten the fetters of an already bound existence. The exploitation of what is at the dispensation of consciousness is a step toward 'loosening' the fetters. Life in the world may thus be said to serve a double function: on the one hand, it perpetuates the cycles of inescapable experiences and, on the other, it provides the necessary atmosphere and framework for the elimination of bondage as such. With the control of the senses, the law of *karman* is itself gradually under control and, with this, the status of man is elevated. It marks the phase of maturity, of a balanced attitude, that goes along with the constant attempt to see things *as they are*. Seeing things as they are, reveals the striking contrast between the insentient categories of experience and the principle of sentience, consciousness as such, at whose disposal they are. Ordinary perception is transformed into 'internal' perception. This latter perception, also a direct and immediate one, makes evident (as already seen) the polarities such as joy and suffering, which characterize the nature of worldly experience. It is particularly in this context that the question arises as to why man *needs* to undergo the apparently unending cycle of polar experiences. To persist in this line of reflection is gradually to delve deeper into the nature and function of each of the categories of experience. It indicates a yogic attitude which is represented in the constant reflection on the nature of things. It may be said, further, that the experiences of inner perception make more urgent the desire to break the link in the chain of fettered existence.

Perception, aided by inference and verbal testimony, serves as a platform which reveals a dimension of reality not readily open to an attitude limited merely to an involvement in worldly experience. Perception is man's most basic instrument of cognition. The significance of the directness and immediacy which, by definition, characterizes the nature of perception is to be exploited to its full capacity. Strengthened by inference and verbal testimony, it transcends its limitation to the perception only of things in the world—a limitation that is not realized in the habitual indulging of one's desires. The conscious inward direction of the senses demarcates them from the power which makes their functions possible. The power of consciousness, intrinsic and inherent to consciousness as such, was seen to be the directing force behind man's involvement in the world. Without a realization of this fact, as Śaiva Siddhānta sees it, the senses succeed in imposing themselves on consciousness, as they are wont to doing because of their close relationship to consciousness. Under their influence, i.e., without a transcendental reflection on what really constitutes their essential nature, consciousness is led; and misled. The appropriate attitude which inference and verbal testimony help bring about, is a 'perception of perception'. That is, a reflection on man's role as a cognitive being makes evident, directly and unmediatedly, the sovereignty of consciousness. Consciousness is not limited the way each sense organ is to its corresponding object, e.g. ears to sound and nose to smell. Consciousness is limited, in its outward expression and manifestation, only to the ability, scope and range of each organ's function, but by pervading all of them it makes their functions possible. Again, that consciousness is necessarily so limited is no reflection on its essential powerful nature. The point is that with inference and verbal testimony, man is provided with the tools with which not only to perceive things as they are but, also, to perceive the power which constitutes the essential feature of consciousness, i.e., man's defining characteristic.

Underlying the role of man as a cognitive being, is the intrinsic validity of cognition and knowledge. Consciousness itself validates its own supremacy over the instruments of cognition at its disposal. This basic presupposition underlies the significance of the Śaiva Siddhānta theory of man as a cognitive being. To ask how we know that we know, is to beg the question, as already seen. The role of consciousness in cognition is its own criterion. Consciousness illumines both itself and the object, through the channel provided by the senses—just as light reveals both itself and the objects around it. The unique feature of consciousness, denied to the organs of perception, is that it can be aware of itself. This may be said to be a logical conclusion of what inference yields as regards the nature of consciousness: consciousness is always a consciousness of something and, logically, it is to be acknowledged that consciousness can be its own 'object'. This stage marks a transcendence of the role of consciousness in the empirical world, though it may be the outcome of a reflection on it. In other words, a reflection on man's role as a cognitive being, points to the possibility of a trained perception of the very basis of this crucial role, which man takes for granted in empirical life. In this perception, the empirical subject-object distinction is interpreted in the light of consciousness alone, i.e., consciousness is the very means which 'perceives' itself as itself, through its own inherent power.

At the empirical level, when the organs of perception are inoperative, the veil of ignorance (the word is used as a synonym for *malam*) enshrouds consciousness. Without the channel forged by the sense organs between the objects of the world and consciousness, the relation or contact between the two is cut. Consciousness is isolated and this isolation indicates a negative status, i.e., consciousness has no scope for the manifestation and expression of its powers; this indicates that it is under subjection. No sooner do the senses respond to the stimulus of their respective objects than it means that the veil of ignorance is lifted, the senses are empowered, and cognition takes place. This is an over-simplification of the overwhelming influence of ignorance and of the complex phenomenon of cognition dealt with in Chapter 3. Suffice it to say for the purposes here that with the beneficent roles of *karman* and *māyā*, consciousness is in a position to experience the objects of the world and, thereby, at least partially, overcome its isolation. At the empirical level, there is generally no control over when and how the veil of ignorance is lifted in cognition. It is a common experience of everyday life and is usually taken for granted as a fact of being in the world. It may be said to *just happen*, as does the sudden perception of a striking object. From the Śaiva Siddhānta perspective, man's role in the world, particularly as a cognitive being, indicates an attempt to unveil consciousness. The oscillation between rending the veil of ignorance and the return of ignorance is the story of man in the world—with which also goes the joy and pain of life's experiences. A reflection on this predicament indicates the possibility of ignorance being completely eradicated through consciousness itself which, when unhindered, naturally and constantly unleashes its powers of volition, knowledge and action.

At the transcendental level, consciousness is conscious of itself, by contrast with a consciousness of what belongs to the nature of insentience. The realization of this nature of consciousness implies an awareness that it animates the organs of the body. It is the power of consciousness that instigates a dynamism in the insentient categories of experience—a dynamism which does not belong to them intrinsically. On account of the close relation between the categories of experience and the principle of consciousness, the *prima facie* view is that the categories inherently possess activity. The error is based on an ignorance of the natures of both sentience and insentience. Also, it may be said that because consciousness permeates the insentient categories that are closely united with it, the ontological distinction between the two is not evident without an intuitive perception. Further, the ignorance about their ultimate distinctive features is responsible for a mutual confusion of the categories of sentience and insentience, on the analogy of the crystal taking on the colour of the object near it. By not discriminating one from the other, consciousness becomes bound and fettered by this ignorance to the point where, even at the empirical level, consciousness has a limited scope. This is to say, as already indicated, that a reflection on man's predicament at the empirical level points to the idea of freedom and liberation from bondage as such. Such an idea can be instilled in man through scripture. Man needs to be taught it in order to overcome the suffering that is due basically to ignorance. In other words, language comes to man's rescue. It is the insentient platform which makes possible the leap from the realm of insentience to that of pure sentience.

The ignorance which acts as the restrictive principle of consciousness is evident, according to Śaiva Siddhānta, not only in man as a cognitive being but, also in the so-called states which consciousness has to undergo on account of it. Of these, the state of wakefulness reveals both the condition of bondage and the condition of the possibility of liberation, i.e., through the power of the word as a category of such revelation. However, life in the world is a series of lapses into the state of ignorance, represented in man's succumbing to the other 'effect' states, such as dream and deep sleep—i.e., apart from the wakeful one in which the discourse on man's predicament and its positive role in possibly bringing about liberation, are meaningful to man. The degree of the desire for liberation is commensurate with the intensity with which the soteriological discipline is undertaken. It calls for a conscious effort on the part of man where the energy utilized in the hankering after what is sensually pleasing, is transformed into a desire for a knowledge of the intrinsic nature of experience as such. Such an effort is characterized by an attempt to constantly reflect on the human situation, i.e., it is an attempt to resolutely be aware of the inescapable involvement in the world and to reflect on the merit of scriptural statements which declare man's bound existence, and consequent suffering, to be due to ignorance concerning man's essential nature. Such an attempt indicates a resilient attitude on the part of consciousness, viz., to return to its natural state which is one of *not* being in subjection but, rather, of consciously commanding the insentient categories at its disposal.

The journey which man undergoes through the different states represents a process intended to culminate in the eradication of ignorance. The root cause of ignorance is *malam* (generally, the two terms ignorance and *malam* may be used synonymously) and man has to rely on the power of grace to be dissociated from its influence—an influence which is represented in the fact of man's possessing limited knowledge and of being involved in experiences in the world. The description of the 'causal' and 'effect' states of consciousness indicates a journey: a journey from an isolated state of consciousness which is overwhelmed by *malam*, to a state of partial manifestation of the powers of consciousness with the aid of *karman* and *māyā* (in which condition the effect states of wakefulness, dream, etc., are of special significance for a philosophical anthropology), to a 'return' to the essential and intrinsic pristine purity of consciousness (via the state of isolation) through the power of grace. It was seen that the concept of *malam* was postulated on the basis of the insight into man's predicament, i.e., of man as a being with limited knowledge, involved in the world, and suffering the effects of the ignorance about the nature of ultimate reality. In short, life in the world is a progressive attempt to be rid of *malam*'s influence.

In the journey to freedom or liberation from fetters which

man undergoes—a journey which may be described as a spiritual one—desire plays a dialectical role. On the one hand, desirelessness or dispassion (*vairāgya*), particularly for worldly experience, is called for and, on the other hand, the desire for liberation is a necessary prerequisite. What this implies is that the desire for what is pleasing in the world (*bubhukṣutva*) is to be transformed into a desire for liberation (*mumukṣutva*). How this is to be reconciled with the elimination of desire as such, since this is what seems to be required ultimately, may be said to be a matter of individual reflection on one's own situation. For man in the world, desire is a motivating factor for continued existence. What seems to be called for in the journey to liberation is initially a 'purification' of desire, i.e., on the basis of the realization that the desire for worldly pleasure fastens man's already existing bonds, a 'redirection' of desire is to be attempted. In other words, by reflecting on the nature and significance of desire—without which, it may be said, man cannot live—desire is turned around, so to speak, in order to pursue goals qualitatively different from worldly ones. The logical conclusion this attitude leads to is, paradoxically, a desire to be without desire. Desire may be said to be rooted in a sense of 'I' and 'mine' which, as already seen, are the most subtle obstructions to liberation. It indicates a duality of subject and object and, hence, is a tacit ignorance of the unity of being. It is particularly in this context that the stress on the supremacy of gnosis is most striking.

It has already been seen that, for Śivāgrayogin, gnosis is the only means for liberation. The entire weight of the discussion on Śaiva Siddhānta philosophical anthropology rests on this emphasis on gnosis. Śivāgrayogin's method of arriving at the unity of being through gnosis is not novel or atypical to Indian thought. The superiority of gnosis was radicalized in Vedānta philosophy by Śaṅkara, several centuries earlier in his radical monism, based on his commentary of the *Brahmasūtra* of Bādarāyaṇa. It may be said that within the philosophical assumptions of Śaiva Siddhānta, Śivāgrayogin's emphasis on the non-difference or unity of being (between the *ātman* and *śivam*) realized through the means of gnosis, on the basis of his commentary on the *Śivajñānabodham*, bears a striking similarity to Śaṅkara's highly estimated efforts. Further, just as Śaṅkara interprets the Vedas in the light of the *jñāna-pāda*, the section which deals with gnosis, so too Śivāgrayogin sees the significance of ritual, etc., in the Āgamas in the light of his emphasis on gnosis. It was also noted that Śivāgrayogin bases his views chiefly on the authority of the *jñāna-pāda* of selected Āgamas. Here too, Śivāgrayogin employs the technique of selection used by Śaṅkara for his own justification of radical monism through gnosis.

The unity of being that Śivāgrayogin's analysis yields is a unity that acknowledges a 'little' difference, on the analogy of a thing and the quality it possesses, and the example of light and its locus was given as a symbolic representation of this unity. The Śaiva Siddhānta understanding of this point has already been discussed and suffice it to say here that the desire which leads to the eradication of desire as such—and thus to a realization of the unity of being—is possible only through gnosis. The activity of the liberated being depends entirely on *śivam* and the sense of 'I' and 'mine' bears no significance at all. The *ātman* becomes *śivam*. *Śivam* is verily said to be the *ātman's* guide as the *ātman* is the guide of the body-functions. The state of the liberated being cannot be said to be one of subjection. Rather, such a being realizes the essential nature of ultimate reality. It is man's intrinsic nature to be guided by the light and power of *śivam* and the liberated being realizes or experiences, through gnosis, the natural unity between consciousness (*ātman*) and the consciousness which underlies consciousness (*śivam*). This natural unity is the basic postulate underlying Śaiva Siddhānta philosophical anthropology. What this point implies is that the Śaiva Siddhānta theory about the nature of man is to be seen in the background of its theory about the nature of ultimate reality. In other words, Śaiva Siddhānta philosophical anthropology has to be read ultimately in the light of Śaiva Siddhānta theology. It has already been indicated that the aim of this study has been to attempt to deal primarily with the former, bearing in mind its position in the latter, as indicated at relevant points in the study.

A question that may be asked now is: what is the special contribution of Śaiva Siddhānta philosophical anthropology to Indian thought? The question may be dealt with in the light of the Śaiva Siddhānta definition of man that emerges from the present study, viz., that man is a bound being expressing and manifesting consciousness in the world in a limited way; a being whose essential nature is to be defined in terms of consciousness; and a being who, through grace, is capable of being liberated from fettered existence. The analysis of the foregoing chapters may be said to elaborate these three aspects of the Śaiva Siddhānta definition of man. What seems to be unique about it is the Siddhāntin's attempt not only to analyze man's essential nature as radically different from the nature of the world—and, indeed, a world in which a scope for liberation is afforded—but, also, to attempt to account for the nature of man's so-called bound existence in the world itself. This study has approached Śaiva Siddhānta philosophical anthropology from the latter standpoint, i.e., by expounding and analyzing the Śaiva Siddhānta description of man in the world, an attempt has been made to bring out the impact of the Śaiva Siddhānta view of the intrinsic nature of man as a being defined essentially by consciousness.

It may be said, generally, the philosophical anthropology of other schools of Indian thought (e.g., Sāṅkhya, Yoga and Advaita Vedānta) emphasizes man's essential nature *at the expense of* man's role in the world. This is to say that the world and man's involvement in it according to the other schools imply a tacit denial of what, according to Śaiva Siddhānta, positively form, shape, or mould the conditions of possible liberation from fettered existence. Man's involvement in the world, according to Śaiva Siddhānta, is due to an act of divine grace for man's sake. Life in the world is no doubt a bound existence, but it is one in which man is given a scope, through fetters, to unbounded expression and manifestation of consciousness. In other words, while regarding man's bound state as being extrinsic to man's essential nature, Śaiva Siddhānta proceeds to describe man as a bound being attempting, thereby, to show how this very bound state is not only a necessary consequence of man's limited freedom but, also, how this freedom can ultimately become unlimited and absolute, through an act of divine grace.

The significance and special contribution of Śaiva Siddhānta philosophical anthropology was discussed specifically with reference to the need to qualify man's essential defining feature as consciousness. It was seen that an adequate definition of man according to Śaiva Siddhānta, has to accommodate both (a) the essential unity between the *ātman*—characterized as consciousness that becomes prey to *malam*—and *śivam*—also characterized as consciousness, but a consciousness which is eternally pure and untouched by *malam*—and (b) the unity of being referred to as man in the world. This is to say that Śaiva Siddhānta attempts to provide a 'complete' definition of man, i.e., it attempts to describe man as a bound and fettered being in the world in a way which accommodates the condition of a possibility of freedom from bondage as such. In other words, what is called a complete definition of man according to Śaiva Siddhānta, takes into account both the 'specific' and the 'general' definitions of man, already discussed.

If gnosis is accepted as the only means for overcoming ignorance and, thereby, being liberated, it may be asked why indeed is there a need to postulate the category of *śivam*. The Śaiva Siddhānta answer would be—in the light of what has already been said—that what is called man's "power of consciousness" does not in fact *belong* to man. If it did, the question would arise as to why in fact we possess a limited knowledge of things and of reality as such and why, indeed, we suffer from its consequences in the world. It is because of this predicament that a 'superior' power which itself empowers man's power of consciousness, needs to be acknowledged—the two being identical with a little difference, in the sense already elaborated. A detailed discussion on the postulation of the category called *śivam* entails, among other things, the proof for the existence of this category, which is beyond the scope of the present study. Suffice it to say that for Śaiva Siddhānta, the existence of *śivam* is what gives credibility to the goals and values of man's life in the world, the highest of which is the aim of liberation from fettered existence, and one which is made possible through *śivam*'s power of grace. The philosophical anthropology of Śaiva Siddhānta thus has to be read in the background of the permeating theology which underlies the system.

## APPENDIX 1: Table of Śaiva Siddhānta Categories

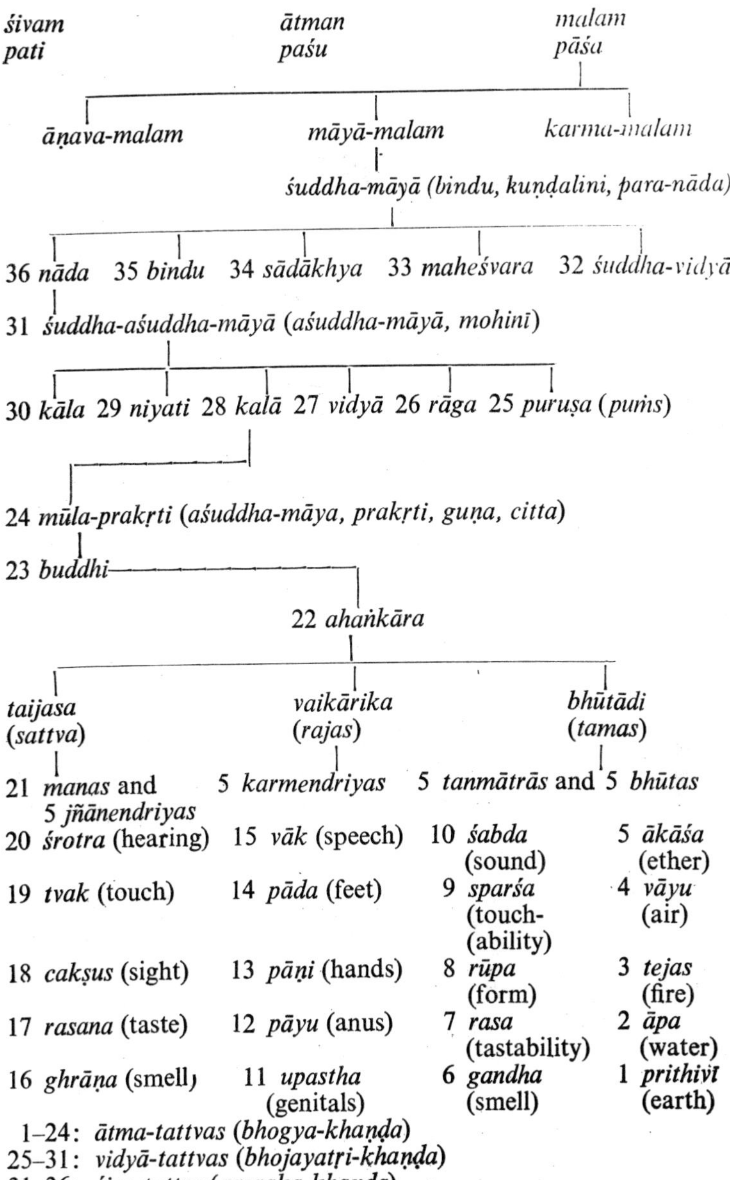

APPENDIX 2:

The text of the *Śivajñanabodham* from *Śivāgrayogin's Śivāgra-bhāṣya* (with a translation in the light of the commentary).

*Strī-puṁ-napuṁsaka-āditvāj-jagataḥ kārya-darśanāt/*
*Asti kartā sa hṛitvaitat-sṛijaty-asmāt-prabhur-haraḥ//*

1. There is an agent of the world on account of seeing [it as] an effect, possessing the female, the male, the neuter, etc. He [the agent] creates it having dissolved it. Therefore, Hara [Śiva] is the lord.

*Anyaḥ san-vyāptito'nanyaḥ kartā-karma-anusārataḥ /*
*Karoti saṁsṛitiṁ puṁsām-ājñayā-samavetayā //*

2. With an intrinsic, unlimited power the agent creates the world for man in accordance with [man's] *karman*; [though] being different the agent is non-different by virtue of pervasion.

*Netito mamatodrekāt akṣoparati bodhataḥ /*
*Svāpe nirbhogato bodhe boddhṛitvād-asty-aṇus-tanau //*

3. There is an *aṇu* in the body on account of: [the cognition of] not-thisness; the excess of mineness; there being consciousness [even] when the senses have ceased [functioning, e.g., in the dream state]; [the recollection of] there being no experience in deep sleep; and on account of there being one [an agent] who perceives when awake.

*Ātma-antaḥ-karaṇād-anyo'py-anvito mantri-bhūpavat /*
*Avasthā-pañcaka-stho'to mala-ruddha-sva-dṛik-kriyaḥ //*

4. The *ātman* is different from the internal organs also [i.e., apart from *citta* and *prāṇa*) associated [with them, though] like a king with ministers. Therefore, it [*ātman*] exists in the five states having its own knowledge and action restricted by *malam.*

*Vidanty-akṣāṇi puṁsā'rthān-na svayaṁ so'pi śambhunā /*
*Tad-vikārī-śivaś-cen-na kānto'yo-vat sa tan nayet //*

5. The senses do not perceive objects by themselves [but] with [the help of] a spirit (*puṁs*) and it [spirit] with [the help of] Śambhu [Śiva]. If [it is said] Śiva is liable to a change [of nature] through this then, it is not so—he [Śiva] leads this [spirit in man] like a magnet an iron.

*Adṛiśyaṁ ced-asad-bhāvo driśyaṁ cej-jaḍimā-bhavet |*
*Śaṁbhos-tad-vyatirekena jñeyaṁ rūpaṁ vidur-budhāḥ ||*

6. If [something is] not seen it would be non-existent, if seen it would be insentient. The wise ones say that the nature of Śambhu is to be known differently from [knowing] these [visible and invisible objects].

*Na-acic-cit-sannidhau kintu na vittas-te ubhe mithaḥ |*
*Prapañca -śivayor-vettā yas-sa ātma-tayoḥ pṛithak ||*

7. In the presence of *cit* there is no *acit*; further, these mutually do not experience each other. The one that knows both *śivam* and the world is the *ātman*, which is different from these two.

*Sthitvā sahendriya-vyādhais-tvaṁ na vetsi-iti bodhitaḥ |*
*Muktvaitān guruṇā-ananyo dhanyaḥ prāpnoti tat-padam ||*

8. Being taught by a guru thus: "Having lived with the hunters, the senses, you do not know yourself," the blessed one, not different [from *śivam*] attains that state [of śivahood], having abandoned these [senses].

*Cid-dṛiś-ātmani dṛiṣṭveśaṁ tyaktvā-āvṛiti-marīcikām |*
*Labdhvā śiva-padac-chāyāṁ dhyāyet-pañca-akṣarīm sudhiḥ ||*

9. Having seen Īśa [Śiva] within oneself through the eye of consciousness (*cit*), having left the mirage of worldly existence, and having obtained the shade of *śivam*'s state, the wise one should contemplate the five [sacred] syllables.

*Śivenaikyaṅgatas-siddhas-tad-adhīna-sva-vṛittikaḥ |*
*Mala-māyā-ādy-asaṁspṛiṣṭo bhavati sva-anubhūtimān ||*

10. Untouched by *malam, māyā*, etc., the perfected one—become one with *śivam*—is one who has self-knowledge, and has [*his*] own activity dependent on that [*śivam*].

*Dṛiśo darśayitā-iva-ātmā-tasya darśayitā-śivaḥ |*
*Tasmāt-tasmin parāṁ bhaktiṁ kuryād-ātmopakārake ||*

11. Śiva is the guide of this [*ātman*] like the *ātman* is the guide of sight [and other sense organs]; therefore, supreme devotion should be had to this one [Śiva] who is the *ātman*'s aid.

*Muktyai prāpya satas-teṣāṁ bhajed-veṣaṁ śiva-ālayam |*
*Itthaṁ vidyāc-chivajñānabodhe śaiva-artha-nirṇayam ||*

12. Having resorted to the virtuous ones, one should worship their habit, which is the dwelling place of *śivam*, for the sake of liberation; thus one should know the established view of matters Śaivite in the *Śivajñānabodham.*

# APPENDIX 3

The transliteration from the Sanskrit of Śivāgrayogin's discussion "defining *cit-śakti's* validity as the means of cognition", translated and exegeted in Chapter 3, pp. 107–117, (*Śivāgrabhāṣya*, pp. 95–98).

*Cic-chakteḥ pramāṇatva-nirūpaṇam*

*Nanu pramāṇasya kiṁ lakṣaṇam. Na tāvat pramitisādhnatvaṁ dīpa-ādiṣv-ativyāpteḥ. Tad-uktaṁ śrīmatpauṣkare* [7:11]:

*Nanu na syāt-kuto mānaṁ yat-tat-pramiti sādhanam |*
*Tan-na-dīpa-dṛg-ādīnāṁ pramāṇatva-prasaṅgataḥ || iti.*

*Tvan-mate cic-chakter-eva pramititvena tat-sādhana-asambhavāc-ca. Nanu kevalā cic-chaktiḥ na pramitiḥ. Kintu tat-tad-viṣaya-avachinnā. Sā ca viṣaya-avacchedasya janyatayā janyeti na sādhana-asambhavaḥ. Na ca dīpa-ādiṣv-ativyāptiḥ sādhana-padasya karaṇa-padatvād-iti cet. Na. Cakṣur-ādy-asannikarṣe'pi viṣayotpatty-anantaram-evacic-chakteḥ viṣaya-avaccheda-sadbhāvena tatra cakṣur-āder-ajanakatvāt. Saṁśayaviparya-āsāder-api tat-tad-viṣaya-avacchinna-cic-chaktirūpatvena tat-karaṇe'tivyāpteś-ca. Karaṇatvasya-anirukteśca. Tathā-hi kiṁ karaṇatvam-ayoga-vyavacchedena phalasambandhitvaṁ vā vyāpāravatvaṁ vā phala-niyata-vyāpāravatvaṁ vā kartṛi-preryatvaṁ veti. Na-ādyaḥ sukha-ādiṣu karmasu ativyāpteḥ cakṣur-ādāv-avyāpteś-ca. Na dvitīyaḥ ghaṭa-dīpa-ādiṣv-ativyāpteḥ. Parāmarśa-ādau vyāpāra-abhāvena-avyāpteśca. Na ca tad-vyāpārakaṁ liṅgam-eva karaṇam. Tasya atīta-anāgata-ādi-rūpatayā janakatvasyaiva-ayogena tad-viśeṣa-karaṇatva-asambhavāt. Ata eva na tṛitīyaḥ cakṣur-vyāpārasya-saṁyoga-āder-andhakāra-ādau phala-ajanakatayā tan-niyama-abhāvena cakṣur-ādāv-avyāpteś-ca. Na ca kāraṇa-antara-sāhitya-avacchinnasya-tan-niyatatvam-asti-iti vācyam. Evaṁ sati sarvasya-api vyāpārasya tathā-vidhatvena phala-niyata-padasya vaiyarthya-āpatteḥ. Karma-ādāv-ativyāpteś-ca. Karma-ādikam-api anena rūpeṇa karṇam-eva kartṛi-karma-karaṇa-ādi-vyapadeśa-bhedas-u-t upādhi-bhedena-api-iti cet. Na. Tathā sati rūpa-ādy-upalabdhi-pakṣaka-karaṇa-janyatva-anumānasya kartr-aādinā'rtha-antara-grastatvena cakṣur-ader-asiddhyāpatteḥ. Karaṇatva-vivakṣā-vaiyarthyāc-ca. Na-api caturthaḥ. Śarīra-ādāv-ativyāpteḥ parā-marśa-ādāv-avyāpteś-ca. Na-api pramā-sāmagrītvam. Cakṣur-ady-avyāpteḥ sāmagryāḥ kāraṇa-samudāya-rūpatayā samudāyasya ca samudāyy-anatirekeṇa-cakṣur-āder-api sāmagrītve meya-mātra-ādīnām-api mānatva-prasaṅgena vivikta-vyavahāra-lopa-prasaṅgaḥ. Tad-uktaṁ śrīmat-pauṣkare* [7:19-21]:

*Nanu prameya-saṁsiddhau sāmagrī kena neṣyate |*
*Pramātra-ādi-ghaṭa-anteṣu satsveva-ghaṭa-niścayāt ||*
*Tat-tat-pramatṛi-meya-ādi-vyavahāra-vilopataḥ |*
*Mātṛi-māna-prameyāṇāṁ-tad-antarbhāvataḥ sthiteḥ ||*
*Teṣāṁ tu vyatirekeṇa sāmagrī ca na dṛiśyate ||* iti

*Sādhana-sāmagry-ādīnāṁ meyatvena mānatvasya-ayuktatvāt. Tad-uktaṁ śrīmat-pauṣkare* [7:12]:

*Yan-meyaṁ na hi tan-mānaṁ yato mānena mīyate | iti*
*Ato na pramāṇa-sāmānya-lakṣaṇaṁ yuktam-iti.*

*Atrocyate tat-tad-viṣaya-avacchinnā cic-chaktiḥ tat-tad-arthe pramā saiva pramāṇam-api. Na caivam viṣayasya sarvadā prakāśa-prasaṅga iti vācyam. Cakṣur-ādi-karaṇaka-buddhi-vṛtty-anudaye mala-āvṛitatvena viṣaya-sambandhasya-asatkalpatvāt. Tad-udaye tu mala-nivṛittyā anāvṛita-viṣaya-sambandhena viṣaya-avacchinna-cic-chakti-kādācitkatayā prakāśa-kādācitkatva-sambhavāt. Yadvā yathā - artha - anubhūti - rūpa - buddhi - vṛitty - upārūḍhatvaṁ viṣayasya cic-chaktyā-sambandha iti kadācid-eva viṣaya-avacchedāt kādācitka-prakāśa-sambhavaḥ. Saṁśaya-ādi-vinirmuktā cic-chaktir-mānamiṣyate iti śrīmat-pauṣkara-sthaṁ* [7:22] *saṁśaya-ādi-vinirmukta-padam-api saṁśaya-ādi-vinirmukta-buddhi-vṛitty-upahita-arthakaṁ tat-tad-viṣaya-avacchinna-param-eva. Cic-chakteḥ saṁśaya-ādi-buddhi-vṛtti-tādātmya - asambhavena tad-vinirmukta-pada-vaiyartha-āpatyā tasya tad-vinirmukta-buddhi-vṛitty-upahita-paratvasya-avaśyakatvāt. Na caivaṁ buddhi-vṛittir-eva-artha-prakāśo'stu alaṁ cic-chaktyā iti vācyam. Buddher-jaḍatvena tad-vṛitter-api-tathātvena saṁvid-rūpāyāś-cic-chakter-eva-artha-prakāśatvāt. Tad-uktaṁ śrīmat-pauṣkare* [7:17]:

*Prākṛitatva-aviśeṣeṇa dṛig-āder-aviśeṣataḥ /*
*Asaṁvid-ātmakatvena na hi buddheḥ pramāṇatā //* iti.

*Atra buddhi-padena tad-vṛittis-tad-abhedād-ukteti dṛiṣṭavyam. Mṛigendre'py-uktam* [11:8]:

*Iti buddhi-prakāśo'yam bhāva-pratyaya-lakṣaṇaḥ /*
*Bodha ity-ucyate bodha-vyakti-bhūmitayā paśoḥ // iti.*

# SELECTED BIBLIOGRAPHY

*Primary Sources*


*Mṛigendra Āgama* (Śrī Mṛigendram). Devakoṭṭai: Śaiva Śiddhānta Paripālana Saṅgraha, 1928.

*Ratnatrayam of Śrīkaṇṭhasūri*. Devakoṭṭai: Śaiva Śiddhānta Paripālana Saṅgraha, 1925.

*Rauravāgama*. Edited by N.R. Bhatt. 2 vols. Pondichéry: Institut Français d'Indologie, 1979.

*Śaivāgamaparibhāṣāmañjarī of Vedajñāna*. Critical edition, with a French translation and notes, by Bruno Dagens. Pondichéry: Institut Français d'Indologie, 1979.

*Śataratna Saṅgraha*. Edited by Pandit Panchanan Sastri. Arthur Avalon Tantrik Texts, vol. XXII. Calcutta: Agamanusandhan Samiti, 1944.

*Siddhānta Prakāśikā of Sarvātmaśambhu*. Published in *The Journal of the Tanjore Maharaja Serfoji's Sarasvati Mahal Library*, edited by A. Panchanathan, vol. xxxiii, nos. 1, 2, and 3, 1984, pp. 1-14.

Śivāgrayogin. *Śivajñānabodham-laghuṭikā*. Pandit Series, vol. 29. Benares: E.J. Lazarus and Co., 1907.

———. *Śivāgrabhāṣya*. Edited by Krishna Sastri. Madras: Sūryanār Koil Ādinam, 1920.

———. *The Śaiva Paribhāṣa*. Edited by H.R. Rangaswamy Iyengar and Vidvan R. Ramasastri. Mysore: Government Press, 1950.

*Śivāyogaratna de Jñānaprakāśa*. Edited, with a French translation and notes, by Tara Michaël. Pondichéry: Institut Français d'Indologie, 1975.

*Śrīśaivasiddāntaparibhāṣā of Kavirājaśekara Sūryabhattāraka*. Edited by Krishna Dikshit. Bangalore: Pratibha, 1958.

*Tattvaprakāśikā of King Bhoja*. Devakoṭṭai: Śaiva Śiddhānta Paripālana Saṅgraha, 1923.

*Tattvasaṅgraha of Sadyojyoti*. Devakoṭṭai: Śaiva Siddhānta Paripālana Saṅgraha, 1923.

*Secondary Sources*

*Aitareya-upaniṣad*. Edited and translated by Swami Sharvananda. Madras: Srī Ramakrishna Math, 1959.

Apte, V.M. *Brahma-sūtra Shaṅkara-Bhāṣya*. Bombay: Popular Book Depot, 1960.

Arokiaswamy, A.P. *The Doctrine of Grace in Śaiva Siddhānta*. Trichinopoly, 1935.

Arunachalam, M. *The Śaivāgamas*. South India, Māyuram Taluk: Gandhi Vidyalayam, 1983.

Ayyar, C.V. Narayana. *Origin and Early History of Śaivism*. Madras University Historical Series, no. 6. Madras: University of Madras, 1939; reprint ed., 1974.

Balasubramaniam, K.M. *Special Lectures on Śaiva Siddhānta*. Annamalai: Annamalai University, 1959.

*Bhāskarī*. 3 vols. Edited by Sri Tribhuvan Prasad Upadhyaya. Vol. 3, *An English Translation of the Īśvara Pratyabhijñā Vimarśinī in the Light of the Bhāskarī with an Outline of the History of Śaiva Philosophy* by Kanti Chandra Pandey. The Princess of Wales Saraswati Bhavana Texts, No. 84. Lucknow: New Government Press, 1954.

Brahma, Nalini Kanta. *Philosophy of Hindu Sādhanā*. London: Kegan Paul, Trench, Trubner and Company, 1932.

Carpenter, J. Estlin. *Theism in Medieval India*. London: Williams and Norgate, 1921; Indian ed., New Delhi: Oriental Books Reprint Corporation (exclusively distributed by Munshiram Manoharlal), 1977.

Cassirer, Ernst. *An Essay on Man*. New Haven and London: Yale University Press, 1944.

Chethimattam, John B. *Consciousness and Reality*. New York: Orbis Books, 1971.

Dasgupta, Surendranath. *A History of Indian Philosophy*. 5 vols. *Southern Schools of Śaivism*, vol. 5. Cambridge: University of Cambridge, 1962.

Datta, D.M. *The Six Ways of Knowing*. Calcutta: University of Calcutta, 1960.

Devasenapathi, V.A. *Śaiva Siddhānta as Expounded in the Sivajñānasiddhiyār and its Six Commentaries*. Madras: University of Madras, 1960: reprint ed., 1974.

———. *Of Human Bondage and Divine Grace*. Annamalainagar: Annamalai University, 1963.

Dhavamony, Mariasusai. *Love of God*. Oxford: Clarendon Press, 1971.

Dunuwila, Rohan A. *Śaiva Siddhānta Theology*. Delhi: Motilal Banarsidass, 1985.

Farquhar, J.N. *An Outline of the Religious Literature of India*. Oxford: Oxford University Press, 1920.

Frauwallner, Erich. *Aus der Philosophie der Śivaitischen Systeme*. Deutsche Akademie der Wissenschaften zu Berlin, Vorträge und Schriften. Heft 78. Berlin: Akademie Verlag, 1962.

Gonda, J. *Die Religionen Indiens*. 2. vols. Stuttgart: W. Kohlhammer Verlag, 1963.

———. *Change and Continuity in Indian Religion*. The Hague: Mouton, 1965.

———. *Viṣṇuism and Śaivism*. Delhi: Munshiram Manoharlal, 1976.

———. *A History of Indian Literature*. Vol. II, fasc., 1. *Medieval Religious Literature in Sanskrit*. Wiesbaden: Otto Harrassowitz, 1977.

Hiriyanna, M. *Outlines of Indian Philosophy*. London: George Allen and Unwin, 1932; 8th impression, 1970.

———. *Indian Conception of Values*. Mysore: Kavyalaya Publishers, 1975.

Hulin, Michel. *Le Principle de l'Ego dans la Pensée Indienne Classique. La Notion d'Ahaṃkāra*. Publications de l'Institut de Civilisation Indienne. Serie 80, Fascicule 44. Paris: College de France, Institut de Civilisation Indienne, 1978.

Iyer, K.A. Subramania, *Bharatṛhari*. Poona: Deccan College, 1969.

Jash, Pranabananda. *History of Śaivism*. Calcutta: Roy and Chaudhury, 1974.

Jha, Hari Mohan. *Trends of Linguistic Analysis in Indian Philosophy*. Varanasi: Chaukhambha Orientalia, 1981.

Kar, Bijayananda. *The Theories of Error in Indian Philosophy*. Delhi: Ajanta Publications, 1978.

Karmarkar, A.P. *The Religions of India*. Vol. 1 Lonavla. India: Mira Publishing House, 1950.

Kaviraj, Gopinath. *Aspects of Indian Thought*. Burdwan: University of Burdwan, 1966.

Kumar, Frederick L. *The Philosophy of Śaivism*. Delhi: Oxford Publishing Co., 1980.

Landmann, Michael. *Philosophical Anthropology*. Translated by David A. Parent. Philadelphia: The Westminster Press, 1974.

Larson, Gerald James. *Classical Sāṁkhya*. Delhi: Motilal Banarsidass, 1969.

Masson, J.L., and Patwardhan, M.V. *Aesthetic Rapture*. 2 vols. Poona: Deccan College, 1970.

Matilal, Bimal K. *Epistemology, Logic and Grammar in Indian Philosophical Analysis*. The Hague: Mouton and Company, 1971.

———. *Logic, Language and Reality*. Delhi: Motilal Banarsidass, 1985.

Mishra, Kamalakar. *Significance of the Tantric Tradition*. Varanasi Ardhanārīśvara Publications, 1981.

Mittal, Keval Krishna. *Materialism in Indian Thought*. Delhi: Munshiram Manoharlal Publishers, 1974.

Monier-Williams, M. *A Sanskrit-English Dictionary*. Oxford: Oxford University Press, 1899; reprint ed., Delhi: Motilal Banarsidass, 1984.

Narasimhachary, M., ed. *Āgamaprāmāṇya of Yāmunācārya*. Gaekwad's Oriental Series no. 160. Baroda: Oriental Institute, 1976.

Oberhammer, Gerhard. *Strukturen Yogischer Meditation*. Veröffentlichungen der Kommission für Sprachen und Kulturen Südasiens. Heft 13. Vienna: Verlag der österreichischen Akademie der Wissenschaften, 1977.

Pandey, R.R. *Man and the Universe*. Delhi: GDK Publications, 1978.

Paranjoti, V. *Śaiva Siddhānta*. 2nd ed. London: Luzac and Co., 1954.

Piet, J.H. *A Logical Presentation of the Śaiva Siddhānta Philosophy*. Indian Research Series VIII. Madras: The Christian Literature Society for India, 1952.

Pillai, K. Raghavan, ed. and tr. *The Vākyapadīya*. Studies in the Vākyapadīya vol. 1. Critical Text of Cantos I and II, with

English translation, Summary of Ideas and Notes. Delhi: Motilal Banarsidass, 1971.

Pillai, J.M. Nallaswami. *Śivajñāna Siddhiyār of Aruṇandi Śivāchārya.* Translated from the Tamil with introduction, notes, glossary, etc. Madras: Meykandan Press, 1913.

Ponniah, V. *The Śaiva Siddhānta Theory of Knowledge.* Annamalai University Philosophy Series IV. Annamalai: University of Annamalai, 1962.

Potter, Karl H. *Presuppositions of India's Philosophies.* Englewood Cliffs: Prentice-Hall, Inc., 1963.

Prasad, Jwala. *History of Indian Epistemology.* Delhi: Munshiram Manoharlal, 1956.

Radhakrishnan, Sarvepalli and Moore, Charles A., eds. *A Source Book in Indian Philosophy.* Princeton: Princeton University Press, 1957.

Radhakrishnan, S., and Raju, P.T., eds. *The Concept of Man.* 2nd ed. Lincoln, Nebraska: Johnson Publishing Company; London: Allen and Unwin Ltd., 1966.

Radhakrishnan. *Indian Philosophy.* 2 vols. London: George Allen and Unwin Ltd., New York: Humanities Press Inc., 1923. 10th impression, 1977.

Raja, K. Kunjunni. *Indian Theories of Meaning.* Madras: Adyar Library, 1963.

Raju, P.T. *Spirit, Being and Self.* New Delhi and Madras: South Asian Publishers, 1982.

Raju, P.T., and Castell, Alburey, eds. *East-West Studies on the Problem of the Self.* Papers presented at the Conference on Comparative Philosophy and Culture held at the College of Wooster, Wooster, Ohio, April 22-24, 1965. The Hague: Martinus Nijhoff, 1968.

Ramakrisnnan, V. *Perspectives in Śaivism.* Madras: University of Madras, 1978.

Renou, L. *Religions of Ancient India.* 2nd ed. New Delhi: Munshiram Manoharlal, 1953.

*Sāṅkhyakārikā of Īśvara Kṛṣṇa.* Edited and translated by S.S. Suryanarayana Sastri, 2nd. ed. Madras: University of Madras, 1935.

*Sarva-Darśana-Saṅgraha of Mādhava.* Translated by E.B. Cowell and A.E. Gough. Chowkambha Sanskrit Series, vol. 10.

London: Kegan Paul, Trench, Trubner and Company, Ltd., 1961.

Sastri, G. *The Philosophy of Word and Meaning*. Calcutta Sanskrit College, 1959.

Sastri, S. Kuppuswami. *A Primer of Indian Logic According to Annambhaṭṭa's Tarkasaṁgraha*. 3rd ed. Madras: The Kuppuswami Sastri Research Institute, 1961.

Sastri, S.S. Suryanarayana. *Collected Papers of Professor S.S. Suryanarayana Sastri*. Madras: Madras University, 1961.

———. *The Śivādvaita of Śrīkaṇṭha*. Madras University Philosophical Series, no. 2. Madras: Madras University, 1972.

Schomerus, H.W. *Der Caiva-Siddhānta: Eine Mystik Indiens*. Leipzig: J.C. Hinrichs'sche Buchhandlung, 1912.

———. *Arunaṇtis Śivajñānasiddhiyār; Die Erlangung des Wissens um Śiva oder um die Erlosung*. 2 vols. *Beiträge zur Südasienforschung*, Südasien-Institut, Universitat Heidelberg, vols. 49a and 49b. Wiesbaden: Franz Steiner Verlag, 1981.

Sen, Debabrata. *The Concept of Knowledge; Indian Theories*. Calcutta: K.P. Bagchi and Company, 1984.

Sharma, Dhirendra. *The Negative Dialectics*. Delhi: Sterling Publishers, 1974.

Shivapadasundaram, S. *The Śaiva School of Hinduism*. London: George Allen and Unwin, 1934.

Siddalingaiah, T.B. *Origin and Development of Śaiva Siddhānta up to 14th Century*. Madurai: Madurai Kamaraj University, 1979.

Sinha, Jadunath. *Indian Epistemology of Perception*. Calcutta: Sinha Publishing House, 1969.

———. *Schools of Śaivism*. Calcutta: Sinha Publishing House, 1970.

*Śiva-Nana-Bōdham; A Manual of Śaiva Religious Doctrine*. Translated from the Tamil with synopsis, exposition, etc., by Gordon Matthews. James G. Forlong Fund, vol. XXIV. Oxford: University Press, 1948.

Sivaraman, K. *Śaivism in Philosophical Perspective*. Delhi: Motilal Banarsidass, 1973.

*Somaśambhupaddhati*. Edited, with an introduction and notes, by Hélene Brunnér-Lachaux. 3 Vols. Pondicherry: Institut Francais d'Indologie, vol. 1, 1963.

*Śvetāśvatāropaniṣad.* 7th ed. Edited and translated by Swami Tyagisananda. Madras: Sri Ramakrishna Math, 1979.

Varadachari, V. *Āgamas and South Indian Vaiṣṇavism.* Madras: Prof. M. Rangacharya Memorial Trust, 1982.

Woods, J.H., Tr. *The Yoga-System of Patañjāli.* Delhi: Motilal Banarsidass, 1966; reprint ed., Harvard University Press, The Harvard Oriental Series, Vol. 17. n.d.

*Articles*

Aiyar, K.A.S., and Pandey, K.C. 'Śaiva Theory of Relation', *Proceedings of the All-India Oriental Conference*, 9 (1940), 603-617.

Aiyar, K.A. Subramania. 'Pratibhā as the Meaning of a Sentence', *Proceedings and Transactions of the Tenth All-India Oriental Conference*, March 1940, 326-332.

Alper, Harvey P. 'Śiva and the Ubiquity of Consciousness', *Journal of Indian Philosophy*, 7 (1979), 345-407.

Arulappa, Antony. 'The Role of Grace in Salvation According to Śaiva Siddhānta', *Studia Missionalia*, Vol. 29 (1980), 273-306.

Balasubramaniam, P. 'On the Epistemic Status of Saṁśaya—A Study with Special Reference to Śaiva Siddhānta', *Indian Philosophical Annual*, XIV (1980-81), 237-253.

Balsubramaniam, R. 'On the Nature and Evidence of Perception', *Indian Phiolsophical Annual*, XIV (1980-81), 215-236.

Banerjee, P. 'Some Aspects of the Early History of Śaivism', *Indo-Asian Culture* (Delhi), 14 (1965), 215-331.

Barnett, L.D. 'Notes on the Śaiva Siddhāntam', *Le Museon* (Paris), n.s. 10 (1909), 27-77.

Bharati, Y.S. 'Śaiva Siddhānta', *Journal of the Annamalai University*, 20 (1956), 25-56.

Biswal, Bansidhar. 'Śaiva Philosophy', *Darsana International*, XXIII, no. 1 (January 1983) 34-42.

Brunner, Héléne. 'Les Categories Sociales Védiques dans le Śivaisme du Sud', *Journal Asiatique*, CCLII (1964), 451-472.

———. 'Analyse de Kiraṇāgama', *Journal Asiatique*, CCLIII (1965), 309-328.

———. 'Analyse du Suprabhedāgama', *Journal Asiatique*, CCLV (1967), 31-60.

———- 'Le Sādhaka, Personnage Oublié du Śivaïsme du Sud' *Journal Asiatique*, CCLXIII (1975), 411-443.

———. 'Le Mysticisme dans le Āgama Śivaïtes', *Studia Missionalia*, 26 (1977), 287-314.

———. 'Importance de la Littérature Āgamique pour l'Etudes des Religions Vivantes de l'Inde', *Indologica Taurinensia*, III-IV (1975), 107-124.

———. 'Le Śaiva-Siddhānta, 'Essence' du Veda', *Indologica Taurinensia*, VIII-IX (1980-81), 51-66.

Devasenapathi, V.A. The Idea and Doctrine of the Guru in Śaivism', *Studia Missionalia*. XXI (1972), 171-184.

———. 'An Outline of the Siddhānta Epistemology', *Indian Philosophical Annual*, XIV (1980-81), 191-202.

———. 'Basic Concepts of Śaiva Siddhānta', *Indian Philosophical Annual*, XIV (1980-81), 39-80.

Filliozat, Pierre-Sylvain. 'Recherches Nouvelles sur le Civaisme', *Annuaire de Collège de France* (1964), 341-347.

———. 'Le Tattvaprakāśa du Roi Bhoja et les Commentaires d'Aghoraśivācārya et de Śrīkumāra', *Journal Asiatique*, CCLIX (1971), 247-295.

———. S.V. 'Caktism', *Encyclopedia Universalis* (1968-73).

———. S.V. 'Civa et Civaïsne', *Encyclopedia Universalis* (1968-73).

———. 'Dualistic School of Śaivism', *Quarterly Journal of the Mythical Society*, Bangalore, India, 69, nos. 3-4 (July-December 1978), 180-190.

Grace, John R. 'Understanding of Man in Śaiva Siddhānta Philosophy', *Śaiva Siddhānta*, II, nos. 3-4 (October-December (1967), 125-136.

Groethuysen, Berhard. 'Towards an Anthropological Philosophy', in *Philosophy and History, Essays Presented to Ernst Cassirer*. Edited by Raymond Klibansky and H.J. Paton. Oxford: Clarendon Press, 1936, 77-89.

Hacker, Paul. 'Saṅkara's Conception of Man', *Studia Missionalia*, XIX (1970), 123-141. Reprinted in *Paul Hacker, Kleine Schriften,* edited by Lambert Schmithausen. Wiesbaden: Franz Steiner Verlag GMBH, 1978, 244-251. Also in *German Scholars on India*, edited by the Cultural Department of the Federal Republic of Germany, New Delhi, vol. 1, published by Chowkhamba, Varanasi, under the title 'A Note on Śaṅkara's Conception of Man', 1973, 99-106.

Halbfass, Withelm. 'Anlhropological Problems in Classical Indian Philosophy', *Beitrage zur Indien forschung*: *Ernst Waldschmidt-zum* 80. *Geburtstag gewidmet.* Berlin: Museum für Indische Kunst, 1977.

Hirudayam, I. 'The Concept of God', *Śaiva Siddhānta*, VII (1972), 37-47.

Irudayaraj, Xavier, 'World view and Salvation According to Śaiva Siddhānta', *Journal of Dharma*, IV, no. 3 (1980), 268-277,

Mahadevan, T.M.P. 'Śaivism, the History and Culture of the Indian People', *Bhāratiya Vidyā Bhavan*, IV (1955), 299-303; V (1957), 441-458; VI (1960), 556-557.

———. Śaivism and the Indus Civilization', *Journal of the Ganganath Jha Institute*, IV, no. 1, 1-9.

Mudaliar, K. Vajravelu, 'The Epistemology of Śaiva Siddhānta', *Indian Philosophical Annual*, XIV (L980-81), 117-122.

Pappé, H.O. 'On Philosophical Anthropology', *Australasian Journal of Philosophy*, 39 (1961), 47-64.

———. S.V. 'Philosophical Anthropology', *Encyclopedia of Philosophy*. (1967).

Pillai, Subramania G. 'Introduction and History of Śaiva Siddhānta', *Journal of the Ganganath Jha Research Institute*, V (1948), 384-389.

Pillai, S.S. 'Śaiva Siddhānta', *Journal of the Annamalai University* XIX (1954), 1-50.

Sastri, S.S. Suryanarayana. 'Truth in the Śaiva Siddhānta', *Journal of the Madras University* II (1929), 111-127. Reprinted in *Indian Philosophical Annual*, XIV (1980-81), 81-100.

———. 'The Philosophy of Śaivism', *Indian Philosophical Annual* XIV (1980-81), 142-157.

Sivaraman, K. 'The Word as a Category of Revelation', in *Revelation in Indian Thought, A Festschrift in Honour of Professor T.R.V. Murti.* Edited by Harold Coward and Krishna Sivaraman. California: Dharma Publishing, 1977, 45-64.

———. 'The Role of the Śaivāgama in the Emergence of Śaiva-siddhānta: Philosophical Interpretation', in *Traditions in Contact and Change*. Edited by Peter Slater and Donald Wiebe Selected Proceedings of the XIVth Congress of the International Association for the History of Religions, Waterloo: Wilfred Laurier University Press, 1983, 53-64.

———. 'The Concept of Transpersonal Revelation in Hindu Philosophical Thinking: The Śaiva Point of View', typewritten 47 pages.

———. 'Treatment of Karma in Śaiva-Siddhānta'', typewritten, 24 pages.

Smart, Ninian, s.v. 'Indian Philosophy', *Encyclopedia of Philosophy* (1967).

Soni, Jayandra. 'The arguments for *Mala* according to Śivāgrayogin', in *Śaiva Siddhānta Perumaṉram; Mutta-Vilā Malar* [80*th Anniversary Volume*]. Edited by P. Thirugnanasambandhan. Madras: Śaiva Siddhānta Perumaṉram (1986), 30-36.

Subramanyam, K. 'The Metaphysics of the Śaiva Siddhānta System', *Proceedings of the All-India Oriental Conference*, III (1924), 569-582.

Sundaramoorthy, G. 'Development of Epistemology in the Sanskrit Works on Śaiva Siddhānta', *Indian Philosophical Annual*, XIV (1980-81), 133-141.

Takedo, Kodo. 'The Śaivadarśana of the Sarvadarśanasaṁgraha', *Journal of Indian and Buddhist Studies*, University of Tokyo, XXI, no. 2 (March 1973), 119-124.

Tirugnanasambandhan, P. 'Concept of Mukti in Śaivism', *Journal of the Madras University*, XLIII, nos. 1-2 (1971), 47-53.

———. 'Contribution of Tamilnaud—Sanskrit Works on Śaivism' *Annals of Oriental Research*, University of Madras (1975), 512-521.

———. 'The Bearing of Śaiva Siḍdhānta Epistemology on its Metaphysics', *Indian Philosophical Annual*, XIV (1980-81), 101-116.

———. 'The Concept of the Soul in Śaiva Siddhānta and Śivādvaita', *Journal of the International Institute of Śaiva Siddhānta* I, no. 1 (July 1985), 43-48.

*Theses*

Fernando, Adrian. 'The Formation of Śaiva Siddhānta: The Theology of Aghoraśiva', Fordham University, 1979.

Nandimath, S.C. "Theology of the Śaivāgamas, Being a Survey of the Doctrine of Śaiva Siddhānta and Vīraśaivism's University of London, 1930.

Rajamanickam, M. 'Development of Śaivism in South India", Madras University, 1950.

Sullivan, H.P. "The Śaiva Siddhānta School of Śaivism", University of Chicago, 1957.

# Index